OECD
MONETARY STUDIES SERIES

EXCHANGE RATE MANAGEMENT AND THE CONDUCT OF MONETARY POLICY

ORGANISATION FOR ECONOMIC CO-OPERATION AND DEVELOPMENT

Pursuant to article 1 of the Convention signed in Paris on 14th December, 1960, and which came into force on 30th September, 1961, the Organisation for Economic Co-operation and Development (OECD) shall promote policies designed:

- to achieve the highest sustainable economic growth and employment and a rising standard of living in Member countries, while maintaining financial stability, and thus to contribute to the development of the world economy;
- to contribute to sound economic expansion in Member as well as non-member countries in the process of economic development; and
- to contribute to the expansion of world trade on a multilateral, non-discriminatory basis in accordance with international obligations.

The Signatories of the Convention on the OECD are Austria, Belgium, Canada, Denmark, France, the Federal Republic of Germany, Greece, Iceland, Ireland, Italy, Luxembourg, the Netherlands, Norway, Portugal, Spain, Sweden, Switzerland, Turkey, the United Kingdom and the United States. The following countries acceded subsequently to this Convention (the dates are those on which the instruments of accession were deposited): Japan (28th April, 1964), Finland (28th January, 1969), Australia (7th June, 1971) and New Zealand (29th May, 1973).

The Socialist Federal Republic of Yugoslavia takes part in certain work of the OECD (agreement of 28th October, 1961).

Publié en français sous le titre:

**GESTION DU TAUX DE CHANGE
ET
CONDUITE DE LA POLITIQUE MONÉTAIRE**

The OECD Monetary Studies were initiated in the early 1970s at the request of the Economic Policy Committee. Each of the first five volumes analysed monetary structures and policies in a selected OECD country[1]. These were then supplemented by a comparative survey: *The Role of Monetary Policy in Demand Management – the Experience of Six Major Countries* (1975). These studies were motivated by the increased importance of monetary policy in economic management and by the frequency with which international capital movements had come to impinge on policy actions.

Two other volumes *Monetary Targets and Inflation Control* and *Budget Financing and Monetary Control*, were published in 1979 and 1981 respectively. The first analysed the significant evolution of monetary management which occurred during the last decade as a result of the widespread adoption of official objectives for the growth of monetary and credit aggregates in the context of inflation control. The second focused on the implications of financing high budget deficits for aggregates-oriented monetary policy and the extent to which increased public sector borrowing may constrain the financing of the private sector.

The present study examines the role of exchange rates in policy formulation. It analyses how the conduct of monetary policy influences exchange rates, and how exchange rate management affects monetary developments. It also assesses the trade-off between domestic monetary objectives and exchange rate stability and considers its implications for policy. The experience in countries of the Group of Ten[2] and Switzerland is examined in detail over the period 1973-83.

This new study has been prepared by P. Atkinson, A. Blundell-Wignall, J.-C. Chouraqui and G. Hacche (the latter as a consultant) of the Monetary and Fiscal Policy Division. Preliminary versions were examined by a group of official experts from central banks and Ministries of Finance. The present volume is published under the responsibility of the Secretary-General. The views expressed therein are those of the authors and do not necessarily represent those of the OECD or its Member governments.

This study was finalized in mid-1984.

---

1. See *Monetary Policy in Japan* (1972); *Monetary Policy in Italy* (1973); *Monetary Policy in Germany* (1973); *Monetary Policy in the United States* (1974); *Monetary Policy in France* (1974).

2. United States, Japan, Germany, France, United Kingdom, Italy, Canada, Belgium, Netherlands, Sweden.

Also available

BUDGET FINANCING AND MONETARY CONTROL (March 1982)
(11 82 01 1) ISBN 92-64-12290-7 124 pages   £5.80   US$13.00   F58.00

MONETARY TARGETS AND INFLATION CONTROL (July 1979)
(11 79 05 1) ISBN 92-64-11963-9 102 pages   £4.60   US$9.50   F38.00

Prices charged at the OECD Publications Office.

*THE OECD CATALOGUE OF PUBLICATIONS and supplements will be sent free of charge
on request addressed either to OECD Publications Office,
2, rue André-Pascal, 75775 PARIS CEDEX 16, or to the OECD Sales Agent in your country.*

CONTENTS

ANNEXES

6

I

INTRODUCTION

The shift from fixed exchange rates to generalized floating during the early 1970s was expected to reduce balance of payments constraints and provide the monetary authorities of major OECD countries with more independence in the conduct of policy than had existed previously. It was hoped that, by relieving the authorities of the commitment to maintain pre-announced parities, monetary policy could be oriented directly toward the attainment of domestic objectives. The experience of the past ten years, however, has not fully borne out this hope. The slow adjustment of trade flows to exchange rate changes and the ability of international financial markets to generate very large movements of capital between countries have meant that exchange rates have been subject to much stronger and more erratic movements than had been envisaged by advocates of floating. These pressures on exchange rates have often resulted in unanticipated costs, leading the authorities to reassess, and in many cases to change, their policy stance.

Monetary authorities have been confronted by two sorts of economic conflicts when policy has been oriented directly toward domestic objectives. First, in many countries the constraint on using monetary policy to support economic activity and employment, which under fixed exchange rates had been the balance of payments, re-emerged under floating rates as an inflation constraint. Thus expansionary policies can result in depreciation and rising import prices which quickly lead to faster increases in domestic prices. Second, when a choice of priorities at the macroeconomic level has been made and monetary policy set accordingly, the resulting exchange rate response has sometimes threatened to lead to resource misallocation and structural distortions. In particular, where monetary policy has taken a strongly anti-inflationary stance, some countries have seen their exchange rates rise to apparently unsustainably high levels. While this has contributed to the desired reduction in inflation, it has placed a large part of the cost of such a policy on those industries most exposed to international competition. However, such costs are sometimes a necessary and inevitable part of the adjustment process and attempts to avoid them may ultimately lead to even greater costs. The main aim of this study is to examine the extent to which the appropriate use of intermediate targets can reduce the costs of instability of output and inflation in relation to the authorities' medium-term objectives for these variables.

If the authorities were able to ascertain the sources of pressure on exchange rates, monetary aggregates, interest rates and other monetary policy indicators, as well as to know the impact and lag profile of the effects of changes in policy instruments, "fine tuning" through a complex set of measures designed to affect final objectives directly would be possible. However, the sources of pressure, (e.g. changes in fiscal stance, foreign monetary policy, wage bargaining, etc.) at any point in time are extremely difficult to determine.

Moreover, the impact of policy changes has a very complex interrelationship with the formation of market expectations about inflation, exchange rates, etc., which may give rise to unstable policy instrument multipliers. These difficulties have led the monetary authorities in many countries to abandon "fine tuning" in favour of more operational policy rules. Since the authorities are unable to affect the final objectives of policy directly, they seek to adjust available instruments to achieve *intermediate targets,* which they believe will influence the economy in a predictable manner in the medium term.

In recent years monetary policies within the Group of Ten and Switzerland have been guided mainly by the adoption of explicit intermediate targets for the money supply and/or the exchange rate. In practice the authorities in most countries have tended to operate a blend of intermediate objectives without strong commitment to a single target particularly (see Annex I), since each may be associated with different costs in the face of alternative pressures. However, while it will be helpful to review such practices, the impact of monetary policy on exchange rates and other variables is best handled at a conceptual level by postulating alternative economic shocks which have been important in the past, and analysing how resulting pressures are conditioned by whether the authorities have been attempting to "peg" the money supply or the external value of the domestic currency.

Interest rate targets, which have at times been important, are not specifically considered. Targets for monetary aggregates have, in most of the larger economies covered in the study, reflected a medium-term orientation of policy towards domestic inflation control. Exchange rate targets, on the other hand, have been implemented mainly where the traded goods sector is particularly important. Operationally these are generally formulated in nominal terms. However, over periods long enough for domestic costs and prices to diverge from those prevailing abroad, such a policy requires the authorities to choose between (*i*) holding the nominal exchange rate, ultimately forcing adjustment on to prices in domestic labour and goods markets; and (*ii*) adjusting the nominal rate to maintain a desired real exchange rate. While the latter practice has not often been formally acknowledged as central bank policy, considerations of competitiveness have frequently led to its implementation in practice. Consequently, the implications of pursuing a real exchange rate objective, which may differ from a nominal target under certain circumstances, are sometimes considered.

Sterilized intervention, whereby the effects of exchange market intervention on domestic monetary conditions are neutralized by offsetting open market operations, permits authorities, in principle, to pursue monetary and exchange rate targets simultaneously. However, whether or not sterilized intervention is an effective means of influencing the exchange rate is highly contentious. The possibilities depend on the degree to which interest-bearing debt denominated in different currencies are substitutes, an issue which is discussed in some detail in Annex II. If such assets in wealth holders' portfolios are imperfect substitutes, then relative asset supplies and currency preferences will affect exchange rates through their influence on risk premia. In this case sterilized intervention, which directly impacts on relative asset supplies, can be effective. With perfect substitutability, on the other hand, such intervention will have no influence on exchange rates because risk premia are always zero. For the most part empirical evidence suggests that risk premia have a zero or at best very small impact on exchange rates (see Annex II). Consequently, in subsequent analysis it is typically assumed that fixing the exchange rate will require the money supply not to be pegged. However, in the case of certain "shocks" (e.g. a shift in currency preferences) it is assumed explicitly that assets are imperfect substitutes and the implications of pursuing a policy of sterilized intervention are analysed.

In Part II of the study broader operational and economic considerations which, in practice, have influenced the choice between monetary aggregates and exchange rates as intermediate targets are discussed. However, having selected the target that the authorities believe will best serve the achievement of their ultimate objectives, the economy may be subject to unforeseen shocks. The costs associated with these shocks will differ according to the intermediate target in place at the time, and to the type of shock in question. These issues are analysed in Part III. The shocks examined include (*i*) domestic wage push; (*ii*) a shift in domestic fiscal policy; (*iii*) shifts in money demand functions; (*iv*) shifts in currency preferences for interest-bearing debt; (*v*) changes in foreign monetary policy; and (*vi*) an oil price shock. Costs are defined in terms of a simple macroeconomic objective function of minimizing deviations from medium-term final objectives for inflation and output growth. Provided the authorities have sufficient information to identify particular shocks, deviations from such medium-term goals may be minimized by altering the priority accorded to the target in place at the time or, where the costs of an alternative target are likely to be ultimately greater, by sticking to the target regardless of the short-run costs. The main implications for the conduct of monetary policy are drawn out in Part IV. Finally, some concluding observations are made in Part V.

II

MONETARY AGGREGATES AND EXCHANGE RATES AS INTERMEDIATE TARGETS

A. OPERATIONAL CONSIDERATIONS

The choice of an intermediate target on which to orient the conduct of monetary policy has obvious operational advantages provided that:

– it can be controlled with available policy instruments; and
– the authorities have up-to-date and reliable information about its past and present behaviour.

These issues are examined for monetary and exchange rate targets, and may constitute important qualifications to some of the implications drawn from the analysis in Parts III and IV.

i) Monetary aggregates

Monetary aggregates have given rise to some difficulties with respect to the above operational requirements. The aggregate in question may, for various reasons related to institutional arrangements for the conduct of monetary policy, be difficult to control[1]. Furthermore, the existence of a stable relationship between money and nominal income may depend on not using the aggregate in question as an intermediate target. If the authorities move to control it, a process of disintermediation may occur which would change the meaning of the measured aggregate. This has, at times, been particularly apparent in countries such as the United Kingdom, France, Italy and Japan where quantitative controls such as credit ceilings have been employed, but it is not confined to such countries.

Finally, statistics on monetary aggregates are usually compiled with a lag, so that up-to-date information on their most recent behaviour is not always available. Even where very short-term (e.g. weekly) figures can be obtained, they are frequently unreliable in that distortions caused by seasonal factors and/or structural change may be overridingly important. As recent experience in the United States has shown, such figures may not have sufficient informational content to be a sound basis for making policy decisions. The above factors have frequently been the basis of suggestions that monetary targets may not always be operationally efficient, so that an alternative intermediate target may need to be employed.

ii) *Nominal exchange rates*

As an observable price set in a financial market the exchange rate has some operational advantages in terms of up-to-date information. However, on a day-to-day basis the difficulty of distinguishing between high frequency "noise" and genuine information about exchange rate trends should not be underestimated. Nevertheless, if the authorities are prepared to abandon the scope for implementing independent monetary policy aimed at directly influencing domestic objectives, essentially allowing external developments to determine domestic monetary conditions, the exchange rate can in most circumstances be controlled (see Part III). By intervening in the exchange market and/or adjusting other policy instruments in support, the authorities may fairly readily achieve pre-determined objectives for the nominal exchange rate, provided they are not manifestly inconsistent with macro-economic fundamentals. In circumstances where major trade and financial linkages are with a country (or countries) pursuing stable policies, attaching the domestic economy to such an environment by fixing the exchange rate may be a more operationally efficient way to ensure monetary stability than attempting to achieve a target for a domestic money or credit aggregate. The decision to form the European Monetary System (EMS) for example, owed much to these considerations in view of Germany's comparatively successful performance during the 1970s.

B. ECONOMIC CONSIDERATIONS

In operational terms exchange rate targets arguably have some advantages over monetary targets. On economic grounds, however, these advantages are less obvious, since intermediate target variables must also have a clearly defined and stable relationship with the final objectives of policy.

i) *Motivation for targeting monetary aggregates*

In recent years inflation control has been accorded a high priority in virtually all OECD countries. A consensus has emerged that inflationary pressures should not be accommodated by the expansion of money and/or credit if the rate of increase of prices is to be reduced in the longer run, and consequently intermediate targets have been set for the rate of growth of relevant monetary aggregates[2]. Previously, monetary policy had tended to focus on interest rates, which influence the economy through their impact on the demand for goods and services. However, stable relationships between interest rates and the demand for goods proved difficult to identify. Moreover, in a period of changing inflation expectations the anticipated *real* interest rate may be subject to changes which are not easily observed by the authorities. Discretionary changes in *nominal* interest rates tended to be insufficiently flexible as a consequence of institutional and political constraints, and frequently resulted in measures being taken which were either inappropriate or "too late". Since policy-makers gave only secondary attention to the behaviour of money and credit aggregates, inflation often became significantly worse before the authorities moved firmly towards restraint.

The usefulness of controlling the rate of growth of a monetary aggregate derives from the assertion that the demand for money, which depends upon nominal income and a few other variables, is more stable than the interest elasticity of the demand for goods and services[3]. Variations in the quantity of money are held to lead to corresponding variations in money income, although these effects may be spread out over a considerable period of time. Real aggregate supply of goods and services is seen as inelastic to nominal income in the longer run, so that monetary growth will eventually tend to determine the rate of inflation. Most of the evidence suggests that the lags involved in this process are long and also variable, so that monetary targeting is most suitably oriented towards medium-term inflation objectives. The relationships involved are too uncertain to warrant policy activism in the short run. Additional benefits of monetary targeting are purported to be the reduction of destabilizing expectations about inflation, which may provide a more suitable environment for wage negotiations, investment decisions, etc. Finally, the switch to monetary targeting reduced, to some extent, many of the institutional constraints leading to interest rate inflexibility. The automatic adjustment of interest rates in the face of real shocks will tend to stabilize the economy, avoiding unnecessary delays associated with an interest-rate-oriented policy.

ii) *Motivation for targeting exchange rates*

The exchange rate directly influences prices and/or profitability of traded goods and services. It is a *relative* price, and as such affects the allocation of resources over the medium term. The impact of sustained movements of the exchange rate on the competitive position of domestic industry vis-à-vis foreign industry in both domestic and foreign markets is the key transmission mechanism. The prosperity of industries most exposed to foreign competition is affected relative to other industries and in absolute terms, and factor shares will tend to shift. An undervalued exchange rate may lead to a transitory period of high profitability in the traded goods sector, possibly causing some enterprises to persist when underlying structural considerations suggest that they should contract: an overvalued exchange rate may have the reverse effects. To the extent that current profitability influences expectations about the future, investment decisions may also be affected. This may lead to under or over-investment in the traded goods sector, so that deviations of the exchange rate from levels which are sustainable in the long run may lead to a misallocation of *fixed* capital: the structure of production may become inappropriate to market shares in world trade that are likely to prevail when the exchange rate returns to a more normal level. It may also become inappropriate to the structure of domestic demand that would prevail in periods of a healthy macro-economy. Such developments may lead to structural distortions for considerable periods of time, so that some small open economies prefer to target the exchange rate.

In the short run, structural considerations may also arise as a consequence of exchange rate *volatility*. This relates less to the actual behaviour of the exchange rate than to uncertainty about its future development. It is frequently asserted that short-run fluctuations in the exchange rate are a problem for firms engaged in international business, either as a consequence of exchange risk, or because of the expense of forward cover. If this were the case, it could lead to a lower level of trade, and to a commensurately inferior allocation of resources. However, empirical findings in this area have generally tended to show that[4]:

 - transactions costs rise in periods of exchange rate volatility, but these are relatively small in absolute terms; and
 - while volatility may create some uncertainty about longer-term trends in the exchange rate, significant effects on international trade have never been successfully identified.

Short-run movements in the exchange rate may also induce changes in the price level. Indeed, a possibility exists that short-run exchange rate variability may exacerbate inflation if depreciations are translated quickly into higher prices and wages, whereas appreciations do not have a symmetric effect. Wage earners, for example, may react strongly to protect real earnings following depreciations, but refuse to accept smaller wage increases following appreciations. Econometric evidence suggests that these asymmetries would not normally be substantial in the case of the United Kingdom[5]. While some evidence exists for a weak "ratchet effect" for non-oil imports in the United States, this hypothesis was not supported by the data in respect to domestic prices[6]. There is likewise little conclusive empirical evidence on this issue for other countries. This finding would seem reasonable on *a priori* grounds. Most recent literature suggests that price behaviour in factor and product markets is characterized by "stickiness", or inertia, in the way they adjust and hence will not be importantly affected by short-run fluctuations in exchange rates that are expected to be reversed[7]. This paper is concerned with more sustained movements of the exchange rate rather than short-run volatility as such.

iii) *Monetary targets, exchange rate objectives and inflation control*

Even in respect of sustained movements it should be noted that the exchange rate will not generally influence inflation independently of the rate of growth of monetary aggregates in the longer run. An exchange-rate-induced increase in the price level, for a given monetary target, will reduce real money balances, increase interest rates and dampen domestic demand, hence putting downward pressure on prices. This effect may take some time to operate, depending on the flexibility of markets, the extent of real wage "resistance", and the way in which price expectations are formed. But in the longer run it will tend to dominate. Consequently, if the objective function of the authorities includes the control of inflation over the longer run, some attempt to contain the rate of growth of the money supply will be required. It should be noted in this context, however, that a depreciating exchange rate may be perceived as a symptom of inflationary monetary policy even where the reasons for depreciation lie elsewhere. In these circumstances inflationary expectations could deteriorate and may constitute a valid argument for stabilizing the exchange rate in the short run, while adjusting monetary policy over a longer period. To the extent that actual prices are affected by movements in the exchange rate in the short run, they may, where a monetary target is in place, be translated into unnecessary costs in the form of lost output.

C. COUNTRY PRACTICES[8]

To a large extent the amount of emphasis given to the exchange rate in the policy formulation process is conditioned by the degree of "openness" of economies in terms of the relative size of their traded goods sector. At one extreme, the relatively small share of foreign trade in GNP in the United States and the reserve currency status of the dollar have meant that US authorities frequently pursued a policy of "benign neglect" of the exchange rate, avoiding intervention on the foreign exchange markets and directing monetary policy towards domestic objectives. In recent years this has been towards inflation control, with the Federal Reserve seeking to control the money supply by operating on non-borrowed reserves. The exchange rate has served primarily as an *information variable*. For example, the depreciation of the dollar in November 1978 provided information that excessive inflationary pressures were developing which, in turn, led to the adoption of restrictive monetary measures.

At the other extreme some countries have adopted the exchange rate as a fairly *explicit target* for policy – aiming to stabilize parities, particularly vis-a-vis the Deutschemark. These include the EMS countries France, Italy, the Netherlands and Belgium, but also other small European countries such as Sweden. Within this group the Netherlands, and to some extent Belgium, pursue a "hard currency" option whereby fixing the exchange rate vis-a-vis the

Deutschemark is normally given priority in formulating monetary policy, and domestic inflation is forced to adjust to the relative low rate in Germany. Depreciation against the DM would tend to increase domestic costs. This approach has a number of operational advantages, which have been discussed above. Moreover, provided dominant countries pursue stable policies, the adoption of such an approach by a small country will tend to permit stable developments to be imported from abroad. This will imply some convergence in performance with major trading partners, but differences may still arise if the economy is subject to various domestic "shocks" – in particular, increased fiscal spending financed by domestic bank credit expansion may be directed at achieving independent objectives for supporting output and employment. This has often been the case in Sweden, where the authorities, as a consequence, have had periodically to devalue the exchange rate in light of domestic requirements.

Amongst the countries targeting the exchange rate, France and Italy are relatively larger in size and attempt also to achieve objectives for domestic money and credit aggregates (M2 and total domestic credit, respectively). The requirement to intervene to manage the exchange rate may lead to inconsistencies with domestic objectives. These may be reconciled in the short run by resort to sterilization operations, quantitative controls on both domestic credit expansion and the foreign exchange market, and compensatory financing. In the longer run, however, such inconsistencies have typically been reconciled by an abandonment of either the exchange rate or domestic monetary policy objectives. In 1976/77 domestic credit expansion was severely squeezed in both countries in order to achieve exchange rate objectives. Since the inception of the EMS both countries have, on a number of occasions, required realignments of central rates vis-à-vis the Deutschemark.

The remainder of the countries covered in the survey use the exchange rate primarily as an *indicator* for monetary policy: Japan, Germany, the United Kingdom, Canada and Switzerland. All have formulated monetary policy in terms of targets for domestic money aggregates, but developments at home and abroad have frequently led to unwanted movements of the exchange rate. Japan, Germany and Switzerland pursued tighter monetary policies than those prevailing abroad from the mid 1970s. This resulted in the trend appreciation of their respective currencies, which reached a climax in 1977/78. Real exchange rates appreciated to the point where they were considered to be in conflict with the ultimate goals of the authorities, and precipitated important changes in policy. In particular, intervention in Germany and Switzerland led to a considerable overshooting of their respective monetary targets. In Japan, on the other hand, heavy intervention was successfully sterilized. Similarly, tighter aggregates-oriented monetary policy to reduce inflation contributed to the real appreciation of sterling from 1977 to 1981, which also indicated the desirability of some moderation of monetary policy to reduce the exchange rate.

Canada and Switzerland are somewhat special cases in that they are closely linked through trade and finance to the United States and Germany, respectively. To avoid depreciation-induced inflation, Canada has frequently adjusted its interest rates in line with movements of rates in the United States. In the period since October 1979 this led to fluctuations in monetary aggregates in the short run, although over longer periods the targets for M1 were generally met. Difficulties in meeting targets mainly arose after 1981, when financial innovations led to distortions in M1[9]. Switzerland is even smaller than Canada, but has a large number of migrant workers which reduce the constraint on policy posed by unemployment, and has generally been more able to orient domestic monetary policy towards inflation control. Since Switzerland's major trading partner is Germany, the pursuance of similar ultimate objectives has led to a *de facto* co-ordination of monetary policies and a reasonable convergence of economic performance which permits sharp movements of their bilateral exchange rate largely to be avoided.

III

THE BENEFITS AND COSTS
OF ALTERNATIVE INTERMEDIATE TARGETS
IN THE FACE OF EXOGENOUS "SHOCKS"

This Part abstracts from the operational issues and specific country practices discussed above, and attempts conceptually to assess the relative costs of pursuing intermediate targets for domestic monetary aggregates and the exchange rate in the face of various exogenous shocks. The objective function of the authorities is assumed to be purely macroeconomic in nature: to control inflation over the longer run and to minimize fluctuations in output. It is assumed that the economy is moving along a path consistent with the medium-term objectives of the authorities when it is subjected to the shock in question. Macroeconomic costs are taken as any movement (divergence from the desired medium-term path) of output and/or prices in the short run. Any initial disequilibrium conditions (excess unemployment or inflation) are therefore abstracted from. It is assumed that foreign monetary policies may be taken as exogenous, unless otherwise specified, and that prices in goods and labour markets are relatively "sticky", whereas financial markets clear more quickly.

Domestic and external shocks will lead to different *ex ante* pressures on the exchange rate. Annex II of the study surveys the major alternative exchange rate models and the econometric evidence. The assumptions of the basic models, which are discussed more fully in the Annex, include:

- The Simple Monetary Model: purchasing power parity is assumed to hold at all points in time; expected depreciation is equal to the expected inflation differential; the interest rate differential is equal to the expected change in the exchange rate; and the price level adjusts to clear the money market. The relationship between the supplies of domestic and foreign money relative to the demands for them determine the exchange rate.
- The "Sticky" Price Monetary Model: as with the simple monetary model, interest-bearing assets are perfect substitutes, so that the interest rate differential in favour of the domestic currency is equal to the expected rate of depreciation at all points in time, but a number of new assumptions are introduced to obtain the result that the exchange rate may overshoot. Purchasing power parity holds only in the long run; expected depreciation adjusts (regressively) depending on movements of the equilibrium real exchange rate (that consistent with the long-run equilibrium current account balance); price adjustments in goods markets are "sticky", and the interest rate moves to clear the money market in the short run. The spot exchange rate adjusts relative to its expected level to ensure that international capital markets remain in equilibrium in the short run.

15

Table 1. **Exchange rate impacts of changes in fundamental variables under alternative théories**[a]

	Simple monetary model	« Sticky » price monetary model	Portfolio balance model
Rise in domestic price level relative to foreign prices	−	−	−
Rise in expected inflation relative to foreign inflation	−	−	−
Rise in domestic interest rate relative to foreign rate	−	+	+
Rise in expected future real exchange rate	+	+	+
Rise in risk premium on foreign currency	0	0	+

a) + indicates appreciation ; − indicates depreciation and 0 denotes no effect. These signs assume that other variables may be taken as given when considering a change in any one.

- The Portfolio Balance Model: adopts similar assumptions to the overshooting model, but instead of assuming that the interest rate differential is equal to the expected change in the exchange rate, assets denominated in different currencies are considered not to be perfect substitutes, i.e. interest rate parity is modified by the inclusion of a risk premium, which depends on currency preferences and relative asset supplies. The role of the latter in exchange rate determination distinguishes it from the other models.

The impacts on the exchange rate of changes in the most important variables directly relevant for these models are summarized in Table 1. In most cases the impacts are of the same sign, with two noteworthy exceptions:

  i)   an exogenous rise in the interest differential in favour of domestic currency causes the exchange rate to depreciate in the monetary model, via the opportunity cost of the demand for money, in contrast to the positive relationship between interest and exchange rates in the other two models; and

  ii) currency preferences and supplies of interest-bearing debt play no role in the monetary and overshooting models, but are potentially important in the portfolio balance model[10].

The first of these qualitative differences is not particularly important, since most evidence suggests that purchasing power parity does not hold at all points in time (see Annex II), giving some grounds to ignore the simple monetary model. The second point, however, is more problematic.

Imperfect substitutability implies that supplies of assets denominated in different currencies and wealth-holders preferences have a role in the determination of exchange rates. This issue may be important for policy, since, in general, supplies of assets denominated in different currencies are affected by:

- current account deficits;
- official intervention; and
- budget deficits.

16

The existence of risk premia provides a theoretical rationale for sterilized intervention, a process which operates to change the currency composition of assets. Aside from this possibility of a role for currency preferences and asset supplies, however, issues about the appropriateness of monetary and exchange rate targets in the face of shocks to the economy may be analysed in a broad macroeconomic framework which does not depend on any particular exchange rate theory.

A. DOMESTIC WAGE PUSH

If a monetary target is in place (money supply pegged) and the nominal rate is permitted to float, a number of adjustment mechanisms will be set into motion by a wage increase. The increase in the wage/price level will cause real money balances to fall, interest rates will rise and output will decline. Higher interest rates will tend to attract foreign capital, although this may be partly offset to the extent that the deterioration of purchasing power parity causes the expected level of the exchange rate to depreciate[11]. The deflation of real demand will have a favourable affect on the current account, whereas the adverse relative cost movement will have an unfavourable impact[12]. The exchange rate will tend to appreciate, in the absence of intervention, as a consequence of the incipient capital inflow. This will be higher *(a)* the more sensitive are capital flows to movements in interest rates, and *(b)* if the current account improves in the short run, since the exchange rate must then appreciate to a sufficiently high level for the *ex post* position to be one of net capital outflow. The rise of the nominal exchange rate will reinforce the real appreciation, and the output loss. The deflation of demand will continue to the point where real wage resistence is reduced and relative prices are restored to normal levels. The nominal exchange rate will eventually return to its original level, but this may take a very long time.

A good example of this type of difficulty was the general breakdown of the pay policy in the United Kingdom in 1979 and the implementation of large public sector wage increases, while aggregates-oriented monetary policy was directed toward controlling inflation. A great many factors were at work, including oil-related influences, but these exogenous wage pressures contributed substantially to the very tight stance of policy and the subsequent upward pressure on the exchange rate. The combination of tight monetary policy and the real appreciation of sterling led to significant costs in the form of lost output and increased unemployment, and eventually led to a shift in emphasis towards a broader approach which gave some weight to the evolution of the real exchange rate (see the note on the United Kingdom in Annex I).

If countries are pursuing a nominal exchange rate target, the severity of the initial impact on output of falling real money balances will depend on whether or not the overall balance of payments improves. If it does, upward pressure on the exchange rate will be offset with a monetary expansion. This will accommodate the wage increase. The appreciation of the real exchange rate will discriminate against the traded goods sector, but by less than if the nominal exchange rate had been permitted to rise. The smaller appreciation of the real exchange rate and the higher level of real money balances imply that the fall in output will be less than under a monetary target. However, the same real adjustment (unemployment in labour markets) would ultimately be necessary to restore relative prices at the given nominal exchange rate (for the same initial degree of wage resistance) as under a monetary target. Since more of this adjustment would have to occur via relative price effects on the current account, it will tend to take longer than the case where the wage shock runs into a target for the money supply, deflating the economy more quickly via reduced real money balances. Consequently, it seems likely that the real exchange rate will remain distorted for a longer period. If, alternatively, the overall balance of payments deteriorates, official intervention to offset downward pressure on the exchange rate would result in a monetary contraction and greater output loss, forcing adjustment through the real sector more quickly. This latter possibility, however, seems less likely.

For a given monetary target the immediate output loss caused by domestic wage push may be increased or reduced in the very short run by stabilizing the real exchange rate through a policy of sterilized intervention to depreciate the nominal rate, provided that interest-bearing debt denominated in different currencies are imperfect substitutes. Real money balances will fall as import prices rise. Moreover, real wage resistance is particularly important in some countries and may be enhanced by widespread formal or informal indexation agreements as in Italy and France, as well as in some of the smaller economies, particularly Belgium and Sweden. A fall in the exchange rate may quickly induce further feedback effects on wage and price increases. The short-run impact on output will depend on:

- the size of the further feedback effects of devaluation on prices in the short run; and
- the elasticity of demand for traded goods with respect to the real exchange rate.

If the elasticity of domestic demand with respect to relative prices is large and the feedback effects of nominal devaluation on domestic costs and prices are small, the attempt to stabilize the real exchange rate may reduce output loss for a given monetary target. On the other hand, where the demand elasticity is small and the feedback effects of devaluation on prices is large, the gain in output stability achieved by a constant real exchange rate may be more than offset by the demand reducing effects on real balances[13]. For a given nominal money supply, the cost effect would lead to a *relatively* more important squeeze on real money balances. If, however, assets denominated in different currencies are perfect substitutes, a policy of sterilized intervention will be ineffective, as discussed above.

If real exchange rate stabilization is pursued without sterilization, monetary accommodation will always enhance output stability in the short run, provided there are no destabilizing expectational effects[14]. The higher are the cost-indexation effects induced by exchange rate changes, the greater will be the degree of monetary accommodation required to stabilize output, and the more destabilizing the policy will be for domestic prices. It is precisely in these circumstances, moreover, that "vicious circle" mechanisms tend to arise, whereby inflation and devaluation reinforce each other. This price instability trade-off may be further complicated if inflationary expectations and/or the credibility of government policy are themselves affected. A policy of indexing the real exchange rate combined with monetary accommodation would probably lead to an unstable situation which would eventually require the approach to be abandoned, and could result in an even larger fall in output in the medium term.

To summarize, domestic wage push is likely to result in short-run output loss unless a policy of stabilizing the real exchange rate is accompanied by monetary accommodation. Such a policy, on the other hand, is likely to have substantial costs in the form of an acceleration of inflation in the longer run. A policy of sterilized intervention will have the least cost, but depends on the uncertain assumption that risk premia are an important determinant of exchange rate movements. Maintaining a money supply or nominal exchange rate target will be more likely to force adjustment through the labour market in the longer run. Such adjustment is likely to be completed more quickly under a monetary target, but with greater

18

initial output loss. An exchange rate target will result in less initial output loss, but real adjustment will be delayed and the real exchange rate will remain distorted for a longer period.

B. FISCAL IMPULSE

In order to abstract from the case of an accommodating expansion of bank credit, the fiscal impulse considered is a sustained increase in general government spending on non-traded goods, financed by issuing debt. The demand for goods will rise, and there will be a tendency for interest rates to increase in order to effect a transfer of funds from private lenders which, in turn, will act to stabilize output. To the extent that interest rates in the rest of the world are unaffected, this will also tend to divert private borrowers abroad and attract foreign lenders to domestic asset markets. The increased demand for goods will be met partly through imports, causing the current account to deteriorate, as well as through increased output. In an *ex ante* sense, capital inflows may exceed the deterioration of the current balance, provided that they are sufficiently interest sensitive, resulting in upward pressure on the exchange rate. The commitment to a monetary target would result in an appreciation of the nominal (and real) exchange rate in order to restore equilibrium in the foreign exchange market. The higher the real appreciation the less will be the impact of the fiscal stimulus on output.

The commitment to an exchange rate target would require the authorities to intervene by selling domestic currency, expanding the money supply. This would essentially accommodate the increased demand for goods resulting in a higher level of money balances and eventually to a depreciation of the real exchange rate. Nominal income would be more sensitive to the rise in the budget deficit than under a monetary target and, with sticky prices, would be most likely to take the form of increased output in the first instance. Depending on the degree of capacity utilization and the nature of inflation expectations, however, the acceleration of monetary growth will eventually cause wages and prices to rise, setting into motion real adjustment through reduced competitiveness. As discussed in reference to a wage shock, this process is likely to take longer than under a monetary target.

If capital is less mobile internationally, interest rates will have to rise by a greater amount in order to displace private borrowers from the capital markets so that the increased budget deficit can be financed under a monetary target. The private sector will economise on its holdings of money balances, so that the income effects under a monetary target will be higher and the exchange rate lower than in the mobile capital case. If the *ex ante* capital inflow at the initial exchange rate is less than the current account deterioration, the exchange rate may actually have to depreciate in order to ensure that the latter is financed. In this case the commitment to an exchange rate target could result in less fluctuation in nominal income than under a monetary target, since the real exchange rate would be higher and the level of money balances lower i.e. the multiplier for nominal income could be correspondingly lower. However, it is likely that this case is of little practical relevance. In the past decade the growing integration of capital markets and high volatility of capital flows imply considerable capital mobility, so that a rise in the budget deficit financed by selling bonds (pegged money supply) would be most likely to cause the exchange rate to appreciate. Indeed, the interest rate implications of high budget deficits in the United States have been a major factor in explaining the strength of the dollar during 1982 and 1983. (See note on the United States in Annex I).

If interest-bearing assets denominated in different currencies are imperfect substitutes, there is a further channel through which a fiscal expansion may cause the exchange rate to be lower than it would otherwise have been. The increased supply of government debt and its possible transfer to foreigners through the current account deficit can imply that wealth holders at home and abroad are required to hold a greater quantity of bonds denominated in domestic currency. The risk premium on foreign currency assets will fall and the exchange rate must be lower for the domestic currency assets to be held. Under an exchange rate target, sterilization will further increase the supply of domestic currency assets and may, via its impact on the risk premium, tend partly to offset the *ex ante* upward pressure on the exchange rate. Again, however, the practical importance of imperfect substitutability may be limited, as was pointed out above.

To summarize, a monetary target will typically result in less fluctuation of nominal income than an exchange rate target in the face of fluctuations of the budget deficit, and will normally imply a temporary distortion of the real exchange rate. An exchange rate target, by accommodating the increased demand for goods, will imply more effects on output and subsequently prices. The latter may lead to a longer distortion of the real exchange rate. This conclusion may be modified to the extent that assets denominated in different currencies are imperfect substitutes, or if administrative controls are effective in imposing impediments to the mobility of capital.

C. UPWARD SHIFT OF MONEY DEMAND

An upward shift of the demand function for domestic money (e.g. transactions deposits) reduces long-run velocity and, in the absence of monetary accommodation, will result in upward pressure on interest rates – a qualitative result which is identical to a wage shock or an increased demand for goods. As before, this will attract capital from the rest of the world. Under a monetary target the exchange rate will appreciate in both nominal and real terms – again qualitatively similar to an increased demand for goods. However, in this case there is no increased absorption to cause the current account to deteriorate, and nominal income unambiguously falls. An exchange rate target, on the other hand, will lead the monetary authorities to sell domestic currency on the exchange market, expanding the money supply. This will accommmodate the shift in money demand, serving to stabilize income. Sterilization, by not permitting the money supply to rise, would tend to maintain pressure on interest and exchange rates. It has been argued that the demand for money function has shifted upwards in the United States towards the end of 1981, so that part of the monetary acceleration in the United States in 1982/83 will not be inflationary and will be associated with a permanent downward shift in velocity[15].

D. SHIFTS IN CURRENCY PREFERENCES

If assets denominated in different currencies are imperfect substitutes, a shift of foreign resident preferences away from foreign bonds (not money) in favour of domestic-currency-denominated securities will tend to reduce the home interest rate and create an excess demand for money for a given money supply target. The risk premium on foreign currency asssets will rise and that on domestic securities will fall. For equilibrium to be restored the domestic currency must appreciate, increasing expected future depreciation. The excess demand for money and the real appreciation of the exchange rate will tend to have a negative impact on output. An exchange rate target, on the other hand, will leave output unchanged. Intervention will cause the overall size of domestic currency assets to rise, since, in this case, it may be conducted with sterilization operations. This will be equivalent to a sale of home securities and a purchase of foreign securities, exactly compensating the source of pressure. This operation would avoid the necessity of permitting the exchange rate to rise and/or the deliberate inducement of falling interest rates via non-sterilized intervention.

It is possible that shifts in currency preferences have been a factor determining exchange rate movements in previous historical episodes, notwithstanding the difficulties referred to above of identifying their importance at an empirical level. For example, it has been argued that upward pressure on the Deutschemark, the Swiss franc and the yen in 1978 was partly a consequence of diversification by dollar holders[16]. In recognizing this the authorities in these countries gave more emphasis to stabilizing the external value of their currencies and intervened heavily on the exchange markets. This led, as noted above, to a substantial overshooting of monetary targets in Germany and Switzerland, whereas Japan was more successful in sterilizing the intervention (see the Japanese, German and Swiss country notes of Annex I).

E.   FOREIGN INTEREST RATE PRESSURES

i)   *General considerations*

A sustained rise in foreign interest rates which does not simply reflect an increase in inflation expectations in that country will induce portfolio holders to substitute towards foreign assets and investors to reduce borrowing from abroad, leading *ex ante* to net capital outflows and/or downward pressure on the exchange rate. The extent of these *ex ante* pressures will depend upon the degree of integration in international capital markets. If priority were accorded to a monetary target, the exchange rate would depreciate to the extent necessary to maintain portfolio equilibrium. The implied depreciation of the real exchange rate will, after some period of time, lead to a rise in export demand, possibly increasing nominal income. The effect on prices would tend to be greater, and that on output commensurately smaller, the larger the effect of increased import prices on domestic wage demands. However, provided that such indexation effects are not too important, there are two reasons for supposing that these disadvantages may not be particularly great. First, the initial rise in foreign interest rates may have represented a contraction of aggregate demand abroad, which could have acted directly to reduce domestic exports. In this case a depreciation would simply be serving to sustain export demand which would otherwise have been lost. Second, any upward pressure on the general price index will interact with the monetary target to push the level of interest rates back towards those prevailing in the rest of the world in the longer run. If wage indexation effects are important, a domestic wage response could reduce real money balances, introducing the counter-intuitive possibility that the overall net effect on output could be contractionary regardless of floating exchange rates.

A policy of stabilizing the exchange rate would lead authorities to intervene, buying domestic currency and running down the level of international reserves. The domestic money supply would contract, reducing real money balances and the level of output, while pushing interest rates back into line with higher world rates. In this example policy is destabilizing in a contractionary sense, the effects of more restrictive policies abroad being imported directly into the domestic economy. However, in small open economies where the demand elasticity with respect to the real exchange rate is large, and/or where domestic wage indexation is important, the authorities may have little choice but to pursue such an approach. The stability of internal monetary developments in this case will inevitably be affected by policies being pursued by major trading partners.

ii) *Illustrative simulations*

The behaviour of US interest rates in late 1979 and the beginning of the 1980s has had important implications for exchange rates and/or monetary policies in other OECD countries – largely as a consequence of the importance of the dollar in trade and international finance. To illustrate the potential impact on exchange rates and interest rates in Europe, a simulation was conducted which assumes[17]:

- a shift in US monetary policy consistent with short-term interest rates declining to two percentage points lower than they would otherwise have been for three years;
- given money supply targets and floating exchange rates in all other OECD economies.

The main features of the results which are reported in Annex III (third year outcomes only) suggest that the US monetary expansion causes the current account to deteriorate and incipient capital outflows which, in turn, cause the effective exchange rate for the dollar to be lower by 6½ per cent by the end of the third year. Real GNP in the United States rises to be ¾ per cent higher as a consequence of lower interest rates and the depreciation of the exchange rate.

The implications of lower US interest rates for Europe vary considerably among countries, depending on size, openness and commitment to currency union arrangements within the EMS.

- The response of Germany to falling US interest rates is the most important channel of influence on Europe. The results suggest that German interest rates will fall to some extent, but the DM will nonetheless be likely to appreciate against the dollar. The effective exchange rate appreciates by 3 per cent by the end of the third year resulting in a small negative impact on output.
- This impact on Germany leads to differential strains within the EMS. Depending on the weight of Germany in each country's trade, *effective* exchange rates in some European countries (such as France and Belgium) may be subject to *downward* pressures.
- If, alternatively, the authorities in European countries respond by simultaneously intervening to fix nominal exchange rates, instability is forced on to domestic money supplies, implying differential impacts on inflation rates within the EMS.

These differential pressures illustrate the difficulties of pursuing currency union arrangements when third country effects (in this case stemming from the United States) are liable to be important. Since the dollar is an important invoicing currency for international trade, particularly with respect to oil, countries may have views on "appropriate" bilateral rates with the United States which conflict with EMS parities. In these circumstances choices and adjustments would have to be made, so that conditionality in the formulation of targets may be important.

The results of a simulated two point cut in German interest rates compared to what they would otherwise have been, assuming fully floating exchange rates, is also reported in Annex III. The effective exchange rate for the Deutschemark depreciates by 10 per cent by the end of the third year. European exchange rates appreciate against the Deutschemark and, in effective terms, lie within a range of 1½ to 4 per cent higher than the control (or baseline) simulation by the end of the third year. Italy, Switzerland and Sweden are more strongly affected because sympathetic market interest rate movements are insufficient to shelter the exchange markets from pressure. Over the relatively short horizon considered, floating exchange rates permit most countries to avoid the increased output and acceleration of inflation in Germany[18]. Such highly divergent movements of exchange rates would, however, be incompatible with parity bands within the EMS. If EMS countries were assumed to intervene to maintain parities vis-à-vis the depreciating Deutschemark, their domestic money supplies would be destabilized in an upward direction. This would also tend to force instability on to inflation and real activity in the EMS countries considered[19].

F.   AN OIL PRICE CHANGE

An oil price change (in this case a *fall* is considered) will tend to influence all OECD countries simultaneously, influencing many variables directly, and possibly inducing some of the various shocks discussed above. It is worth noting that from an international perspective, the same disturbance can appear as an entirely different shock to different countries. For example, a wage shock in one country may appear as a foreign monetary shock to other countries if it is not accommodated by faster monetary expansion. Since there is a large combination of possible disturbances which may be induced by an oil price fall, and any one of these combinations will appear different to different countries, an attempt to take them into account would prove highly intractable. Consequently, except where otherwise stated, the following discussion describing the adjustment process under alternative monetary regimes assumes an absence of the other shocks analysed above.

Assuming that prices of oil-substitutes respond sympathetically, an oil price fall will imply a direct positive effect on real incomes, both wages and profits, in the private non-energy sectors of OECD countries. Energy producing sectors, on the other hand, and governments (since tax revenues in most OECD countries are to varying degrees related to energy prices) will experience real income losses. These real income losses will be larger the more important the energy producing sectors. Those countries in which the losses exceed the gains will experience overall terms of trade (and hence real income) losses and conversely for those countries in which the gains exceed losses. Since the OECD is, on balance, an energy importer, the losses of oil exporters outside the OECD will exceed the gains of non-OECD oil importers.

In the absence of direct nominal wage responses to the fall in energy prices, short-run developments with which monetary policy must cope will depend on *(i)* the relative speeds with which the various gainers and losers adjust their real expenditure to the change in their real income; *(ii)* the impact of the associated financial adjustments made by the various sectors (and countries) as they adjust their expenditure; and *(iii)* the extent to which the changed pattern of expenditure and financial flows impact differentially on different countries.

Two factors in particular will be of importance with regard to *(i)* and *(ii)*. First, governments must make a choice about their responses to the changed budgetary situation. They may reduce their expenditure in line with their revenues, raise other taxes to replace the shortfall (transferring the income losses to the private sector), increase their borrowing, or some combination of these. Second, non-OECD oil producers, to the extent that they do not fully reduce their expenditures in line with their incomes, will generate a set of capital outflows from the OECD area, in the form of higher borrowing, reductions in existing assets or reduced lending due to lower surpluses. In effect, there will be a recycling of the reductions in oil producers' surpluses (or increases in their deficits).

In aggregate, any failure of expenditure to adjust to real income changes will be matched by counterpart financial flows which will influence credit markets. Thus any tendency for

23

gainers to adjust their expenditure to the change in real income faster than losers, which would have a direct expansionary impact on real demand, will be matched by a tendency for the associated financing needs to tighten credit markets, leading to further adjustment of aggregate expenditure. The reverse is true where losers adjust faster. Two other forces will influence developments: *(i)* the fall in energy prices will tend to lower the general price level in all countries, which, by itself, will work to raise real money supplies, lower the general level of interest rates, and hence encourage real expenditure; and *(ii)* any change in the general level of interest rates due to the induced financial flows will influence the demand for real money balances, and hence the velocity of money, in an accommodating manner. While the net effect of these interacting forces is likely to be small but expansionary (due to the impact of lower prices on real money supplies and the associated tendency for interest rates to be lower), the effect on each country, individually, may be substantial and either expansionary or deflationary. Consequently, in the absence of policy adjustments, there will be a tendency for exchange rates to move.

Under a regime of monetary targeting, the induced changes in financial flows will influence interest rates directly, setting up further adjustments in expenditure and generating further capital flows. Those countries for whom the net impact of these forces on demand for their exports, their own demand for imports, and capital flows, is such as to lead to an incipient balance of payments surplus will experience a higher exchange rate. In the absence of an increase in the demand for money, there will be an increase in demand for home output. The rise in the exchange rate will tend to reduce this by discouraging exports and encouraging import penetration. If an increase in the demand for money did occur (i.e. if interest rates were lower) the impact of the rising exchange rate on the general price level would tend to restore a balance. Conversely, countries experiencing falling exchange rates will find their exports encouraged and import penetration discouraged, while the impact on the price level lowers real balances.

Under a policy of fixing the weighted effective nominal exchange rate, a country experiencing a tendency toward surplus will intervene in the exchange market, allowing a faster monetary expansion which will accommodate higher demand. Monetary ease will allow domestic expenditure and imports to rise and/or it will permit interest rates, and hence capital inflows, to fall, so that the tendency toward surplus will stop. The levels of output and expenditure, however, will probably be higher. The only adjustment mechanism set into motion will be the tendency for higher demand to induce wage and price rises, which will have the effect of raising the real exchange rate. The ultimate adjustment in this case will therefore be the same as in the case of adherence to a monetary target. But in the latter case the adjustment is likely to be faster (because the exchange rate will adjust faster than money wages), to involve less transitory impact on output, and to entail a movement of the general level of prices in the opposite direction.

If the nominal exchange rate is fixed against the currency of some dominant country (or bloc of countries such as in the EMS arrangement) adjustment will depend importantly on developments in that country. If, for example, the dominant currency country experiences a tendency toward overall payments surplus, the smaller country may experience monetary deflation and a rising real exchange rate regardless of whether it faces higher or lower demand for home output. If the incipient impact of the oil price fall is expansionary, the rising real exchange rate and the slower monetary growth will reinforce each other, accelerating the adjustment process. On the other hand, if the initial tendency is deflationary, the immediate increase in the nominal exchange rate will mean that the price deflation required to achieve the necessary real depreciation of the exchange rate will be greater than in the case of a stable nominal effective exchange rate, by the extent of the nominal appreciation.

24

IV

IMPLICATIONS FOR THE CONDUCT
OF MONETARY POLICY

Table 2 summarizes the main benefits and costs of alternative intermediate targets in the face of the various shocks which were discussed in Part III[20]. If policy has a medium-term orientation and the main objective of the authorities is to minimize price and output disturbances, a money supply target combined with floating exchange rates will have considerable advantages when the economy is subjected to:

- wage disturbances;
- fluctuations in the budget deficit; and
- changes in foreign monetary policy.

The destabilization of inflation and inflation expectations will generally be avoided under a monetary target – whereas the endogeneity of money under an exchange rate target risks accommodating inflation pressures. Unnecessary output fluctuations will also be minimized. In the case of fluctuations in budget deficits and changes in foreign monetary policy these results are well known[21]. For a wage shock the output loss is that which is necessary to restore relative prices through reduced wage resistance.

Two qualifications to these propositions should be noted. First, real wage resistance will increase the output costs of pursuing a monetary target. A greater initial real adjustment will be required to achieve the appropriate set of relative prices for most of the above disturbances. In the case of a foreign monetary policy disturbance, real wage resistance can also reduce the degree of independence afforded by flexible exchange rates. For example, a rise in foreign interest rates, incipient capital outflows and exchange rate depreciation may lead to a nominal wage response to the fall in real wages in the domestic economy. Real balances will be lower and interest rates higher than they would otherwise have been, exerting more deflationary pressures. A second qualification is that movements of the real exchange rate under a monetary target, even where these are temporary, may result in structural distortions which persist after the exchange rate has returned to more "normal" levels. These structural concerns may be considered as more important than the simple medium-term macroeconomic objective function assumed above, particularly in economies which are small and closely linked with main trading partners.

An exchange rate target achieved through non-sterilized intervention has unambiguous advantages in the case of shifts in the demand for money function. It would be more appropriate to achieve an exchange rate target through sterilized intervention where pressures arise as a consequence of changes in preferences for interest-bearing debt denominated in

Table 2. **Macroeconomic benefits and costs of alternate policy targets in the face of selected shocks**

	Wage shock	Fiscal impulse	Upward shift of money demand	Increased foreign preference for domestic currency assets	Rise in foreign interest rate
Monetary Target	*Benefits* : inflation stabilizing, rapid real adjustment to reduce wage resistance and restore real exchange rate. *Costs* : probable temporary appreciation of real exchange rate.	*Benefits* : stabilizes short-run output and price effects. *Costs* : short-run output loss and real exchange appreciation.	*Benefits* : None. *Costs* : short-run output loss and real appreciation.	*Benefits* : None. *Costs* : short-run real appreciation and ambiguous output effect.	*Benefits* : isolation from direct money supply effects of changes in foreign monetary policy, minimizing output and price responses. *Costs* : temporary distortion of exchange rate and possible fall in real money balances via increased prices, particularly if wage indexation is important.
Exchange rate target	*Benefits* : less short-run output loss due to partial monetary accommodation. *Costs* : less real adjustment, resulting in longer distortion of real exchange rate ; possible inflation expectations effects.	*Benefits* : initial real exchange rate effect confined to possible small price rise. *Costs* : monetary accommodation leads to more important output and subsequent price effects, which may be enhanced by expectations mechanisms ; the latter would imply subsequent real exchange rate distortions.	*Benefits* : output, price and real exchange rate stability. *Costs* : none.	*Benefits* : output, price and real exchange rate stability. *Costs* : none.	*Benefits* : initial stability of the real exchange rate. *Costs* : monetary contraction, output loss, and possible subsequent price expectations and real exchange rate effects.
Real exchange rate target	*Benefits* : no short-run output loss due to full monetary accommodation to depreciate exchange rate. *Costs* : upwardly unstable inflation-inflation expectations effects.	*Benefits* : same as exchange rate target. *Costs* : if prices begin to rise intervention to depreciate the nominal rate will lead to upwardly unstable inflation-inflation expectations effects.	Same as exchange rate target.	Same as exchange rate target.	Same as exchange rate target unless there are induced wage/price effects.

different currencies. The maintenance of a monetary target in the face of such shifts, while permitting the exchange rate to float, will lead to otherwise avoidable output, price and real exchange rate effects.

A. INTERVENTION PRINCIPLES FOR MACROECONOMIC STABILITY

The above discussion suggests that an approach to policy based on either monetary aggregates or exchange rates may lead to policy errors, depending on the nature of shocks to the economy. Since the economy may be subjected to various shocks simultaneously, only some of which may be offset by intervention policies, the analysis suggests that a policy of managed floating will be optimal in normal circumstances[22]. Where, as in many of the major economies, monetary targets are already in place, intervention could be defined as appropriate in principle when medium-term macroeconomic stability will best be served by divergences from the target in response to exchange rate pressures:

- Where exchange rate pressures arise from fluctuations in money demand, official intervention in the exchange market could be permitted to influence the money supply.
- Where exchange rate pressures arise through shifts in currency preferences, because interest-bearing debt instruments denominated in different currencies are imperfect substitutes, intervention accompanied by sterilization operations would be most appropriate. This would permit the currency composition of assets to adjust to altered preferences, offsetting any tendency for risk premia to change, and there would be no need to diverge from the monetary target.
- Where pressures arise through domestic real and pricing shocks and/or changes in foreign monetary policy, intervention should be avoided, with priority being accorded to the domestic monetary target – unless factors other than medium-term macro-economic stability are given weight in the objectives of the authorities.

At an operational level the appropriate implementation of exchange market intervention will depend heavily upon the availability of information to identify shifts in money demand and/or currency preferences. This is examined below.

B. AVAILABILITY AND INTERPRETATION OF INFORMATION TO IDENTIFY SHIFTS IN MONEY DEMAND AND CURRENCY PREFERENCES

i) *Interest rates and exchange rates as indicators*

One important source of information consists of observable economic variables whose behaviour may be used to diagnose or "indicate" instabilities in asset demands. Interest rates could perform this function for the authorities, for example, if they were always positively related to money demand. For a given level of nominal income, a rise in interest rates might indicate an upward shift of the demand for money function. However, interest rates may also move because inflationary expectations have changed, leading to an incorrect policy response. Upward pressure on interest rates due to an increase in the expected inflation rate would, if interpreted as a shift in money demand, lead the authorities to increase the supply of money.

This would involve accommodating an acceleration of inflation expectations. These problems with interest rates have led to the suggestion that exchange rates could be used as an alternative or supplementary indicator. The asset market view of exchange rates suggests that a shift in the demand to hold domestic money should be reflected in the value of domestic money in relation to foreign money. To the extent that this prediction is reliable, a policy that led the authorities automatically to increase the money supply when the exchange rate was tending to appreciate via this channel, and vice versa, would offset any destabilizing pressures associated with monetary targeting.

If it were considered desirable to offset fluctuations in money demand in this way, the use of the exchange rate as a supplementary indicator to interest rates could prove less likely to lead to policy errors. If the exchange rate is depreciating when interest rates are rising, this may be indicative of the presence of increasing domestic inflation expectations. This would require judgements about whether it is appropriate to *tighten* money conditions, instead of loosening them as might be the case if nominal interest rates were used as indicators on their own. However, while indicators may be used to distinguish the case of inflation expectations, ambiguities arise in the more general case of distinguishing an upward shift of the demand for money function from an increase in the demand for goods or a price level shock when the money supply is pegged. In both cases interest and exchange rates would tend to rise. Since information about the demand for goods and prices is available with a considerable delay, financial market indicators may prove difficult to interpret. A rise in rates may subsequently be shown to have been the consequence of a real or pricing shock. An incorrect diagnosis of an upward shift in money demand may lead to inappropriate exchange market intervention in the intervening period.

If interest-bearing debts denominated in different currencies are imperfect substitutes, shifts in currency preferences will affect interest and exchange rates. For given supplies of assets, such a shift, e.g. from dollar assets into foreign currency assets, would imply increased risk premia on the former and reduced risk premia on the latter. This will tend to cause dollar interest rates to rise relative to those abroad and the external value of the dollar to depreciate. This configuration would be distinguishable from an upward shift in money demand (interest rate rise and appreciation), and may indicate the need for sterilized intervention. However, this scenario would be difficult to distinguish from an upward shift of inflation expectations in the United States, causing the exchange rate to depreciate, combined with an upward impact on interest rates.

In summary, interest rates and exchange rates as indicators of the source of shocks will generally involve ambiguities because certain pairs of shocks lead to the same configuration of outcomes. In general one would need to have as many independent indicators as there are shocks, since different pressures may be active simultaneously. For example, a rise in money demand may occur simultaneously with an increase in budget deficits, inflation expectations, and a shift in preferences for interest-bearing debt in favour of domestic currency. Interest rates would be likely to rise, but depending on the relative importance of inflation expectations, the exchange rate could move in either direction. However, if used in conjunction with other information, such financial market indicators may be useful in certain situations.

ii) *Econometric models*

Structural econometric models with fully specified real, pricing and financial sectors provide information about a wide range of behavioural relationships in the economy. If forecasts from such models, for example, begin consistently to over-predict the income velocity of money, this may be taken as evidence of an upward shift of the money demand function. Such consistent overprediction has been widely reported for the demand for M1 in the United States during 1979 and 1980. There are, however, a number of well known conceptual difficulties which impinge upon the usefulness of models as a source of information:

- The econometric model may be misspecified, particularly in modelling expectations.
- The parameters of the model may be unstable because optimal decision rules of economic agents change in response to changes in policy variables.
- There are very few world models which take account of international interdependence. The assumption that the rest of the world may be taken as given in many of the models available to policy-makers may make them particularly unsuitable for examining issues concerning shifts in currency preferences between countries, etc.

Invalid assessments about shifts in money demand functions and/or changes in currency preferences based on an inappropriate econometric model may lead to policy errors. Their use in policy making must inevitably be confined to background information, which may be overriden by judgemental decisions.

iii) *Surveys*

Sample surveys of banks' and other financial institutions' sources and uses of funds provide a useful means of improving the statistical verification of hypotheses about shifts in money demand functions and/or currency preferences in the short run. Such procedures may be subject to small sample bias, but have the advantage of building up statistical information in a very short period.

C. EXPECTATIONAL PROBLEMS AND "CREDIBILITY"

One further potential difficulty in implementing the above principles is that asset demand functions may not be independent of the exchange market intervention rule. For this reason alone, it may be difficult to implement decisions that would link the supply of domestic currency to its external value. The rule itself may affect the way in which exchange rates behave, possibly invalidating its usefulness. This may be particularly problematic in countries where the past performance of monetary policy reflects a persistent failure to achieve stated objectives, and where financial markets are fairly sophisticated. A flexible strategy with conditional targets, however well conceived, may be misinterpreted by the public, and may lead to significant expectational effects. This will be particularly the case if market participants do not accept the monetary authorities' assessment, for example, that the source of exchange rate pressure is a shift in currency preferences. Market participants may have a different interpretation of the source of pressure, and their expectations will affect the actual exchange rate.

An alternative to an exchange market intervention rule with conditional monetary targets is to announce a point target for the monetary base while allowing some flexibility with regard to broader aggregates through the endogeneity of the money multiplier, as is the case in Switzerland. Prior to 1978 the authorities had targeted M1, the demand for which was strongly influenced by exchange rate expectations, risk, etc. making the multiplier relationship with the monetary base (the operating instrument at that time) difficult to forecast. By setting a target for the base itself, this endogeneity of the multiplier can be used to introduce short-run automaticity of money supply responses to movements of money demand caused by shifts in preferences for the currency denomination of deposits. Extremes of pressure would tend to be avoided, while the base target would serve to emphasize the longer-run commitment of the authorities to controlling the money supply and inflation. However, this approach has a number of disadvantages:

- The slippage between the monetary base and the money supply may be insufficient to offset major changes in preferences for the currency denomination of deposits. In this case the target for the base would have to be diverged from in order to avoid unnecessary costs, possibly invalidating its usefulness as a guide for longer-run expectations.
- domestic real and pricing shocks may also be accommodated in the short run, delaying necessary real adjustment.
- If shifts in preferences for interest-bearing debt are important, automatic money supply responses will not be wholly appropriate, as discussed above.

V

CONCLUDING REMARKS

If exchange rate instability was induced purely by currency substitution involving shifts in preferences for demand deposits among countries, this would be equivalent to symmetrical shifts in national money demand functions. In this case non-sterilized intervention should be used in the countries involved. For example, country A may experience exchange rate overshooting in respect to the currencies of countries B and C. Country A should undertake non-sterilized sales of its own currency on the exchange market to expand its money supply above its targeted level, while intervention in countries B and C could also be used to reduce their money supplies[23]. Such policies would avoid the need for any divergence of output and prices from the authorities' medium-term final objectives for these variables.

Alternatively, if shifts in demand for interest-bearing debt denominated in different currencies are the main source of exchange rate pressure, then, given the supplies of such debt, risk premia would change. In the above example, risk premia on debt denominated in the currencies of countries B and C would rise and those on country A assets would fall. In the absence of a matching shift in the supplies of interest-bearing debt, this would imply that interest rates should rise in countries B and C and fall in country A if exchange rate movements are to be avoided. This could be achieved by non-sterilized intervention. However, in this example a policy of sterilized intervention would permit both interest rates and exchange rates to remain constant. The changes in the relative supplies of interest-bearing debt denominated in different currencies implied by sterilized intervention would match the shift in preferences, offsetting any tendency for risk premia to move. This would be more appropriate, since it would not require a deviation from domestic monetary targets.

The analysis above suggests that non-sterilized intervention policy should not, in general, be used to offset exchange rate pressures caused by domestic real and pricing shocks, or when the stance of foreign monetary policies change. The tightening of monetary policy in country A to reduce inflation, for example, would probably cause its exchange rate to overshoot during a transitional period, particularly if this was accompanied by increased budget deficits (as was the case in the United States in 1981/82). If inflation rates were not excessive in countries B and C, it would be inappropriate to force monetary contraction on these countries. In the same way it would be inappropriate for countries to import inflation engendered by looser foreign monetary policies. Sterilization would avoid the implied loss of domestic monetary control in these examples. However, except where changes in preferences for interest-bearing debt denominated in different currencies are identified as the source of pressure in the first place, sterilized intervention will not normally be effective for dealing with sustained pressures on the exchange rate. This is because risk premia are unlikely to be important determinants of exchange rates in practice. Where exchange rate pressures arise through divergent national monetary policies, changes in budgetary positions, wage settlements, etc., it seems difficult to avoid the conclusion that costs will be least if the exchange rate is permitted to float.

Any attempt to implement the intervention principles discussed above, it should be recalled, will be heavily constrained by the difficulty of identifying sources of pressure on the exchange rate. Information is extremely difficult to interpret in practice, and judgemental factors will always be important in making decisions. It should also be stressed that the above principles are valid only for the simple macroeconomic objective function assumed. If other factors are important, notably structural resource allocation considerations, they will be less appropriate.

NOTES

1. These difficulties are surveyed in some detail in OECD (1982).

2. A detailed account of the transition to aggregates-oriented monetary policies may be found in OECD (1979).

3. This issue will not be discussed here, but is surveyed in a previous Secretariat publication: OECD (1982).

4. See, for example, Group of Thirty (1980) and T. Gylfason (1978).

5. See Brown, R.N., C.A. Enoch and P.D. Mortimer-Lee (1980).

6. See Truman, E.M. (1981).

7. This feature plays an important role in the literature on exchange rate overshooting surveyed in Annex II. See Robert J. Gordon (1981) for a survey of theoretical explanations and empirical support for these propositions.

8. References to country experiences in this subsection are intended only as a brief overview of the role of the exchange rate in policy formulation. Detailed information is presented on a country by country basis in Annex I. These country notes analyse particularly interesting episodes with respect to policy responses to exchange rate pressures in each of the countries covered by the survey: namely the Group of Ten and Switzerland.

9. Towards the end of 1982 targets for M1 were abandoned on this account.

10. A possibility exists that such assets would matter in the other models if wealth appears in the demand for money function. See W.H. Branson and W. Buiter (1981).

11. A possibility exists that the wage rise would increase the long-run expected price level leading to a fall in the expected equilibrium exchange rate. This would offset the need for the exchange rate to rise. Since the stance of monetary policy remains unchanged, however, the assumption of a relatively static expected exchange rate level seems most reasonable. It is assumed that the interest rate effect dominates any influence on the expected level of the exchange rate.

12. A possibility exists that the rise in wages may increase incomes and domestic demand in the short run. This is unlikely to be important because it will be at the expense of profits, dividend income, etc., and may also result in a reduction in the number of persons employed. In any case, any such short-run effect on flows must be dominated by the stock real balance effect over longer periods.

13. This type of result is discussed in J.B. Taylor (1979) and R. Dornbusch (1981) in the context of rational expectations models with long-term overlapping wage contracts. Sterilized intervention is implied in the case of no monetary accommodation.

14. This point is discussed in R. Dornbusch (1982).

15. This is discussed at more length in OECD (1983).

16. Dornbusch, R. (1980).

17. This has been conducted with the Secretariat's Financial Interlink model which has been built along the lines of the portfolio balance approach to capital flows and exchange rates. A brief description of this model, which is still in an experimental stage, supporting tables and technical details on the simulations are provided in Annex III.

18. Over longer periods of 4 or 5 years, the effects of exchange rate changes on prices are greater.

19. Because all intervention in the Financial Interlink model is assumed to take place in dollars (see Annex III), it is not technically feasible to conduct a simulation for specifically EMS bilateral interventions at this stage.

20. Except for an oil price shock which affects many countries asymmetrically and induces some of the other shocks considered in Table 2. See Argy (1982) for a similar ranking of alternative policy regimes in the face of exogenous shocks.

21. See J.M. Flemming (1962); R.A. Mundell (1968); W. Poole (1970); Dale W. Henderson (1979).

22. See Dale W. Henderson (1979).

23. Professor R.I. Mckinnon (1981) (1982) has recently proposed exactly such a coordinated intervention rule. In terms of the analysis of this study, such a coordinated rule should not be applied to all cases of exchange rate pressure – the appropriateness of intervention (non-sterilized and sterilized) depends on the precise source of pressure. For example, if high budget deficits in the United States have forced interest rates to levels which remain attractive compared to other countries, then exchange rate pressures caused by incipient capital inflows should not be offset by the monetary accommodation of these deficits.

Annex I

COUNTRY EXPERIENCES

UNITED STATES

The dollar is, by a large margin, the most widely used currency internationally. It acts as an important international unit of account in at least two ways. First, a significant share of international trade is denominated in dollars, mainly raw materials and, in particular, oil. Second, the dollar is the standard in terms of which many countries define, and against which they peg, their own currency. The dollar is also the most important international medium of exchange, both with respect to the settlement of private transactions and as the vehicle for exchange market intervention. Given these features and the greater breadth and depth of capital markets in the United States, which greatly facilitates the placement of large investments, internationally held financial assets are preponderately denominated in dollars.

Since March 1973 there has been no formal arrangement for the dollar's exchange rate. Before the breakdown of fixed exchange rates the dollar had already acquired a central role as the main reserve currency in the system, a role which has diminished only slightly since (see Table below). The very large build-up of dollar-denominated assets in official portfolios has been accompanied by an even more rapid increase in external private holdings, of which many are in the form of eurodollars and dollar denominated eurobonds. The increasingly international character of the dollar has made its external strength very sensitive to shifts in the portfolio preferences of international borrowers and lenders, including, importantly, many central banks.

The importance of foreign trade to the United States, although it has grown rapidly, is much less than for most OECD countries[1]. The largest trading partner of the United States is by far Canada, which has often felt constrained to tailor its monetary and exchange rate policies to those prevailing in the United States[2]. While substantial interest or inflation differentials and associated exchange rate movements vis-a-vis Japan and some European countries have occasionally emerged, their immediate impact on the American economy has been limited, reflecting the low share of US output devoted to trade with these countries.

OVERVIEW OF THE BEHAVIOUR OF THE EXCHANGE RATE
SINCE THE EARLY 1970s

By the early 1970s it was clear to most observers that some downward adjustment of the external value of the dollar was necessary to compensate for the United States' loss of competitiveness during the 1960s. The devaluations of 1971 and 1973 and the further depreciation during spring and summer of 1973 reflected this need. As American inflation was somewhat below foreign inflation during this period (Chart 1) these devaluations were translated into substantial real depreciations (as measured either by relative unit labour costs or consumer prices). From mid-1973 to late 1976 the dollar was comparatively stable, although, given the favourable behaviour of differential inflation, this again resulted in a small real depreciation as measured by relative unit labour costs. During 1977-78 the dollar suffered a second period of persistent weakness, depreciating significantly, both in nominal and real terms, particularly in terms of the Japanese yen and major European currencies. Since then the dollar has recovered and appreciated in real terms, which, at least until 1980, can be seen as a correction for the excessive weakness of 1978. But the nominal appreciation between late 1980 and late 1982 seems to have gone well beyond any such correction, particularly as the adverse inflation differential which had emerged in 1978 continued into 1981. The consequence was that by mid-1981 the real value of the dollar was approaching levels that had not prevailed since before the 1973 devaluation.

The only period during which the current account appears to have been an important influence on the exchange rate was 1977-78 when large deficits occurred during one of the dollar's weakest periods. The deterioration of the current account during the early 1970s may have also played a role in the dollar's weakness during that period, but neither the deterioration nor the deficits were very large. The large surpluses of 1973-75, on the other hand, were not reflected in a persistently strong dollar, and its recent strength seems much greater than could be explained by the small current surpluses which have emerged. Interest differentials at times appear to have played an important role in the dollar's behaviour, notably during 1980-81. In general, however, interest differentials do not seem to have had a strong influence, and in 1977-78, the relationship with the exchange rate was even perverse.

At various times, other factors, which are difficult to measure, have also influenced the dollar. For example, it rose sharply in late 1973 following the October oil embargo when the feeling was that the United States was comparatively well-placed to cope with this in view of her high degree of self-sufficiency in energy. As this view came to seem less convincing, early in 1974, the dollar fell back again. During periods of sustained weakness, i.e. 1970-73 and 1977-79, a desire on the part of some groups of international investors to change the currency composition of their portfolios was at least a contributing factor in the dollar's weakness. During the latter period, for example, the flow of OPEC funds invested in the United States was steadily reduced almost to zero, recovering only at the end of 1979[3]. The reversal in the

Currency composition of foreign exchange reserves

Per cent, end of period

	1973	1976	1977	1978	1979	1980	1981	1982
U.S. dollar	76.1	79.7	79.4	76.9	73.7	68.7	71.1	71.4
Pound sterling	5.6	2.0	1.6	1.5	1.9	2.9	2.2	2.2
Deutschemark	7.1	7.0	8.2	9.9	11.5	13.8	12.3	11.6
French franc	1.1	0.9	1.0	0.9	0.9	1.2	1.1	1.1
Swiss franc	1.4	1.4	2.0	1.4	2.2	3.1	2.9	2.7
Netherlands guilder	0.5	0.5	0.4	0.5	0.7	0.9	0.9	0.8
Japanese yen	0.1	0.8	1.2	2.5	2.9	3.5	3.8	3.9
Other	8.1	7.8	6.2	6.3	6.0	5.9	5.6	6.3
Total	100.0	100.0	100.0	100.0	100.0	100.0	100.0	100.0

Source : IMF Annual Report, 1983.

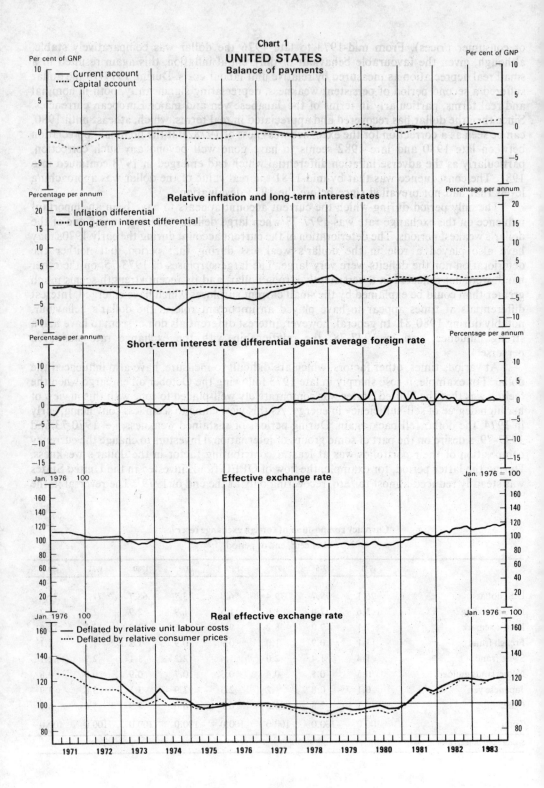

Chart 1

UNITED STATES
Balance of payments

Per cent of GNP

- Current account
- ⋯ Capital account

Per cent of GNP

Percentage per annum

Relative inflation and long-term interest rates

- Inflation differential
- ⋯ Long-term interest differential

Percentage per annum

Percentage per annum

Short-term interest rate differential against average foreign rate

Percentage per annum

Jan. 1976 = 100

Effective exchange rate

Jan. 1976 = 100

Jan. 1976 = 100

Real effective exchange rate

- Deflated by relative unit labour costs
- ⋯ Deflated by relative consumer prices

Jan. 1976 = 100

1971 1972 1973 1974 1975 1976 1977 1978 1979 1980 1981 1982 1983

dollar's fortunes since late 1980 may similarly owe something to a change in these preferences related to *(i)* the election of a new administration committed to a more conservative approach to financial policies; and *(ii)* the increased risks associated with other currencies.

EXCHANGE RATE DEVELOPMENTS AND THE CONDUCT OF MONETARY POLICY

Monetary policy in the United States has been directed towards domestic objectives for most of the past decade. During the early 1970s and again during 1976-78 the expansion of real domestic demand had top priority, while the restrictive phases which began in 1973 and 1979 were aimed at reducing inflation. The shifts in the stance of policy have generally occurred when the objective receiving priority has appeared to have broadly been achieved while performance regarding other objectives was threatening to become unacceptable. While these domestically-oriented policies have had implications for the exchange rate, only at the end of 1978 and throughout 1979 did considerations of the exchange rate importantly influence policy. But even in this case, the weakness displayed by the dollar during 1978 and periodically during 1979 was taken as an indication of underlying domestic financial imbalance. Consequently, policies followed at the time were still primarily domestically-oriented.

Although foreign central banks have often intervened heavily in the exchange market to influence their exchange rates vis-a-vis the dollar, the United States has only occasionally resorted to intervention on its own account. Such intervention has rarely been large, and the breadth of American capital markets is such that any impact on the monetary base has been easily offset (Chart 2). A more detailed discussion of the impact of intervention by either the United States or foreign monetary authorities is provided in a brief appendix to this note. Very little attempt has been made to use other instruments to influence the exchange market directly. Restrictions on capital movements, which had increased steadily since 1963, were abolished in January 1974, partly to remove the distortions which they generated but partly also in recognition that they had not been very effective.

a) *Periods of external weakness*

During the two periods (the early 1970s and 1976-78) when policy was directed towards strengthening real domestic demand the current account deteriorated as domestic expenditure rose. The size of the external deficits which emerged, however, was not large (Chart 1) in comparison to the outward capital movements which accompanied them. These portfolio readjustments were at least partially motivated by a concern that the policies then being pursued would prove inflationary and that this would be reflected in future depreciation of the dollar. Furthermore, during the early 1970s a belief existed that the dollar suffered from a legacy of overvaluation and many people felt an adjustment in the real exchange rate was necessary.

In both periods considered the dollar's depreciation proved to be a forewarning of, and a contributor to, a deteriorating performance with respect to inflation which ultimately led to a change in the overall stance of policy. However, during the early 1970s the weakness of the dollar on the exchange market was not, by itself, a major factor in this shift in stance. Partly this reflected a view that the United States economy was comparatively insulated from the rest of the world, and partly it reflected a perceived need for a significant real exchange rate realignment. Only in the late 1970s did the exchange rate play a major role in persuading the

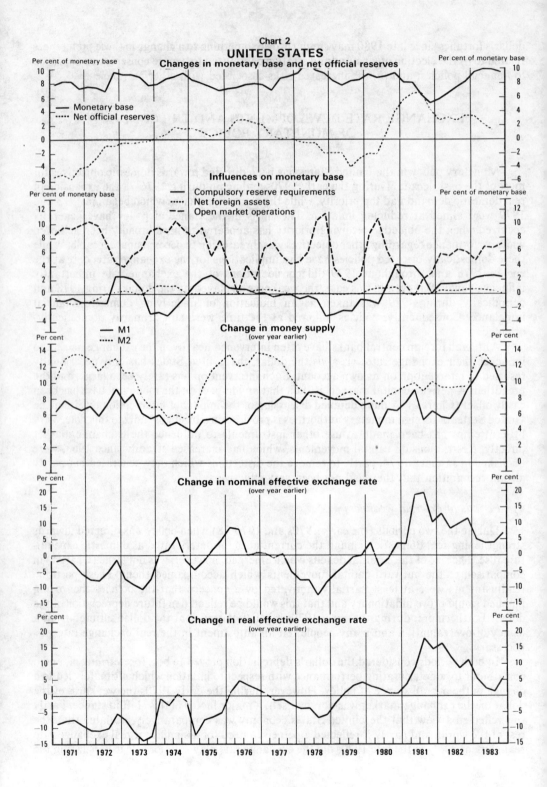

Chart 2
UNITED STATES

Per cent of monetary base

Changes in monetary base and net official reserves

Per cent of monetary base

— Monetary base
····· Net official reserves

Influences on monetary base

Per cent of monetary base

— Compulsory reserve requirements
····· Net foreign assets
--- Open market operations

Per cent of monetary base

Change in money supply
(over year earlier)

Per cent

— M1
····· M2

Per cent

Change in nominal effective exchange rate
(over year earlier)

Per cent   Per cent

Change in real effective exchange rate
(over year earlier)

Per cent   Per cent

1971 1972 1973 1974 1975 1976 1977 1978 1979 1980 1981 1982 1983

authorities to adopt a more restrictive posture. This was to some extent a consequence of the greater exposure of the United States economy to international developments, as reflected in the increased share of foreign trade in economic activity, but, perhaps more importantly, a consequence of a greater recognition of that exposure.

Several measures were taken in November 1978 to reduce severe downward pressure on the dollar. First, interest rates were increased and over the next few months growth of the monetary aggregates was sharply reduced. Second, the Administration embarked on a programme of borrowing in foreign capital markets to build up a significant balance of foreign currencies which could be used to support the dollar in the exchange market. Third, these measures were announced forcefully in an effort to influence the market's confidence by making clear the government's commitment to support the dollar. Although the dollar was to weaken again, particularly against European currencies, during the latter part of 1979, the support package of November 1978 proved to be a turning point in the dollar's fortunes.

b) *Periods of external stability or strength*

When the stance of policy has been geared towards control of inflation the exchange rate has tended to move around a steady or even rising trend. During the restrictive period which began in 1973 the eventual stabilization of the dollar occurred mainly as a by-product of the domestically oriented anti-inflation policy. The real exchange rate which emerged broadly consolidated the adjustments of 1971-73.

The recent restrictive period has proved different. After the support package of November 1978 the dollar strengthened for a period but, in terms of European currencies, weakened again during the latter part of 1979. An important contributing factor here may have been an adverse market response to a reacceleration of monetary growth. In October 1979 the Federal Reserve responded by implementing a new set of operating procedures with which it aimed to improve its control of the money supply by regulating the supply of bank reserves more tightly on a short-term basis. This involved allowing the federal funds rate to fluctuate far more freely than earlier. During 1980 the authorities frequently intervened in the exchange market, with some bias towards buying foreign currency to build up larger balances. Since the present Administration came into office in 1981 the policy of the United States has been to avoid interfering with market forces, and to intervene only in exceptional circumstances to steady the exchange market.

In the event, the exchange rate rose sharply to a level which created difficulties for those industries in the United States most exposed to international competition, and which, in real terms, may prove to be unsustainable. The monetary policy which led to this situation, however, has had substantial benefits in terms of inflation control, which may explain, particularly given the small share of foreign trade in American GNP, the length of time for which the US monetary authorities maintained a tight stance. Some easing occurred during the summer of 1982 and continued until the summer of 1983, but the dollar exchange rate has remained persistently strong.

CONCLUDING REMARKS

The US authorities have rarely permitted exchange rate considerations to be the main determinant of the thrust of their policies. Similarly, they have devoted little effort or resources to resisting exchange market pressures by intervening in the market or by devising supplementary instruments. Given the relatively small, albeit growing, role that foreign trade,

41

particularly with countries outside North America, has played in the United States' economy, assessments of the costs and benefits of orienting monetary policy towards domestic rather than external objectives have tended overwhelmingly to favour the former. However, the economy's exposure to international developments has been growing, largely as a consequence of the fact that its integration with the rest of the world has been increasing rapidly while the dollar has retained its position as the predominant international currency. It thus may become more and more difficult to neglect external considerations in the conduct of monetary policy.

The exchange rate has, at times, proved to be a useful indicator of economic and financial imbalances in the United States. While in the short run it has displayed a degree of volatility, persistent pressures over a sustained period have tended to be a prelude to changes in performance with respect to inflation. This tendency for the exchange rate to act as a leading indicator reflects the sensitivity of the exchange market to sustained changes in monetary conditions. While this provides no grounds for orienting policy toward exchange rate stabilization, it suggests that the emergence of any persistent weakness or strength of the dollar should be regarded with caution, as it may be indicative of economic developments which might require adjustments by policy action.

Appendix

THE RELATIONSHIP BETWEEN OFFICIAL INTERVENTION IN THE EXCHANGE MARKET AND THE MONEY SUPPLY IN THE UNITED STATES

The role of the dollar as an international reserve currency, in conjunction with the relatively low priority that has often been attached to the exchange rate by the US authorities, has meant that intervention to stabilize the dollar's exchange rate has largely been undertaken by foreign monetary authorities. Since their reserves have not generally been held as vault cash or as deposits at Federal Reserve banks but as marketable US government securities (mainly short-term), the impact of such intervention on the monetary base has normally been offset by securities transactions in the open market.

When the United States intervenes on its own behalf[4] the impact on the monetary base will similarly be nullified if the authorities carry out an offsetting operation in the securities market. Since the day-to-day conduct of monetary policy has for many years been formulated in terms of either the overnight interest rate on banks' reserves (i.e. the federal funds rate) or the quantity of these reserves, such an offsetting securities operation would normally occur. Consequently, sterilization of the impact of exchange market intervention on the monetary base, regardless of which central bank conducts the operation, is routine.

Potentially, some complications may still arise in the overall conduct of monetary policy. The offsetting securities operations have an impact on the financial markets for the particular types of securities involved. This may influence the term structure of interest rates and/or the relationship between interest rates on private and government debt instruments of the same maturity. These effects may in turn affect the private sector's demand for various types of financial assets, including those that make up the monetary aggregates. Since the relationships between either the monetary base or banks' reserves and the main monetary aggregates have considerable elasticity due to *(i)* differing reserve requirements against the various types of deposits, and *(ii)* the inclusion of substantial non-bank liabilities in definitions of M2 and M3, targeted aggregates can be influenced by intervention despite insulation of the base.

The importance of the considerations above, however, is probably comparatively minor. First, the extent of official intervention in the exchange market, even when heavy in absolute amount (as in 1971 or 1978), has been small compared to the overall size of US financial markets. Second, the problem of anticipating the relationship between the money aggregates and the monetary base, or banks' reserves, is one of anticipating the private sector's response to a wide array of economic forces, many of which cannot be foreseen. The influence of exchange market intervention on domestic financial markets is just one of these unforeseeable forces, and does not fundamentally alter the problem of achieving monetary control in an uncertain world.

NOTES

1. Exports and imports of goods and services, as shares of GNP, amounted in 1982 to 11.5 and 10.7 per cent, respectively. In most other countries considered in this study the comparable figures exceed 20 per cent.

2. See the note on Canada.

3. The real value of the flow of OPEC investments in the United States appears to have been fairly stable, 1978-1979 apart, ranging from $7.6 billion in 1982 to $12.7 billion in 1974 (1975 prices). The failure to add significantly to holdings during 1978 and most of 1979 implied a reduced share of a growing portfolio.

4. The New York Federal Reserve Bank often acts as agent for foreign central banks, undertaking exchange and security operations on their behalf.

JAPAN

Until late August 1971, and from December 1971 until February 1973, the Japanese monetary authorities were committed to maintaining (within small margins) a fixed parity for the yen against the dollar. Since February, 1973 there has been no formal commitment to any pre-announced parity. In view of the inflationary environment in other countries it is seen as desirable for the yen to appreciate so long as this takes place in a gradual and orderly fashion. The Bank of Japan feels that intervention has an impact on exchange rates, although this may be limited if it is not supported by monetary and other economic policies. Intervention can, for example, have an announcement effect as regards the authorities' policy stance, and it may add an element of uncertainty in circumstances where speculation has fed on itself to the point where virtually all market participants have the same view as to the likely movement of the exchange rate. Consequently, the authorities have frequently intervened heavily, both to smooth day-to-day fluctuations and to resist more persistent pressures, particularly where these are in a downward direction.

The exchange rate's significance to Japan may be understated by the relatively low ratio of foreign trade to national income[1]. While a comparatively small share of resources in the Japanese economy is oriented toward producing for export, this sector includes many of the more rapidly expanding industries. Furthermore, the need to import raw materials, particularly oil, creates a degree of structural dependence on trade.

OVERVIEW OF THE BEHAVIOUR OF THE EXCHANGE RATE
SINCE THE EARLY 1970s

Changes in the nominal exchange rate (Chart 1) during the early 1970s reflected mainly the agreed parity realignment of December 1971 and an appreciation immediately following the decision to float the yen in February 1973. Since there was little differential between inflation in Japan and in the rest of the world, the real exchange rate appreciated during this period roughly in line with the nominal appreciation. For the next few years, until early 1977, the real exchange rate was relatively stable around the level prevailing after the shift to floating in February 1973, as some yen depreciation offset an adverse inflation differential. Since the beginning of 1977 both the nominal and real exchange rates have fluctuated widely, and by early 1983 the real exchange rate, as measured by unit labour costs, was roughly at the level which prevailed immediately after the Smithsonian agreement in 1971. Any forces working to stabilize the real exchange rate at some longer-term equilibrium have evidently been persistently overridden by other disturbances.

Until 1980 the current account had been strongly correlated with the behaviour of the exchange rate, which has tended to rise when the current account has been strong and conversely. Interest rate differentials also influenced the exchange rate, particularly in the

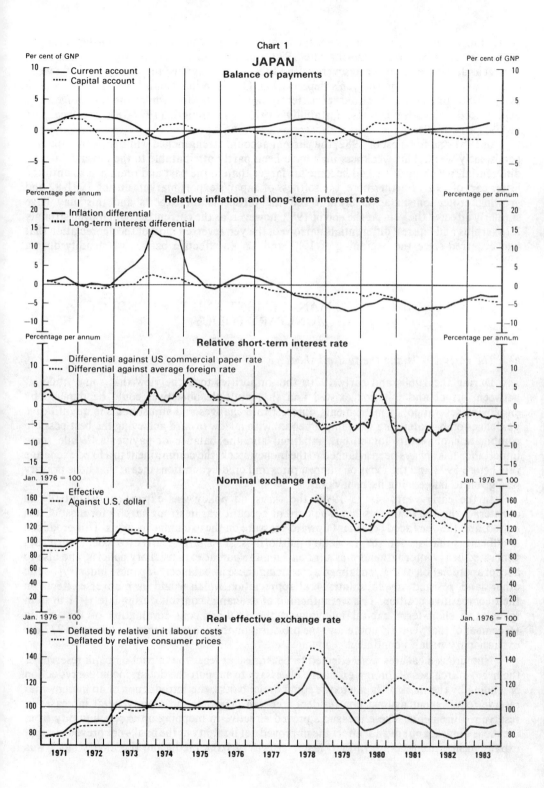

Chart 1

JAPAN

Per cent of GNP

Balance of payments

- Current account
- Capital account

Percentage per annum

Relative inflation and long-term interest rates

- Inflation differential
- Long-term interest differential

Percentage per annum

Relative short-term interest rate

- Differential against US commercial paper rate
- Differential against average foreign rate

Jan. 1976 = 100

Nominal exchange rate

- Effective
- Against U.S. dollar

Jan. 1976 = 100

Real effective exchange rate

- Deflated by relative unit labour costs
- Deflated by relative consumer prices

1971 1972 1973 1974 1975 1976 1977 1978 1979 1980 1981 1982 1983

short run. In the long run, however, they have shown no persistent relationship with the exchange rate's behaviour. During late 1973 and 1974 there appears to have been some impact as Japanese interest rates were raised substantially against the background of a weak current account, limiting the yen's depreciation. On the other hand, from early 1975 until early 1980 differentials moved persistently against Japan, while the exchange rate experienced successive periods of stability (1975-76), strength (1977-78), and weakness (1979, early 1980).

In 1981 and for most of 1982, the current account strengthened while the yen remained persistently weak. This weakness may have been partly attributable to the adverse interest differential, which by 1981 had become far larger than in the past and remained so until the latter part of 1982. Furthermore, the softness of Japan's export markets during 1981-82 and growing protectionism adversely affected the prospects for exports and this may have similarly affected the yen. At the end of 1982, however, as the current account moved strongly into surplus and interest differentials narrowed, the yen reversed most of the depreciation that had occurred since the beginning of 1981 and, on an effective basis, rose steadily during 1983.

EXCHANGE RATE MANAGEMENT AND THE CONDUCT
OF MONETARY POLICY

a) *The early 1970s and the first oil shock*

During the 1960s and early 1970s the authorities took the view that some trade-off between output and inflation existed and that multiple objectives could be pursued by employing several policy instruments. Interest rate changes and adjustments in quantitative guidelines on bank lending were implemented with a view toward achieving the best possible combination of results for output, inflation, and the balance of payments. While some importance has always been attached to the money stock, the commitment to a fixed exchange rate before 1973 and the focus on interest rates and credit conditions meant that little priority was given to influencing its behaviour.

In the early years of the 1970s the thrust of policy was expansionary, initially to counteract the 1969-70 recession. The current account was in strong surplus for most of this period, and the yen faced persistent upward pressure on the exchange markets. This produced a difficult situation for the monetary authorities. The large current account surpluses generated heavy international pressures on Japan to pursue expansionary policies, and also to accept appreciation of the yen, aimed at reducing these imbalances. Japanese industry, on the other hand, resisted any substantial real appreciation which would have adverse effects on their competitive position. The strengthening of exchange controls during late 1971 to stem speculative short-term capital inflows and the 16.9 per cent revaluation of the yen in December of that year did not relieve the pressures on the exchange rate, and during 1972 the expansionary policies continued.

Numerous measures were effected to neutralise at least the impact on bank reserves of the heavy purchases of foreign exchange necessary to support the dollar, including reduction of lending by the Bank of Japan to the commercial banks, the introduction of an incremental reserve requirement against non-resident free-yen deposits, and more general increases in reserve requirements. These measures proved effective in mopping up excess liquidity from the money market but did not affect the improved net liquidity of the banks nor prevent a rapid expansion in bank lending. In fact, faster growth of bank credit and the money stock was

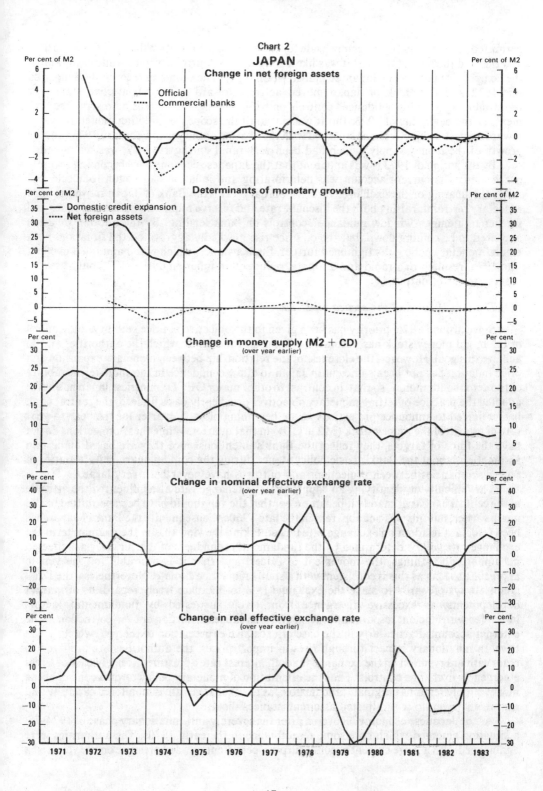

Chart 2
JAPAN

Change in net foreign assets

Per cent of M2 (left and right axes)

— Official
······ Commercial banks

Determinants of monetary growth

Per cent of M2

— Domestic credit expansion
······ Net foreign assets

Change in money supply (M2 + CD)
(over year earlier)

Per cent

Change in nominal effective exchange rate
(over year earlier)

Per cent

Change in real effective exchange rate
(over year earlier)

Per cent

1971 1972 1973 1974 1975 1976 1977 1978 1979 1980 1981 1982 1983

permitted, at least initially, to compensate for the anticipated deflation due to the revaluation, and this had the advantage that it was likely to reduce the current surplus while maintaining the competitive position of Japanese industry (Chart 2). The economy recovered strongly by mid-1972 and the Bank of Japan moved actively toward a more restrictive stance by re-introducing "window guidance" controls on bank lending and increasing reserve requirements at the beginning of 1973. But it was not until the scope for directing monetary policy toward domestic objectives was enlarged with the floating of the yen in February 1973 that the growth of the money supply, which had been very rapid during 1971-72, was restrained.

By the spring of 1973 it was apparent that the Japanese economy was becoming severely overheated. The current account was deteriorating and inflation had begun to accelerate. After the floating of the exchange rate in February 1973 the Bank of Japan moved toward monetary restraint, raising both the discount rate and reserve requirements several times and further tightening "window guidance" controls on bank lending. By the autumn inflation appeared to be coming down, but the oil price rise markedly aggravated the situation. As a result, monetary policy was tightened further. Such a stance, which was maintained in effect into 1975, resulted in a rapid and dramatic reduction in inflation during 1975 but at severe costs in terms of output.

b) *The late 1970s and the second oil shock*

Since around 1975, priority has been given to the objective of price stability, and control of the broad money stock has become one important means by which the authorities aim to achieve this goal. However, the closeness of the relationship between monetary expansion and price inflation has not been sufficient in Japan to allow confidence in the short-term stability of the demand for money, so that, in contrast to other major OECD countries, Japan has never adopted the practice of setting monetary objectives on a yearly basis. Indeed, the central bank has preferred to announce projections at the beginning of each quarter for the year-to-year rate of growth of the money stock (M2 + CDs) in that quarter. While these projections do not have the force of targets, they reflect the Bank's intentions since they are based on certain assumptions about the Bank's basic policy stance during the coming quarter. As a matter of fact, discrepancies between projections and outturns have never been very large.

The difficulty of identifying an "appropriate" exchange rate also influenced the attitude of the central bank. Ultimately it became clear that the yen should have been permitted to rise much earlier, but this was not apparent in the late 1960s. Consequently the Bank of Japan has been reluctant to adopt an exchange rate target, taking the view that in the medium term the exchange rate will be determined by the fundamental soundness of the currency as reflected in, among other things, the movement of prices, and that it is desirable for the yen to appreciate so long as this is consistent with a stable monetary climate. Nevertheless, the Bank is not always prepared to leave the exchange rate to fluctuate freely regardless of market developments, as excessive divergence from levels suggested by fundamental factors interferes with efficient resource allocation and also causes distortion or over-correction in the external account. Particularly in the case of excessive depreciation of the yen, which would have an inflationary impact through rises in import prices, the authorities are prepared to react with intervention on the exchange market, interest rate adjustment, and, in case of a real emergency, exchange controls. Thus the orientation of monetary policy toward control of the money supply remains pragmatic and flexible, as the exchange rate is monitored carefully and the weight given to it is adjusted as circumstances dictate.

As the Japanese economy recovered after the severely anti-inflationary phase of 1974-75, a situation emerged which bore some resemblance to the early 1970s. The authorities were again faced with a large current account surplus, persistent upward pressure on the yen, and a tendency for real domestic demand to be deficient. Fiscal measures were taken to sustain domestic demand and the central bank provided support by lowering the discount rate in several steps and by virtually abandoning effective ceilings on bank lending. At the same time the authorities allowed the yen to appreciate in view of underlying payments trends, particularly the current account surplus, despite the adverse impact of such appreciation on real demand. A number of measures were taken to moderate volatile capital inflows, including the introduction of an incremental reserve requirement against non-residents' free-yen deposits and a ban on non-resident purchases of bonds with maturities of five years and one month or less. Their impact was limited, however, in the face of a substantial weakening of the dollar against other major currencies.

Thus a real appreciation of the yen of nearly 30 per cent occurred as official intervention, although at times heavy, was not very effective in the face of serious erosion of confidence in the dollar. The impact on bank reserves of such intervention was neutralized by actions such as reductions in lending by the Bank of Japan to the banking system and a diminution of its bill purchases from the market. Moreover, in contrast to 1971-72, real interest rates remained positive throughout 1977-78, and the basic framework of guidelines on major banks' lending was retained, although the general stance of monetary policy was designed to support the recovery of domestic demand. As a result monetary expansion remained moderate, reflecting the importance attached by the Bank of Japan to limiting the growth of the money supply. Despite concerns about the weakness of demand real growth proceeded steadily in the range of 5-5½ per cent per annum during this period.

Against this background, the Japanese economy responded to the second oil shock in 1979 very differently than it had to the first. The appreciation of the real exchange rate and the subsequent strengthening of domestic demand had already led to a disappearance of the current account surplus and had begun to reverse itself. As this occurred the authorities became concerned that inflation, which had been markedly reduced, would re-accelerate. The authorities attempted to restrain the depreciation by intervening in the exchange market. They also progressively dismantled the deterrents to capital inflows that had been used earlier, and on two occasions they implemented further measures to encourage inflows. These changes proved to be of only limited effect, however. Inflation showed signs of accelerating from November and the Bank moved quickly to keep the situation under control by preventing any acceleration of the money stock. The discount rate was raised in several steps and "window guidance" ceilings on bank lending were tightened. These measures reinforced the restraining impact of exchange market intervention on monetary growth, and the money stock decelerated until late 1980 (Chart 2).

The oil price rise, together with more general increases in world commodity prices late in 1979, exacerbated the inflation problem somewhat, as did the continuation of yen depreciation until spring 1980 when the agreement of several major central banks to intervene jointly in support of the yen stabilized the situation. Domestic inflation accelerated somewhat until 1980, but this largely reflected the real terms of trade loss implied by the oil price rise. After the once and for all effect of this loss had been absorbed, inflation fell back to the 2 per cent region. Despite the deflationary impact of the oil shock and the non-accommodating stance of monetary policy, real output continued to grow at about 4 per cent until the middle of 1981.

c)   *The period after the second oil shock*

An interesting feature of the Japanese experience after the second oil shock was the steady strengthening of the yen from spring 1980 despite the rise of US interest rates to very high levels, late that year. In view of the low inflation rate that had been achieved, the

Japanese authorities felt that some relaxation of monetary policy was possible to encourage the recovery of domestic demand. Interest rates were reduced steadily from the latter part of 1980 until March 1981. Despite these moves the yen remained firm for a time against the background of an improving current account. From the spring, however, the exchange rate against the dollar began to ease[2], due in part to exceptionally high US interest rates, and until the latter part of 1982 it remained persistently weak as export markets softened and protectionism mounted. Although the yen recovered late in 1982, the current account strengthened and inflation remained low, concern about protectionism in major trading partners has limited the scope for any relaxation of monetary policy which might adversely affect the yen.

CONCLUDING REMARKS

Before the first oil shock the Japanese authorities gave priority to maintaining a fixed exchange rate in the face of strong upward market pressures. While this was consistent with domestic objectives during the early 1970s, it involved acquiescing in an unusually rapid rate of monetary growth for more than two years. The results might well have been adverse in any case but in conjunction with the oil shock the policy resulted in a situation which was highly unsatisfactory with respect to inflation. Confronted with broadly similar conflicts prior to the second oil shock the authorities gave priority to domestic monetary control and confined their efforts to stimulate domestic demand to what could be done within that constraint. The result was that overall macroeconomic performance held up well in the face of the second oil shock. With inflation held to very low rates the Japanese economy is poised to face the rest of the 1980s in better shape than most other OECD economies.

The real exchange rate has fluctuated sharply, however, and this has undoubtedly posed problems for some industries and resulted in some misallocation of resources. The low exchange rate which prevailed until late 1982 was particularly a problem in this respect, as it tended to aggravate protectionist pressures in trading partners. Furthermore, concern about the exchange rate had removed the scope for further relaxation of monetary policy to stimulate domestic demand. Thus, despite the broadly satisfactory performance in the wake of the second oil shock, conflicts between internal and external objectives continue to confront the Japanese authorities.

NOTES

1. In 1982, exports of goods and services only accounted for around 17 per cent of GNP while imports represented about 16 per cent.
2. The exchange rate has been firm against European currencies, so the divergence between the yen's effective rate and the rate against the US dollar has been significant since 1981 (see Chart 1).

GERMANY

Since March 1973 the Deutschemark (DM) has been permitted to float against major currencies, with the Bundesbank deciding the extent of any intervention on the exchange market. The latter has mainly been oriented towards stabilizing the bilateral rate against the dollar. However, from early 1979 Germany has been a member of the European Monetary System (EMS), which requires the authorities to intervene in order to meet contractual obligations when bilateral rates vis-à-vis currencies of other member countries reach certain threshold levels. Since 1974 the Bundesbank has also announced annual targets for the rate of growth of the central bank money stock (CBM)[1], which influences the growth of the broad money supply. This intermediate target variable is controlled indirectly through variations of the central bank's own lending rate to the commercial banks, and other short-term liquidity operations[2]. The target has been formulated in terms of a range since 1979.

While no specific targets or guidelines have been set for bilateral rates against other major currencies, the openness of the Germany economy (particularly the strong export-orientation of domestic industry) has made the exchange rate of considerable concern to policy-makers[3]. Exchange rate trends have been important in the case of Germany, given its low inflation performance, and have sometimes been exaggerated by the emergence of the DM as an important international reserve currency. In particular, the DM has sometimes played the role of a substitute reserve currency with respect to significant movements of the US dollar.

OVERVIEW OF THE BEHAVIOUR OF THE EXCHANGE RATE SINCE THE EARLY 1970s

The main presumed determinants of exchange rate movements are shown in Chart 1. The inflation differential moved sharply in favour of Germany during 1973-74 and remained above 5 per cent per annum until 1982. The nominal exchange rate appreciated sharply after the switch to floating in 1973, but subsequently remained relatively steady until well into 1976. Subsequently, it began a prolonged period of appreciation until 1980. The behaviour of the real exchange rate has typically been dominated by that of the nominal rate, with the exception of the mid-1970s when the favourable inflation differential operated to improve German competitiveness.

The relationships between the current account, the interest rate differential and the nominal exchange rate show no broad consistent patterns. However, at times, movements in the interest rate differential have clearly been positively associated with the timing of exchange rate movements (which can be seen more clearly from Chart 2). This was so in the early 1970s, and subsequently during the 1980s. The weakness of the current account in 1979

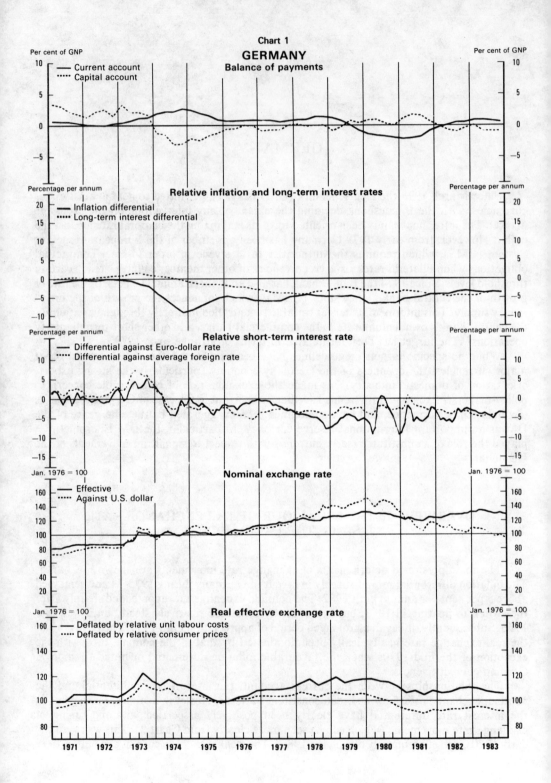

Chart 1

GERMANY
Balance of payments

Per cent of GNP

— Current account
...... Capital account

Percentage per annum

Relative inflation and long-term interest rates

— Inflation differential
...... Long-term interest differential

Percentage per annum

Relative short-term interest rate

— Differential against Euro-dollar rate
...... Differential against average foreign rate

Jan. 1976 = 100

Nominal exchange rate

— Effective
...... Against U.S. dollar

Jan. 1976 = 100

Real effective exchange rate

— Deflated by relative unit labour costs
...... Deflated by relative consumer prices

1971 1972 1973 1974 1975 1976 1977 1978 1979 1980 1981 1982 1983

and 1980 provides a strong contrast with the surpluses over most of the 1970s. It is also interesting to note that the reversal of the prolonged upward trend in the nominal and real exchange rates coincide with this period.

EXCHANGE RATE MANAGEMENT AND THE CONDUCT OF MONETARY POLICY

a) *The period prior to the EMS*

The German authorities have always placed considerable emphasis on domestic monetary policy and inflation control. This was true even in the early 1970s under the system of fixed exchange rates. Indeed, tight monetary conditions relative to those prevailing abroad and expected appreciation of the DM were largely responsible for the substantial capital inflows which, immediately prior to the switch to floating, threatened the independence of domestic policies. The commitment to intervene required offsetting measures in order to sterilize these inflows (Chart 2), resulting in substantial upward pressure on interest rates[4]. The ability to further squeeze bank reserves without endangering the operations of the banking system was limited, already having surpassed historical norms, and the inconsistency between fixed parities and independent monetary policy became increasingly apparent. The Bundesbank chose largely to abandon intervention in favour of domestic monetary control.

The experience with floating was quite favourable in its early stages. Intervention was confined to moderating fluctuations vis-à-vis the US dollar, but was not used to counter "fundamental market trends". The current account was in surplus throughout this period, and the nominal exchange rate remained relatively stable. As the inflation differential moved in Germany's favour in response to the initial appreciation of the exchange rate in 1973 and to the non-accommodating stance of monetary policy in the face of the first oil price shock, the real exchange rate depreciated throughout 1974 and 1975. From 1976, however, both the nominal and real exchange rates began a sustained period of appreciation. This largely reflected the low inflation/low monetary growth record in Germany, possibly enhanced by the advent of monetary targeting, and the favourable current account position. It was also partly the result of portfolio diversification by dollar holders[5].

At first the loss in competitiveness was borne fairly readily by German firms, but by mid-1977 the exchange rate began increasingly to concern policy makers. In late 1977 and particularly during 1978, the Bundesbank began actively to intervene in order to prevent further appreciation. These difficulties were increased by the pressures on the dollar after mid-1978, and the DM began more and more to play the role of a substitute reserve currency. Dollar assets were shifted on a large scale into a small number of strong currencies of which the Deutschemark was perhaps the most important. The liquidity creating effects of intervention policies at this time led to a significant overshooting of the target for CBM. This reflected the opinion of the Bundesbank that the exchange rate had significantly diverged from an "appropriate" path and had to be deliberately counterbalanced by maintaining easy conditions in the domestic money market. At the same time Germany was under considerable international pressure to maintain low interest rates as a part of a concerted reflationary action programme. Unutilized rediscount quotas were maintained at relatively high levels, and interventions in the money market implied interbank rates that were close to the Bundesbank's own historically low lending rates.

53

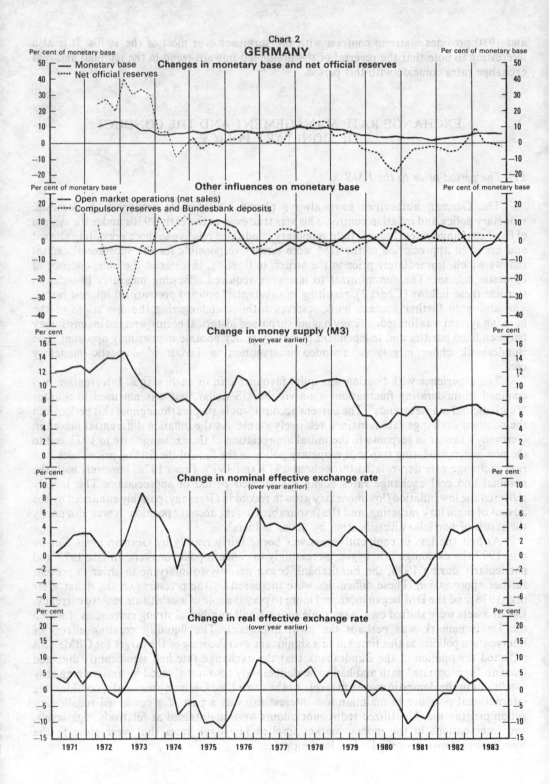

Chart 2
GERMANY

Per cent of monetary base

Changes in monetary base and net official reserves

— Monetary base
...... Net official reserves

Per cent of monetary base

Other influences on monetary base

— Open market operations (net sales)
...... Compulsory reserves and Bundesbank deposits

Per cent

Change in money supply (M3)
(over year earlier)

Per cent

Change in nominal effective exchange rate
(over year earlier)

Per cent

Change in real effective exchange rate
(over year earlier)

1971 1972 1973 1974 1975 1976 1977 1978 1979 1980 1981 1982 1983

This policy did not amount to an abandonment of domestic inflation objectives. The previous upward pressure on the exchange rate had acted to dampen domestic inflation. Moreover, the German authorities have adopted the view that temporary deviations from monetary targets will not destabilize the economy, provided the reasons are sufficiently well explained to the public. The authorities have typically attempted to avoid "base drift". In setting the targets for CBM in the years following 1978, for example, the Bundesbank has attempted to reduce the monetary carryover created in that year. However, to give monetary policy more flexibility in coping with unforeseen developments, particularly with respect to the external sector, year on year monetary targets were subsequently formulated in terms of target ranges (1979: 6-9 per cent; 1980: 5-8 per cent; 1981, 1982 and 1983: 4-7 per cent respectively). The authorities have attempted to explain which end of the target range they aimed for, and the reasons why they have chosen to do so.

b) *The period since the inception of the EMS*

The expansionary policies of 1978 gave Germany a head start in the international trade cycle, causing its imports to increase while exports remained sluggish. Trade was also adversely affected by the preceding sustained real appreciation of the DM. Consequently, Germany entered the EMS at a time when its current account had begun significantly to deteriorate. In the course of 1979 this was further accentuated by the second oil price shock, given Germany's heavy dependence on imported energy, and the failure of OPEC spending to favour German products. These developments, together with the possible inflationary consequences of the previous monetary overshooting, figured in the Bundesbank's decision to aim towards the lower end of the monetary target range in 1979. Banks' unutilized rediscount quotas were kept close to zero, and their refinancing needs were met with Lombard credits at higher Bundesbank interest rates.

In the early part of 1979 the overall strength of the dollar led to intervention in order to prevent a depreciation of the DM, which was broadly consistent with the aim of reducing bank liquidity. However, the renewed weakness of the dollar later in the year, together with a shift of the interest rate differential in favour of Germany, began to lead to tensions within the EMS. In this respect the Bundesbank has generally taken the view that any failure to achieve the desired convergence of bilateral parities as a consequence of persistent inflation differentials should lead to a rapid realignment of central rates of European currencies. Germany conducts over 40 per cent of its foreign trade with EMS countries, and this approach is regarded as the best way to maintain its own low inflation performance[6]. Consequently, the EMS underwent its first major realignment in September 1979, the DM being revalued by 5 per cent against the Danish crown and by 2 per cent against all other currencies.

This situation was quickly reversed by the beginning of 1980, when the DM began to come under strong downward pressure. The main factors were:

– the large German current account deficit, and
– the rapid rise of US interest rates in the wake of the shift to the new monetary control procedure by the Federal Reserve[7].

In response, the Bundesbank again chose to aim towards the lower half of the target range. Money market rates were forced significantly above the Bundesbank's own lending rates, and cash shortages were relieved only at penal rates. At the time, however, the tasks of domestic monetary policy were complicated by the sharp *volatility* of US interest rates. Their continued rise in the first quarter of 1980 led to expectations of an increase in interest rates in German capital markets. Agents tended to shift out of deposit liabilities not included in the definition of M3 (e.g. bank bonds), and monetary growth expanded fairly rapidly. The Bundesbank chose not to react too quickly, in the belief that the rise in US rates was a temporary phenomenon, and the growth of CBM at first remained close to the top of the target range.

The Bundesbank's relaxed attitude was in fact validated in the second quarter of 1980, when US rates dropped sharply. The interest rate differential moved in Germany's favour, monetary growth quickly shifted towards the bottom of the target range, and subsequently fell below it. The DM briefly strengthened at this time, but the alleviation of pressures proved to be short-lived. From July until the end of 1980 US interest rates again rose sharply, and the dollar began a period of steep ascent against most European currencies. This development, together with the underlying pressures implied by the huge German current deficit, caused the DM to weaken significantly, both against the dollar and in effective terms. At times it moved to the weakest position within the EMS. Already undershooting its stated monetary target range of 5 to 8 per cent, the Bundesbank began heavily to intervene to support the exchange rate while, at the same time, partially offsetting further negative effects on money creation mainly through changes in minimum reserve requirements. By the end of 1980 reserve outflows resulting from supporting interventions within the EMS and sales of dollars amounted to some DM 30 billion. But these measures proved largely ineffective in offsetting exchange market pressures, and a crisis in confidence emerged by the beginning of 1981.

The Bundesbank, fearing a depreciation-induced inflationary spiral, began to accord considerably more weight to external factors in the formulation of domestic monetary policy. The target range had been lowered to 4 to 7 per cent, in order to give more scope for restrictive policies, and from 20th of February banks' access to day-to-day Bundesbank market rates to sufficiently high levels. The rate charged for the newly introduced Special Lombard facility was finally advances was temporarily suspended in order to force money established at 12 per cent, 3 percentage points above the previous Lombard rate, and credit on this basis was recallable at 24 hours notice. In response to these exceptional measures the DM quickly moved to the strongest position within the EMS, and the Bundesbank was required to support other currencies, notably the Belgian and French francs. However, the DM continued to remain in a weak position against the dollar in the first half of 1981, and the offsetting nature of interventions implied that international reserves declined by very little. The strengthening of the DM continued in the second half of the year, as the current account deficit turned around, and it has been revalued in successive EMS realignments in November 1981, June 1982 and March 1983. It has remained relatively strong within the EMS throughout this period, and has gradually appreciated in effective terms.

During 1980 and 1981 it will be recalled that the growth of CBM remained at the bottom of the target range, and sometimes below it, mainly as a consequence of the external situation. The very high level of interest rates by the spring of 1981 was regarded as necessary for achieving a recovery of the DM: firstly by permitting the large current deficit to be financed without requiring excessive depreciation, and subsequently by helping to reverse the adverse trade balance. But this did not represent a permanent shift in priorities away from domestic policy goals. As the external situation was normalized in late 1981 and early 1982, the Bundesbank began actively to test the scope for lowering domestic interest rates. Banks' dependence on Special Lombard credits were reduced through open market operations, which tended to force market interest rates below the Bundesbank's own lending rate. As expectations in financial markets did not seem to respond unfavourably, the Lombard rate was gradually reduced, and conditions in domestic money markets were permitted to ease. During most of 1983 CBM was above the ceiling of its target range, which tended to support real activity. As the economy showed clear signs of recovering monetary conditions were tightened somewhat: interest rates were raised, the overshoot in CBM was gradually reduced and the target range for CBM in 1984 was lowered.

CONCLUDING REMARKS

German monetary policy has been based primarily on intermediate targets for the growth of CBM, with the ultimate aim of maintaining inflation control. However, this approach has not been implemented in a rigid manner and external considerations have, from time to time, been accorded considerable priority. This was true at the time of upward pressure on the DM in 1978, and again in 1980/81 when pressures were in a downwards direction. Official intervention played a useful role in easing liquidity conditions to meet external objectives in 1978, but partially sterilized intervention proved largely inadequate for alleviating exchange rate pressures during 1980.

There is some recognition on the part of German authorities that the type of pressure on the exchange rate may be important in determining the nature of the policy responses. Certainly the type of pressure during 1978 differed from that of 1980/81. In the former period pressures largely arose from portfolio diversification from abroad, and it proved sufficient to increase the supply of the Deutschemarks on the exchange markets to meet the increased demand. During 1980, however, partially sterilized intervention did not address the more fundamental pressures arising from the marked deterioration of the German current account. In these circumstances it became clear that firmer signals of the Bundesbank's intention to reverse the depreciation of the DM were required. The special money market measures taken by the Bundesbank in February 1981 could be interpreted in this light.

Finally, it should be noted that the flexible approach to monetary targeting in Germany has never implied the abandonment of domestic policy goals. Any deviations from targets related to external considerations are carefully explained to the public in order to avoid destabilizing expectations cycles. Moreover, after the external pressure has subsided, the Bundesbank has made considerable efforts to avoid "base drift" in an upwards or downwards direction. The tightening of domestic monetary policy after 1978 and the easing of policy in 1982 were partly related to such considerations.

NOTES

1. Currency plus commercial banks' required reserves at constant 1974 reserve ratios.
2. For more detailed accounts of the operation of monetary management see OECD (1979, 1982).
3. In 1982 exports and imports of goods and services represented, respectively, 33.4 per cent and 31.2 per cent of GNP.
4. It is interesting to note that the actions on bank liquidity by the Bundesbank did not involve open market operations (panel 3 of Chart 2). At this time short-term capital markets were extremely limited and the Bundesbank did not possess sufficient debt instruments to sell.
5. It has been has argued that holders of dollars became more aware of the different characteristics of the returns on assets denominated in different currencies and gradually began to diversify as they acquired more and more experience with floating. See Dornbusch (1980).
6. This implies that any convergence of parities within the EMS would have to be based on the lowest, i.e. German, inflation rate.
7. See the note on the United States.

FRANCE

Since the introduction of floating exchange rates in early 1973 the French monetary authorities have sought to control the movement of the franc on the foreign exchange market so as to ensure its stability in the short term. This policy has been reflected in France's joining the European monetary agreements (the "snake" and then the EMS) set up in order to limit fluctuations in the currencies of the participating countries. The importance attached to the stability of the exchange rate is attributable to the growing share of foreign trade in France's economic activity[1] and to the fears that a depreciation of the franc would push up domestic prices, while an appreciation would reduce the competitiveness of exports. In the presence of external shocks, such as a rise in the oil price, stabilization of the exchange rate has thus been seen to be an essential element in the fight against inflation. This has had a considerable influence on the thrust of monetary policy, especially since 1976, but it has had no major effect on the methods of monetary control.

OVERVIEW OF THE BEHAVIOUR OF THE EXCHANGE RATE

a) *Exchange rate developments since the early 1970s*

Several phases of the behaviour of the franc on the foreign exchange market during the 1970s and early 1980s may be distinguished:

1971 to 1973. In December 1971 the general realignment of exchange rates agreed in Washington resulted in an 8.6 per cent appreciation of the franc against the dollar, but, given the adjustments of other currencies, its effective rate was virtually unchanged. From April 1972 the franc took part in the European arrangement to limit fluctuations against other participating currencies[2] (the "snake") more narrowly than required by the Washington agreement. The franc's effective exchange rate remained more or less stable in 1971 and 1972 and appreciated during the first half of 1973. At the end of 1973, the acceleration of inflation and the deterioration of the trade balance, both of which were made worse by the effects of the first oil shock, resulted in heavy downward pressure on the franc so that, in January 1974, it had to leave the snake and float.

1974 to July 1975. After falling steeply during the first half of 1974, the franc's exchange rate recovered in the second half of the year and more or less regained its autumn 1973 level. This was facilitated by the improvement in the current balance following the slowdown in growth due, in particular, to a tighter monetary policy. The franc continued to recover in the first half of 1975 and in July of that year it rejoined the European snake.

July 1975 to March 1976. The introduction of a programme to stimulate the economic activity in the second half of 1975 was accompanied by a large external deficit and a rapid

58

expansion of domestic credit. As a result, from the end of 1975 the franc came under downward pressure and again had to leave the snake in March 1976.

March 1976 to March 1979. The franc fell steeply from March to September 1976, the effective exchange rate declining by some 10 per cent. The introduction of a stabilization programme in autumn 1976 (the "Barre Plan") resulted in a gradual improvement of the current balance of payments, so that by the end of 1977 it was back in equilibrium and in 1978 and 1979 it showed a surplus. During these three years the franc's effective exchange rate was remarkably stable (except during the months immediately prior to the parliamentary elections in the spring of 1978). The franc appreciated against the dollar but depreciated against the Deutschemark, which was a favourable development regarding both the terms of trade (because of the oil bill) and export competitiveness.

March 1979 to 1983. During this last period the franc participated in the European Monetary System, set up in March 1979. Until the end of 1980 the franc held up well against the other EMS currencies[3], and was in fact the strongest of them throughout most of 1980. This performance was facilitated by the weakness of the Deutschemark following the marked deterioration of Germany's current balance after the second oil shock[4]. In spite of a relatively high inflation rate, operators on the foreign exchange markets were apparently also favourably influenced by the continued restrictive stance of monetary policy, the reduction in the budget deficit and the first benefits from an ambitious energy programme.

Upward pressures on the dollar and the approach of the presidential elections caused the franc to weaken in early 1981. This weakness was exacerbated by the introduction in the spring of that year of an expansionary economic policy aimed at curbing the growth of unemployment by stimulating domestic demand. Intervention by the central bank enabled the franc's parity within the EMS to remain unchanged until October 1981, when it was devalued by 3 per cent while the Deutschemark was revalued by 5.3 per cent. The cyclical divergence caused by the fact that the orientation of economic policy in France was out of line with that prevailing in the other main EEC trading partners resulted in a substantial worsening of the trade balance. Consequently, and also because of continuing inflationary pressures, the franc weakened further at the beginning of 1982 and in June was once again devalued within the EMS, this time by 5.75 per cent (the Deutschemark was revalued by 4.25 per cent). This new devaluation was accompanied by anti-inflation measures. Downward pressures on the franc again emerged however, towards the end of 1982 and in early 1983; these resulted in a realignment of parities within the EMS in March 1983, whereby the franc was devalued by 2.5 per cent and the Deutschemark revalued by 5.5 per cent.

b) *Main determinants of the exchange rate's behaviour*

Of the factors that have influenced the franc's behaviour, it would appear that developments in the foreign balance have played a major role (see Chart 1). Indeed, as noted above, the weakening of the franc at the end of 1973, during 1976 and over the period 1981-82 was closely connected with a deterioration in the current account; on the other hand, the improvement in the foreign balance in 1975 and 1977 helped the franc to recover while the current account surpluses of 1978 and 1979 were partly responsible for its firmness on the foreign exchange market.

Movements in the franc's exchange rate seem also to have been influenced by inflation differentials though, to judge by the absence of any very close relationship between these variables, this influence has probably not been decisive in the short term. Over a large part of the period considered, price rises were steeper in France than in other countries. On three

59

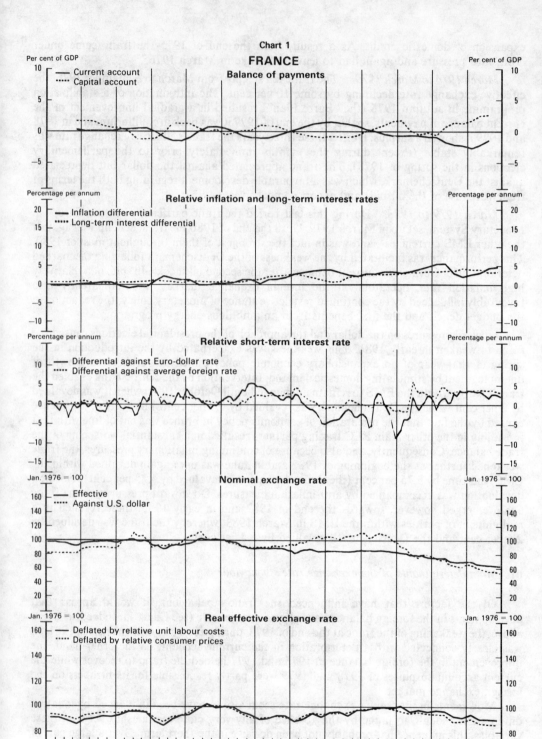

Chart 1

FRANCE

Balance of payments

Per cent of GDP

— Current account
····· Capital account

Relative inflation and long-term interest rates

Percentage per annum

— Inflation differential
····· Long-term interest differential

Relative short-term interest rate

Percentage per annum

— Differential against Euro-dollar rate
····· Differential against average foreign rate

Nominal exchange rate

Jan. 1976 = 100

— Effective
····· Against U.S. dollar

Real effective exchange rate

Jan. 1976 = 100

— Deflated by relative unit labour costs
····· Deflated by relative consumer prices

1971 1972 1973 1974 1975 1976 1977 1978 1979 1980 1981 1982 1983

60

occasions – 1974, 1976 and 1981-82 – this differential was accompanied by an even larger depreciation of the franc's nominal effective exchange rate. By contrast, from 1977 to 1980 the franc's nominal effective exchange rate remained relatively stable in spite of a comparatively higher rate of inflation. Consequently, the real effective exchange rate tended to appreciate, implying a deterioration of the competitiveness of French industry.

The relationship between movements in the franc and short-term interest rate differentials is apparently not systematic, which may be due to the fact that a number of factors have simultaneously affected the behaviour of the exchange rate. Throughout the period under review, money market rates were actively adjusted, relative to rates abroad, in order to influence capital movements and thereby the behaviour of the franc on the foreign exchange market (see below). Thus, in 1974, 1976 and 1981-83 the French monetary authorities engineered a significantly positive interest differential so as to counteract downward pressures on the franc. During 1974 and 1976 the franc responded favourably to this situation, mainly as a result of large inflows of capital and of the accompanying measures introduced to bring down inflation and restore current payments equilibrium. On the other hand, during 1981-83 the substantial rise in short-term interest rates relative to other countries was not sufficient to stem the depreciation of the franc, which is why measures were announced to make the stance of economic policy more restrictive after the devaluations of June 1982 and March 1983. It should also be pointed out that from 1977 to 1980 the franc remained stable and was even strong at various times (see above), despite the almost constantly negative short-term interest rate differential. This suggests that other factors, related to the overall stance of economic policy, played a dominant role at those times.

EXCHANGE RATE MANAGEMENT AND THE CONDUCT OF MONETARY POLICY

During the period under consideration, efforts to stabilize the exchange rate involved the use of four main instruments: interest rate adjustment, direct intervention by the central bank on the exchange market, exchange controls and borrowing abroad. In addition, at various times, restrictive measures were applied to limit the growth of the money supply and to contain the budget deficit.

a)   *Interest rate adjustment*

The effect of the managed floating of the franc was to strengthen the tendency towards more flexible short-term interest rates that started in the early 1970s. Indeed, in 1971 the central bank began to regulate money market rates rather than adjusting the discount rate in the context of its refinancing policy. To the extent that the commercial banks continued to rely heavily on the central bank to satisfy their cash requirements[5], the Bank of France's rate of intervention on the money market became the key to the structure of short-term interest rates (including the banks' base rate) and at the same time an indicator of the stance of monetary policy. In practice, except during certain periods, the Bank's intervention rate followed the movement of rates on foreign money markets and the Eurodollar market fairly closely, but provided for a (variable) positive or negative differential when the franc was on a downward or upward trend on the exchange market. This policy was designed to maintain exchange rate stability and protect the foreign exchange reserves[6].

Adjustment of short-term interest rates for external purposes has sometimes posed problems because of conflicts with internal objectives. This was the case in 1972 when, in order to limit capital inflows, relatively low interest rates had to be maintained in spite of the

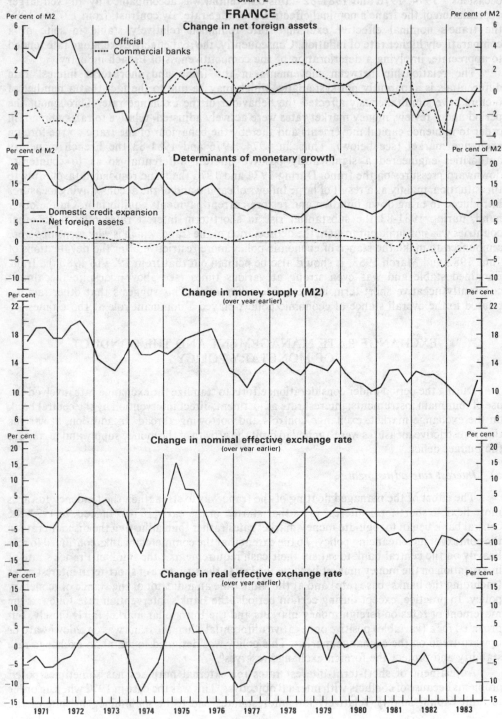

Chart 2

FRANCE

Change in net foreign assets

Per cent of M2

— Official
---- Commercial banks

Determinants of monetary growth

Per cent of M2

— Domestic credit expansion
---- Net foreign assets

Change in money supply (M2)
(over year earlier)

Per cent

Change in nominal effective exchange rate
(over year earlier)

Per cent

Change in real effective exchange rate
(over year earlier)

Per cent

1971 1972 1973 1974 1975 1976 1977 1978 1979 1980 1981 1982 1983

resurgence of inflationary pressures. Likewise, in 1979, in order to prevent speculative movements when the EMS was set up, and in 1981-82, in order to discourage capital outflows, it proved necessary to raise interest rates in spite of the authorities' wish to reduce the cost of credit in order to revive investment. In these circumstances the authorities sometimes tried temporarily and partially to cut the link between the cost of bank credit and money market rates[7]. Thus, in 1981, for example, they tried to reduce banks' operating costs by lowering compulsory reserve ratios and by altering the regulations governing the interest rates on deposits so as to reduce the proportion of banks' liabilities earning market rates. In so doing, the authorities' aim was to lessen the impact of the rise in money market rates on the banks' base lending rate. Since mid-1981 this type of measure has made it possible to keep the banks' base lending rate at a level close to or slightly below the the money market rates.

b) *Official intervention on the foreign exchange market*

Since 1973 when a managed floating of the exchange rate was introduced, the Bank of France has continued to intervene actively on the foreign exchange market. However, a distinction must be drawn between its intervention due to European commitments – which has at times been substantial – and discretionary intervention undertaken by the central bank to adjust the exchange rate in order to go along with, or even smooth, market movements[8]. On balance, judging from the movements of official reserves shown in Chart 2, the overall scale of intervention seems to have remained fairly small, except in 1973-74, 1976, 1981-82 and the beginning of 1983, periods which were characterized by heavy downward pressures on the exchange rate. This was due to the fact that because the authorities wished to maintain a minimum level of reserves they tended to influence indirectly the supply and demand for foreign exchange to avoid intervening in the market. The techniques used to this effect included, in addition to interest rate adjustments as described above, exchange control measures and borrowing by non-banks (see below).

The impact of official intervention on money creation has on the whole been fairly weak (see Chart 2) for one of two reasons:

    i)   either the domestic counterparts of the money supply have varied spontaneously in the opposite direction to the foreign counterpart (as in 1974-75 and 1978-79);

    ii)   or the authorities have acted to sterilise the monetary effects of external disequilibrium by adjusting compulsory reserve ratios, lending to the government, and open market operations.

Experience would suggest, however, that the authorities have tended to neutralise the consequences of a fall in foreign exchange reserves more than those of an increase. This was why, in the early 1970s, the commercial banks took advantage of the creation of liquidity stemming from capital inflows to increase their lending while at the same time they ran down their debt to the central bank. Furthermore, it would seem that the monetary impact of increases in foreign exchange reserves during some periods (1975, 1977-78) was greater than the impact of earlier falls in reserves (1974 and 1976), which would suggest that sterilisation was not entirely symmetrical. This reflects the fact that the reconstitution of foreign exchange reserves, which was deemed positive, was accepted without the authorities seeking to contain the domestic sources of money creation.

c) *Exchange controls*

In order to restrict outward exchange movements the French monetary authorities have frequently used administrative measures[9]. For the most part these have been aimed at capital movements, although restrictions have also been applied on foreign currency transactions for

63

travel purposes. Regulations include, first of all, prohibition of franc loans to non-residents to limit outflows of capital and to prevent any expansion of the Eurofranc market. With regard to the behaviour of residents, which is by far the main influence on capital movements, regulations have applied – with varying force depending on the period – both to banks (particularly to their net foreign positions) and to transactions by the non-bank sector. The latter are at present subject to overall regulations (applying in particular to direct investment, security and foreign currency transactions), coupled with measures to limit leads and lags in respect of commercial payments. In certain circumstances too, the authorities have been prompted to supplement their direct control of short-term capital movements with financial disincentives. Thus from May 1970 to October 1973, and again from November 1980 to May 1981, special reserve regulations were applied to non-residents' deposits in order to discourage capital inflows; from August 1970 to October 1973, moreover, banks were not permitted to pay interest on such deposits. In addition, from August 1971 to March 1974 a two-tier foreign exchange market operated to prevent both inflows and outflows of capital[10].

It is difficult to assess accurately the effectiveness of exchange control at times when the franc has been under pressure. As the first line of defence of the exchange rate, this type of control has certainly had the effect of limiting the scale of direct central bank intervention on the foreign exchange market, and has thus helped to protect official reserves. In 1981, and to a lesser extent in 1982, it limited capital outflows and, by inducing residents engaged in international trade to borrow in foreign currency from the French banking system, it facilitated the financing of the balance of payments deficit. When having to contend with large-scale speculative movements, however (as in 1970-71, 1974, 1976, 1981-82 and early 1983), exchange controls were not sufficient to stem upward or downward pressure on the franc, and in some cases even proved ineffective. Furthermore, exchange control has damaging effects in that it tends to worsen firms' operating conditions and hurts their competitiveness. With regard to commercial transactions, the provisions aimed at restricting leads and lags or reducing forward purchases of foreign currency soon proved moreover to be of limited scope since the authorities generally sought to avoid penalising foreign trade. Even so, this type of restriction has been strengthened considerably in recent years.

d) *Foreign borrowing*

With the foreign indebtedness of the banking sector increasing only slightly during the period in question, it was foreign borrowing by firms (medium and long-term) which was chiefly responsible for reducing the drain on foreign exchange reserves[11]. In allowing enterprises – and particularly those in the nationalised sector – to borrow on foreign markets, the monetary authorities had three objectives: to finance the current account deficit (particularly after the two oil shocks), to provide finance for enterprises and, in especially 1981-83, to support the franc. Foreign borrowing by public and private companies helped to increase the supply of foreign currency on the exchange market when there was downward pressure on the franc, thus limiting the amount of foreign currency sales by the central bank. It may therefore be considered that exchange rate management has been more active than official intervention alone might suggest.

Apart from public enterprises, the government too has sometimes been a direct foreign borrower. On two separate occasions – in 1974 and 1982 – the French government negotiated the opening of credit lines on the Eurocurrency market with the object of bolstering its foreign exchange reserves. The first line of credit was for $1.5 billion but was not used; the second, totalling $4 billion, appears to have been drawn in tranches at the discretion of the monetary authorities. In addition, in May 1983 the government arranged a $3.7 billion loan from the European Economic Community.

Firms' foreign indebtedness is not necessarily neutral from the view point of money creation[12]. Once converted this indebtedness results in resident firms having francs at their disposal, while it also improves the "external" counterpart of the money supply which, otherwise, would have contracted more. In formulating their money supply growth targets (see below), the authorities usually make the assumption that liquidity created as a result of foreign borrowing makes up for that destroyed because of the external deficit. In practice, however, foreign indebtedness and the current account deficit are not perfectly synchronized, so that the monetary neutrality of foreign borrowing is not always guaranteed. When the current deficit does not move as forecast, adjusting foreign borrowing can prove difficult since it takes time to set up such borrowing. If therefore the current account deficit is bigger than initially forecast, foreign exchange reserves will tend to diminish by the same amount. If it is smaller, the foreign borrowing "surplus" will tend to be reflected either in an increase in official reserves or in an increase in French banks' net foreign asset position (since the borrowed funds go into resident accounts).

e) *The "announcement" effect of monetary targets and budget forecasts*

Since they consider that rapid monetary growth is likely to feed inflationary pressures, and hence the depreciation of the franc on the foreign exchange market, the authorities have decided, from 1976 onwards, to set quantitative limits on M2 growth. Targets for this aggregate have been published every year, with the object on the one hand of making inflation control policy more credible in the eyes of domestic and foreign economic agents and, on the other hand, of making the conduct of monetary policy more stable[13]. From 1977 to 1979 monetary targets were very close to nominal GDP forecasts. This was because the government's prime concern was to stabilize the domestic liquidity ratio (i.e. the ratio of M2 to

Monetary growth and budget balance : targets, forecasts and outturns

	Period	Target	Outturns
Growth of M2 (per cent)	Dec. 1976-Dec. 1977	$12\frac{1}{2}$	13.9
	Dec. 1977-Dec. 1978	12	12.2
	Dec. 1978-Dec. 1979	11	14.4
	Dec. 1979-Dec. 1980	11	9.8
	Dec. 1980-Dec. 1981	10[a]	11.4
	Dec. 1981-Dec. 1982	12.5-13.5	12.0
	Dec. 1982-Dec. 1983[b]	9	

		Forecasts[c]	Outturns
Net borrowing. (−) or lending (+)	1975	+ 6.2	−32.5
by general government	1976	−25.2	−8.2
(billions of francs)[d]	1977	−13.0	−15.7
	1978	−18.1	−40.0
	1979	−41.6	−16.7
	1980	−41.9	+ 7.2
	1981	−52.7	−57.2
	1982	−83.0	−92.3
	1983	−115.5	−120.5[e]

a) Raised implicitly to approximately 12 per cent in the second half of the year to allow for the implementation in June 1981 of a more expansionary economic policy which attached priority to reducing unemployment.
b) For 1983 the target was expressed in terms of three month moving averages centred on December of 1982 and 1983.
c) Forecasts included in the draft budget presented in the autumn of the previous year.
d) Central government, local authorities and social security.
e) OECD estimate.

GDP), which had been rising continuously in the course of previous years. Subsequently the authorities sought gradually to reduce monetary growth, but in 1981, faced with a changed economic situation and new government priorities, they raised their initial quantitative targets. Over the whole of the period considered, control of monetary growth continued to rest mainly on quantitative limits on bank credit, in accordance with the system set up in late 1972[14]. It was also facilitated, between 1976 and 1980 in particular, by strict control of bank lending to the Treasury, coupled with a cautious fiscal policy to limit the budget deficit.

On the whole, as the table above shows, monetary growth targets have always been slightly exceeded by the end of the year, except in 1980. Since, however, nominal GDP also rose a little more than forecast, the domestic liquidity ratio remained stable. This result was achieved, however, with a real rate of growth in activity which was lower than initially envisaged by the authorities, while the rate of inflation was faster than anticipated. With regard to budget forecasts, the general government deficit was often in excess of initial estimates. This was due mainly to the faster than expected slowdown in activity which resulted in slower growth of tax revenues and a large increase in transfer payments due to mounting unemployment. However, this trend did not have damaging consequences for monetary growth except in 1975 and 1981-82 when, owing to the substantial increase in the budget deficit, there was a considerable rise in bank lending to the government.

CONCLUDING REMARKS

The economy's growing foreign trade dependence and the consequences of the oil shocks (the increased cost of energy imports) explain why exchange rate stability has remained an important objective for the French authorities since the move to floating exchange rates in 1973. To help achieve this objective over the long term, the authorities have sought since 1976 to reduce monetary growth through the adoption of explicit targets for the broad money supply (M2). This has involved an increased risk of conflict between the internal and external objectives of monetary policy.

The experience of the 1970s and early 1980s would suggest, however, that such conflicts have remained limited. Two observations may be made in this respect:

i)   With downward pressure on the franc caused by fundamental factors (such as a deterioration of the current account), priority could not continue to be given to exchange rate stability. In such circumstances – as in 1974, 1976, 1981-82 and early 1983 – the authorities were obliged to allow the franc to depreciate or to devalue. This decision was only taken, however, after considerable effort had been made to support the franc on the foreign exchange market, entailing substantial losses of official reserves.

ii) Whenever upward or downward pressure on the franc had seemed temporary, exchange rate stability has been maintained primarily by adjusting interest rates in light of those prevailing abroad. In order, however, to retain a degree of independence for monetary policy, they have used a number of other instruments: adjustment of quantitative credit restrictions, exchange controls, occasional intervention in the foreign exchange market coupled with measures to sterilise the impact on domestic liquidity and, above all, since 1974, foreign borrowing by public enterprises. Some of these measures (foreign borrowing in particular) prevented monetary policy from becoming too restrictive as from the mid-1970s. In 1971-72, on the other hand, foreign exchange regulations and sterilisation of capital inflows did not prove sufficient to prevent monetary policy from turning out to be more accommodating than seemed desirable.

More generally, the French experience shows that the pursuit of exchange rate stability means that the stance of economic policy has to remain similar to that adopted by Germany for two reasons: the importance of trade with that country and attachment to the European monetary agreements limiting the margins within which currencies could fluctuate. The fact that this constraint influenced economic management in France during the second half of the 1970s is not unrelated to the stability of the franc's exchange rate during that period. Conversely, the downward pressures on the franc in 1973-74, 1976 and 1981-82 were partially due to the more flexible stance of economic policy in France than in Germany, which was reflected in diverging economic situations in the two countries.

NOTES

1. From 1970 to 1982 the share of imports of goods and services in GDP rose from 15 to around 24 per cent; that of exports increased from 15 to almost 22 per cent.

2. Deutschemark, Belgian franc, Dutch guilder, Sterling and the Irish pound (until June 1972), Italian lira (until February 1973) and (beginning March 1973) Norwegian and Danish Kroner.

3. Deutschemark, Dutch guilder, Belgian franc, Italian lira, Irish pound, Danish krone.

4. See the note on Germany.

5. For further details, see OECD (1974, 1979)

6. In practice, during the first half of the 1970s the central bank followed the fluctuations in the one-month Eurodollar rate closely as part of its policy of intervention on the money market. Subsequently, the monetary authorities oriented their short-term interest rate policy more toward rates prevailing in European markets. This orientation became more pronounced with the establishment of the EMS in 1979. In doing this, the authorities' essentially intended to stabilize the franc against the major European currencies, its rate against the US dollar moving in line with the fluctuations of the latter against the EMS currencies (in particular the Deutschemark).

7. It is worth noting that a degree of delinkage has become permanent because nearly half of medium- and long-term credit is extended at subsidised rates (these rates differing with the type of credit).

8. This was the case, for example, during the pre-election period of spring 1978: the downward pressures on the franc in early February (with the approach of the parliamentary elections) were absorbed at the cost of some modest intervention and a limited slide in the exchange rate. By the end of March the foreign exchange reserves were reconstituted and the franc's effective exchange rate regained its end-1977 level.

9. For a more detailed description see OECD (1974), Annex 1.

10. Under this system, most current transactions were made at the market rate for the commerical franc which fluctuated within fixed margins around the central rate, while capital transactions were made at the market rate for the financial franc which was determined by supply and demand. Official intervention was in principle limited only to the commercial franc market. In early 1974 the authorities decided to extend the managed floating of the franc – introduced a year earlier – to the commercial market. As a result, the two-tier market was abolished shortly afterwards.

11. Net foreign borrowing by French enterprises between 1974 and the third quarter of 1983 can be estimated at a total of some $53 billion.

12. The same is not true of foreign borrowing by the government, the franc counterpart of which is automatically sterilised by the central bank.

13. For more details see OECD (1979), pp. 45-47.

14. This system involves establishing recommended norms for the growth of credit granted by banks and financial institutions; where these norms are exceeded, progressively increasing penalty reserves apply to total outstanding credit distributed by these institutions.

UNITED KINGDOM

Some four months after the Smithsonian agreement of December 1971, which left the effective exchange rate for sterling approximately unchanged, the United Kingdom joined the European "snake" arrangement whereby participating countries were obliged to keep movements of their currencies against each other within tight margins. Almost immediately, however, in June 1972, sterling came under heavy downward pressure and, after heavy support, intervention rates were suspended. The high degree of integration of the British economy with the rest of the world meant that the exchange rate remained a matter of concern, and, at least until May 1979, intervention in the exchange market was at times substantial. But no formal commitment to a fixed parity for sterling has ever been re-established.

A particular aspect of the British situation, which weighed heavily with policymakers for many years, was the existence of a large stock of external sterling debt, mainly in the form of marketable government bills and bonds, which was subject to withdrawal whenever the exchange rate appeared vulnerable. Under arrangements made in 1977 the United Kingdom attempted to reduce the level of those balances held as official reserves by offering to replace them with special foreign currency bonds. Relatively few of these balances were funded in this way, however, and as sterling strengthened during 1979-80 these balances were built up further.

OVERVIEW OF THE BEHAVIOUR OF THE EXCHANGE RATE SINCE THE EARLY 1970s

After sterling was allowed to float in June 1972 it alternated between periods of stablity and weakness until late 1976, with its overall depreciation (in effective terms) amounting to nearly 40 per cent (see Chart 1). As the differential between inflation in the United Kingdom and in other countries was in general high and variable the real effective exchange rate depreciated far less. During 1972-73 and during 1976 the real exchange rate, as measured by unit labour costs, fell rapidly. But during 1974-75 it appreciated almost to the level prevailing before June 1972. From the end of 1976, and particularly from early 1979, until early 1981 sterling was persistently strong despite a substantial adverse inflation differential. The result was that the real exchange rate, in terms of unit labour costs, nearly doubled during this period. Some of this appreciation can be seen as a correction for the excessive depreciation during 1976, providing some support for the view that purchasing power parity asserts itself over the medium term. But the appreciation of 1979-80 put the real exchange rate far above anything that had been experienced during the 1960s or '70s. Some downward adjustment of

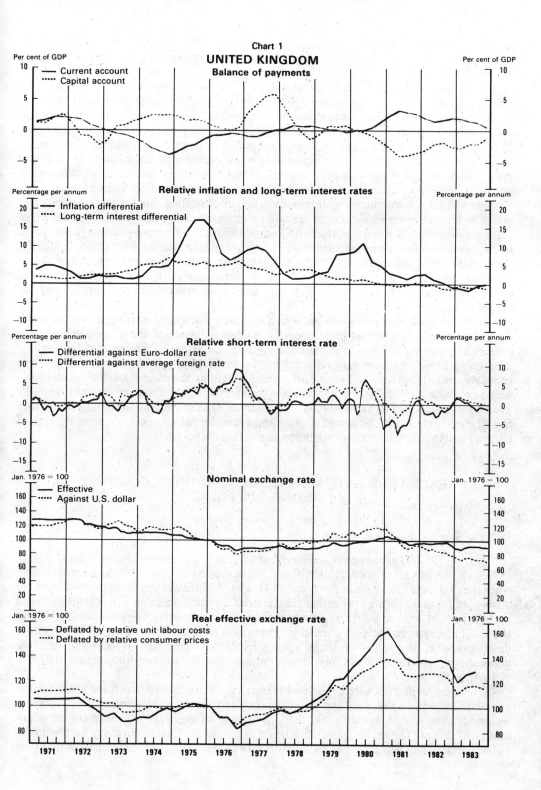

Chart 1

UNITED KINGDOM

Per cent of GDP

Balance of payments

Per cent of GDP

— Current account
····· Capital account

Relative inflation and long-term interest rates

Percentage per annum

— Inflation differential
····· Long-term interest differential

Relative short-term interest rate

Percentage per annum

— Differential against Euro-dollar rate
····· Differential against average foreign rate

Nominal exchange rate

Jan. 1976 = 100

— Effective
····· Against U.S. dollar

Real effective exchange rate

Jan. 1976 = 100

— Deflated by relative unit labour costs
····· Deflated by relative consumer prices

1971 1972 1973 1974 1975 1976 1977 1978 1979 1980 1981 1982 1983

sterling occurred during 1981, and again at the end of 1982. This somewhat improved the competitiveness of the economy, but at the end of 1983 the real exchange rate was still high by historical standards.

It has proved difficult to explain sterling's behaviour with econometric methods[1]. This implies that there has been no regular relationship between the exchange rate and the main observable variables which theoretical considerations suggest might be its principal determinants. At times the current account may have been an important influence, as in 1972-73 when it deteriorated from a large surplus to a large deficit, and in 1980 when a movement into a strong current account surplus contributed to a nominal and real appreciation. Similarly, between 1978 and mid-1980, when interest rate policy was directed to domestic monetary objectives, a clear positive association existed between exchange rate changes and short term interest differentials in favour of sterling. But for most of the period under review these variables cannot provide an explanation. In particular, the very large current deficit in 1974 was associated with a surprisingly strong nominal exchange rate and a real appreciation despite no important offsetting favourable interest differential. Similarly, the record interest differential of 1976 was a reflection of sterling's weakness, rather than a source of strength. Finally, no strong or regular relationship exists between either domestic credit expansion or the growth of the money supply, however defined (Chart 2), and the exchange rate.

A factor, not directly measurable, which may have influenced sterling at various times, has been changes in portfolio preferences. The adverse impact of the oil price rise on the current account in 1974 was in effect offset by some oil exporters' preferences for sterling, even though this may have only reflected inertia in their cash management, and this was probably crucial to the stability of the exchange rate at the time. Conversely, sterling's weakness during 1975-76 was exacerbated by a reversal of these preferences and the associated reduction of oil exporters' sterling balances. During 1979-80 the influence of North Sea oil, to the extent that this moved sterling into a superior risk-class of currencies at a time of oil price instability, may have contributed to sterling's strength.

EXCHANGE RATE MANAGEMENT AND THE CONDUCT OF MONETARY POLICY

a) *The first oil shock, and its aftermath*

During 1972-73 expansion of real demand was the main concern of the authorities, and, in view of previous experience, priority was given to domestic objectives[2]. As a consequence, when the exchange rate came under pressure in June 1972 the authorities permitted it to float downward for more than a year rather than restrict domestic demand. It was initially hoped that the current account would respond to real depreciation to restore equilibrium, stabilising the exchange rate. In the event, the rapid expansion of domestic demand, together with a deterioration of the terms of trade arising from the commodity price boom and the depreciation, produced a sharply deteriorating current account throughout 1972-73 (Chart 1).

These developments were considered transitory, and because it was feared that further depreciation would undermine the incomes policy introduced in November 1972, an effort was made to moderate sterling's fall, but still without affecting the expansionary monetary and fiscal stance. The exchange cover scheme to encourage foreign currency borrowing by public sector bodies was reintroduced in March 1973 and during the second half of that year

70

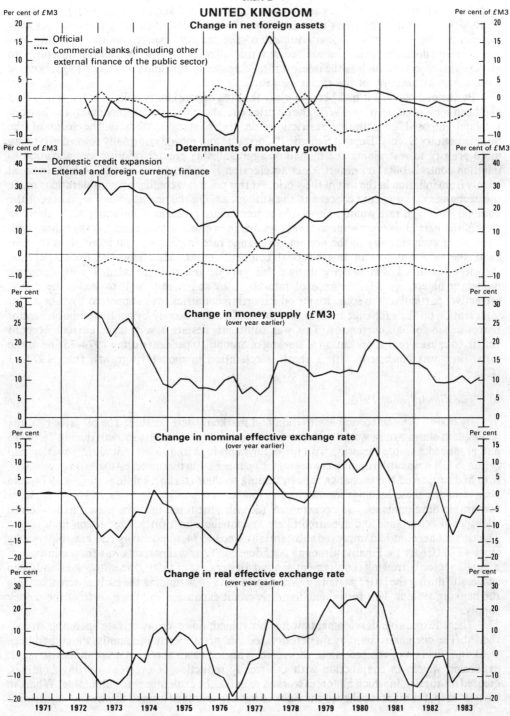

Chart 2

UNITED KINGDOM

71

official intervention was heavy. The exchange rate continued to depreciate until the latter part of the year, when it steadied. The combination of depreciation and the world commodity boom resulted in very rapid increases in import prices which threatened to (and eventually did) undermine the counter-inflationary impact of the incomes policy. As the economy was overheating, domestic priorities shifted toward inflation control. Monetary measures to achieve this objective, such as the interest rate increases in July and November 1973, became consistent with stability of the exchange rate.

By the end of 1973 it had become clear that the expansionary policy stance of 1972-73 had been somewhat overdone. With the oil price rise about to make its impact felt the Bank of England imposed quantitative restrictions on the banking system in the form of the Supplementary Special Deposit Scheme ("Corset")[3] and moved informally toward attaching more priority to restraining the monetary aggregates as greater priority was accorded to inflation control. Inflation nevertheless accelerated sharply and by mid-1974 had diverged widely from inflation in the rest of the world. At this point two conflicting considerations made the exchange rate an acute concern to the authorities. On the one hand any weakness of the nominal exchange rate would aggravate the immediate problem of inflation, particularly in view of the partial *de facto* wage indexation scheme in effect at that time. On the other hand, strength or even stability of the nominal exchange rate implied a rapid increase in the real exchange rate and loss of international competitiveness. Managing the exchange rate, therefore, assumed first priority during this period, and did not conflict with domestic monetary objectives. Maintenance of interest rates sufficiently high to make the pound attractive, particularly to some major oil-exporting countries, was supported by substantial intervention on the exchange market, which was financed largely by continued public sector borrowing in foreign currencies. This was sufficient, despite a very large current account deficit, to cause a real appreciation of sterling of around 10 per cent during 1974-75 and at the same time was consistent with a sharp deceleration in monetary growth from 1972-73 (Chart 2).

b) *The difficulties of 1976*

By early 1976 the economic situation had markedly deteriorated. The oil price rise, the subsequent slowdown in world trade, and the restraint on monetary growth during 1974/75 had produced a severe recession with unemployment high and rising. Although inflation had begun to fall it was still running in excess of 20 per cent. Furthermore, oil exporting countries, who had supported the exchange rate by adding to their sterling holdings during 1974, had been reducing these holdings for much of 1975 and were continuing to do so. However, some favourable developments had occurred. A recently instituted incomes policy had received widespread acceptance and appeared likely to contribute to a further reduction in inflation. The current account had improved substantially since 1974, temporarily reaching balance by early 1976 (Chart 1). Finally, although confidence in financial markets was fragile in view of a public sector borrowing requirement around 10 per cent of GDP, the authorities had been successful during the latter part of 1975 and early in 1976 in funding the budget deficit outside the banking system. This restrained domestic credit expansion and the growth of the money supply.

These favourable developments were threatened, however, as private spending streng-thened. The current account again deteriorated and private credit demands, which had been weak in reflection of the recession, recovered. This led to an acceleration of domestic credit expansion which, in conjunction with the steady reduction of overseas sterling holdings, created a situation in which all forces worked to make the exchange rate vulnerable. When, in early March, the market believed the Bank to have encouraged a small downward adjustment

72

of the exchange rate to maintain competitiveness a downward spiral ensued. Short-term interest rates were raised several times during the spring and summer, and a quantitative target for the annual growth of the broadly defined money supply (M3) was announced in July. However, measures sufficiently strong to stabilize the situation were resisted until the autumn for fear of aggravating the recession.

A major problem concerned unease about the financial situation. The actual and prospective budget deficits were regarded as uncomfortably large by financial markets, likely to result in excessive monetary growth and a subsequent reacceleration of inflation. These fears were reinforced by the deteriorating current account and the weakness of sterling during the spring, and resulted in some reluctance on the part of the markets to fund the budget deficit outside the banking system. The consequent need to finance the budget deficit by expanding domestic credit made the markets' fears self-fulfilling during the summer when the money supply accelerated sharply, well above the quantitative target for M3 announced in July. From early September the exchange rate came under renewed heavy pressure. As in 1973, the depreciation threatened both to undermine the anti-inflationary intent of an incomes policy and to lead to structural distortions due to an excessively undervalued exchange rate. Finally, therefore, priority shifted toward stabilizing the pound, in order to support the inflation control programme. Despite the recession further increases in interest rates were imposed, restrictions on capital movements were tightened, and finally the Government announced its intention to draw on its remaining standby credit tranches from the IMF.

Market sentiment rapidly shifted to the view that sterling's decline had been excessive. At the same time the rise in interest rates had made sterling assets attractive. From late September the authorities were able to resume funding of the budget deficit outside the banking system, which had a favourable impact on domestic credit expansion and the money supply, and capital flows began to move back into the United Kingdom. The exchange rate recovered steadily through November and sterling remained persistently strong during 1977.

c) *Coping with appreciation*

During 1977, the authorities were reluctant to allow the exchange rate to rise too far, preferring to consolidate some of the gains in competitiveness made during the previous year. They therefore intervened to buy foreign exchange and build up the official reserves. The result was persistent upward pressure on the money supply which necessitated heavy sales of government debt to the non-bank private sector in order to remain within the monetary target for sterling M3[4]. These debt sales drained the financial system of funds that would otherwise have been available to other borrowers, and this in turn attracted more capital from abroad. As a consequence, during the summer and early autumn intervention on the exchange market to prevent an appreciation of sterling became very large. Capital inflows showed no signs of abating, despite substantial reductions in interest rates during the course of the year, while concern mounted that it would be difficult to continue selling large amounts of gilt-edged securities to non-bank financial institutions. The authorities were thus faced with a choice between the exchange rate and the money supply as the intermediate target whose achievement should receive priority. In October they chose the latter, and the exchange rate was permitted to appreciate despite the likely impact on competitiveness.

The budget in spring 1978 was expansionary despite overshooting of the monetary target during the fiscal year 1977-78, and in June the corset was reintroduced to assist with monetary control. The corset led to disintermediation by the banking system which enabled the economy to circumvent, to some extent, the restrictive intent of the target. The economy expanded rapidly until the spring of 1979. The exchange rate was stable during most of 1978 but during 1979-80, as inflation control returned to top priority, there was to be persistent upward pressure on sterling.

An important influence on the exchange market during this period was oil. Production of North Sea oil, which began in 1975, made real national income and the current account relatively insensitive to shifts in the price of oil. Thus, when the second oil crisis occurred the United Kingdom was less vulnerable than other countries and sterling assets may have appeared comparatively attractive as a hedge against the risk of future oil price increases. Despite these pressures on the exchange rate monetary policy attached increasing priority to the achievement of targets for the growth of £M3. Intervention was confined to smoothing operations through most of the period after March 1979, and the abolition of restrictions on capital movements in October 1979 only temporarily slowed the appreciation, which, by the end of 1980, exceeded 50 per cent in real terms, as measured by unit labour costs (Chart 1). In terms of lower inflation, which was the principal objective, the apparently excessive strength of sterling had substantial benefits.

However, a number of factors worked to frustrate the policy, at least in the short term and, in consequence, a severe squeeze developed on the real economy. A large increase in indirect taxes in the budget of June 1979 had the effect of raising prices substantially and encouraging wage increases. This interacted with some public sector wage and price rises and the oil price increase to produce an inflation rate which approached 20 per cent. Despite the persistent failure to meet targets for £M3, and even allowing for bank disintermediation induced by the corset, monetary expansion was insufficient to accommodate price rises of this magnitude without generating severe deflationary pressures. The strength of the exchange rate, to which this financial squeeze clearly contributed, had the effect of putting the burden of the recession on those sectors most vulnerable to international competition, principally manufacturing.

By mid-1980 there were signs that the recession was deepening, and serious concern was developing about its longer-term effects on large parts of the manufacturing sector. In view of developments in the real economy, and in recognition of the tightness of monetary conditions suggested by monetary indicators other than £M3 (including M1) and by the behaviour of the exchange rate, the stance of policy was eased. Interest rates were adjusted downward in several steps despite the tendency for foreign rates to rise. For a period this failed to halt sterling's appreciation, but as the adverse interest differential widened and as oil prices weakened in 1981 a substantial downward adjustment took place. By 1982 the orientation of policy was closer to what it had been during 1974-75. Although the authorities had no specific exchange rate objectives they were concerned to maintain a relatively strong exchange rate to assist with inflation control but also to ensure that adverse effects on international competitiveness were not too severe. Attention was still paid to monetary aggregates and a commitment to keep these under control was maintained, but the target itself was loosened and was made to apply to several aggregates rather than a single one.

CONCLUDING REMARKS

There have been three episodes during the past decade when monetary policy has given priority to domestic objectives while the authorities have been prepared to accept, to some extent, the consequences for the exchange rate. Partly due to factors such as fiscal policy and oil price rises, the movement of the exchange rate went further than was anticipated or regarded as tolerable. The overshooting was always of some assistance with respect to the ultimate objective being accorded first priority at the time (real demand in 1972-73 and 1976, inflation in 1979-80), and this may explain much of the authorities' reluctance to respond.

In each of these instances the exchange rate contributed to, or at least provided forwarning of, unacceptable performance with regard to other objectives. Ongoing reappraisals of the balance between costs and benefits of maintaining the existing policy stance inevitably led to the conclusions that an adjustment would be appropriate. Changes in the relative priority given to inflation and unemployment were important factors, as the shifts in late 1973 and 1976 involved acceptance of a negative impact on unemployment while that of 1981 implied some easing of the previous anti-inflationary stance. But the shifts were also partly motivated, particularly in 1981, by concerns that an unrealistic real exchange rate would lead to structural distortions.

At the operating level, an important lesson from these experiences is that the behaviour of the exchange rate may at times be a good indicator of the stance of monetary policy. By taking the information embodied in exchange market conditions into account the authorities have sought to improve the conduct of policy. As such, the role of the exchange rate in the formation of monetary policy has increased since the late 1970s, although it has not regained the priority which it had before 1972.

NOTES

1. See Hacche and Townend (1981).
2. See the Budget statement by the Chancellor of the Exchequer in March 1972.
3. See OECD (1982), p. 78 for details.
4. As part of its agreement with the IMF the UK monetary authorities imposed ceilings on domestic credit expansion for the fiscal years 1977/78 and 1978/79. This supplemented the announcement of monetary targets in terms of sterling M3, but when external conditions improved the latter were given priority.

ITALY

Italy switched to floating exchange rates in January 1973, first with a two tier (commercial/financial) float and subsequently shifting to a uniform flexible rate in March 1974. Given the openness of the economy[1], authorities have always been concerned with movements in the external value of the lira, so that official intervention on the exchange market and/or externally-oriented changes in domestic monetary policy have been frequent. Since early 1979 Italy has been a member of the European Monetary System (EMS), though with wider bands than other participants, which has tended to formalise the "triggering" of intervention policies between parity readjustments. Since 1974 the Bank of Italy has also sought to target total domestic credit, i.e. from both bank and non-bank sources, but not the growth of the money supply. The monetary authorities have attempted to regulate credit via operations on the monetary base (e.g. variations of discount rate, Treasury bill sales, etc.), but the potential for conflicts in using this operating variable to achieve domestic objectives while official intervention is used to achieve exchange rate objectives may be important. Partly as a consequence of this, quantitative ceilings on bank credit expansion (until recently excluding foreign currency denominated loans) have also been extensively applied[2].

OVERVIEW OF THE BEHAVIOUR OF THE EXCHANGE RATE SINCE THE EARLY 1970s

The main presumed determinants of exchange rate movements in the case of Italy are shown in Chart 1. The general picture has been a steady deterioration of the inflation differential since 1973, which has been partly due to the monetary accommodation of excessively large public sector deficits and to the operation of wage indexation since 1975. The nominal effective exchange rate has tended to adjust afterwards in a series of discrete "jumps" to offset the gradual deterioration in competitiveness. Consequently, while there has been no prolonged tendency for the real exchange rate to appreciate, there has rarely been a sustained gain in competitiveness associated with devaluations. Deteriorations in the current account balance have frequently acted as "detonators" of exchange rate crises. This was the case in the 1973/74 period, in 1976, and during 1980/81. Aside from an adverse movement in 1973, short-term interest rate differentials have generally been in Italy's favour. Large positive swings in 1974, 1976 and since 1980, have tended to reflect domestic monetary responses to exchange market pressures.

76

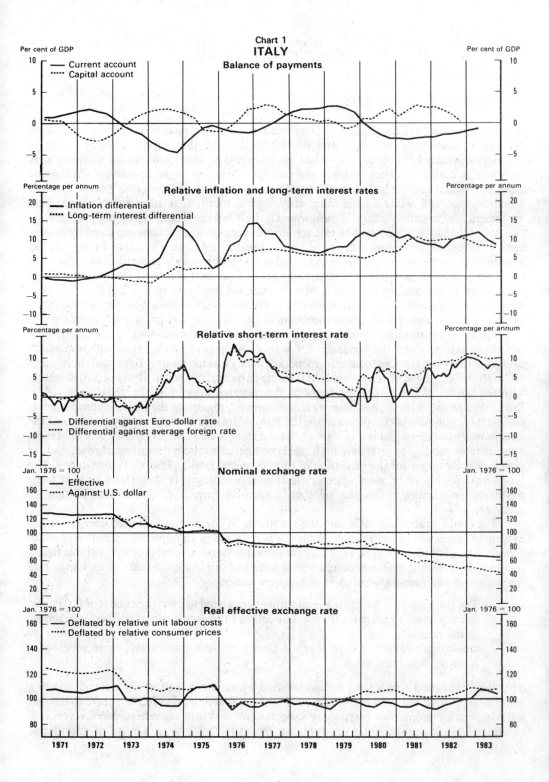

Chart 1
ITALY

Per cent of GDP / Per cent of GDP

Balance of payments
— Current account
···· Capital account

Percentage per annum

Relative inflation and long-term interest rates
— Inflation differential
···· Long-term interest differential

Percentage per annum

Relative short-term interest rate
— Differential against Euro-dollar rate
···· Differential against average foreign rate

Jan. 1976 = 100

Nominal exchange rate
— Effective
···· Against U.S. dollar

Jan. 1976 = 100

Real effective exchange rate
— Deflated by relative unit labour costs
···· Deflated by relative consumer prices

1971 1972 1973 1974 1975 1976 1977 1978 1979 1980 1981 1982 1983

EXCHANGE RATE MANAGEMENT AND THE CONDUCT
OF MONETARY POLICY

a) *The period prior to the EMS*

By the end of 1972 the Italian economy was experiencing a modest recovery in response to previous expansionary monetary and fiscal policies, and the current account began to deteriorate in early 1973 (Chart 1). As interest rates rose in other European countries, notably Germany, a conflict between internal and external objectives began to emerge. On the one hand the authorities wished to avoid increases in interest rates in order not to forestall economic recovery, while on the other they were committed to the EEC exchange rate agreement (the so-called "snake" arrangements). Italy left the "snake" in January, adopting a two tier exchange rate system. The rate for current account transactions was fixed by central bank intervention, reflecting a desire to avoid imported inflation, while that for the capital account was permitted to float freely. A spread quickly opened up between the two rates, with the floating rate immediately depreciating by about 6 per cent. This was followed by a sharp devaluation of the commercial rate in March, once the fixed rate system had finally broken down, in spite of intervention by the authorities. The main factors were the deterioration of the current account, and the adverse movements of the inflation and interest differentials.

The Italian authorities have always been concerned with the inflationary consequences of lira depreciation, given the tendency for wages and export prices rapidly to respond to exchange rate changes. Consequently, monetary policy was moderately tightened throughout 1973. However, for the year as a whole, a sizeable current account deficit was recorded which, with the advent of the first oil price shock, deteriorated even more sharply in early 1974. Downward pressure on the exchange rate built up and, regarding the earlier depreciation as sufficient for purposes of competitiveness, the Bank of Italy intervened heavily throughout the year in order to defend the lira (Chart 2). At the same time monetary policy was tightened, interest rates moving to relatively high levels compared to those prevailing abroad, and, as noted above, a target for the expansion of total domestic credit (TDC) was introduced. The latter was thought to be more appropriate than a money supply target at a time of large payments imbalances, given the significant negative impact of official intervention on monetary growth.

The credit squeeze in 1974 and the sharp rise in the cost of imported energy largely explain the recession of 1975 which, in turn, was reflected in an improved current account in the second half of the year. The exchange rate actually began to strengthen, but at this time a number of significant events occurred which were to complicate the tasks of exchange rate management and monetary policy in subsequent years:

- The government's borrowing requirement expanded to over 18 per cent of GDP, as a consequence of expansionary fiscal measures (and automatic stabilizers) in response to the recession; and
- employers and trade unions reached agreement on a considerably more widespread form of wage indexation.

The fiscal expansion was largely accommodated by monetary policy, and contributed to a sharp consumption-led recovery in late 1975 and the first half of 1976. The current account quickly deteriorated, as did inflationary expectations, and this was reflected in a reversal of capital inflows and substantial pressures on the exchange rate in a wave of speculative activity.

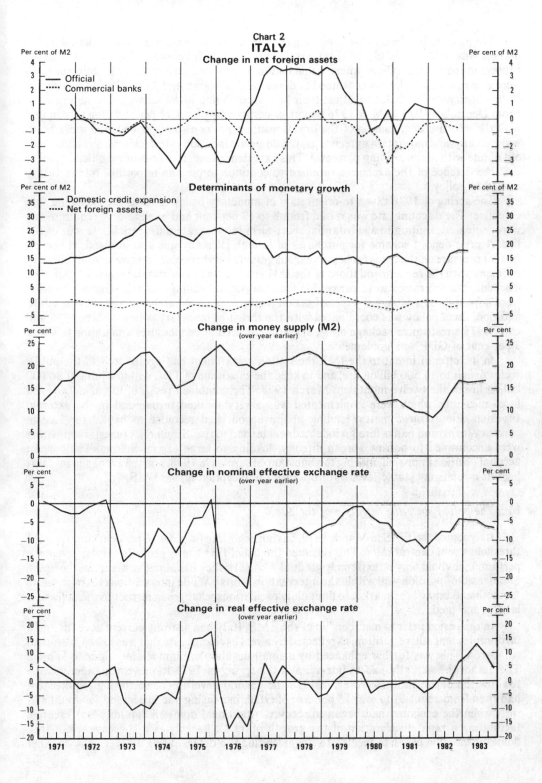

Chart 2
ITALY

Per cent of M2

Change in net foreign assets

- Official
- Commercial banks

Determinants of monetary growth

Per cent of M2

- Domestic credit expansion
- Net foreign assets

Per cent

Change in money supply (M2)
(over year earlier)

Per cent

Change in nominal effective exchange rate
(over year earlier)

Per cent

Change in real effective exchange rate
(over year earlier)

1971 1972 1973 1974 1975 1976 1977 1978 1979 1980 1981 1982 1983

The lira was devalued at the beginning of 1976. Pressures were so great that the exchange market was temporarily closed from 21st January to 28th February. When it re-opened, support in the form of official intervention had to be provided on a large scale. Interest rates were also raised, but the lira continued to depreciate in March and April. During this period Italian businessmen tended to adjust their lira prices in line with exchange rate movements. From December 1975 to May 1976 export prices rose by about 18 per cent, roughly in line with the effective depreciation of the lira. Consumer prices also responded, and locked into widespread wage indexation agreements, the domestic inflation rate accelerated rapidly, well out of line with major trading partners[3]. This experience tended to re-confirm official opinion that the defence of the exchange rate had to continue to play an important role in future monetary policy.

The spring of 1976 saw a re-orientation of monetary policy towards the exchange rate objective. The discount rate was raised from 8 to 12 per cent and bank reserve requirements were increased, leading to a substantial short-term interest rate differential in favour of the lira. A prior deposit scheme for purchases of foreign currency was also imposed. However, further pressure on the lira later in the year suggested that these measures were insufficient. In harmony with the recommendations of the IMF, monetary policy was tightened further. The discount rate was raised to 15 per cent in October, tighter ceilings on bank credit expansion were imposed and a temporary special tax on foreign currency purchases was introduced. In addition, fiscal policy was coordinated with the thrust of monetary policy. In late 1976 and early 1977 a restrictive package of tax and administered price measures amounting to about 3 per cent of GDP was implemented.

In its letter of intent to the IMF the Italian government had agreed to hold the public sector deficit to 16 500 billion lire, and to keep the expansion of TDC within a limit of 30 000 billion lire in the twelve months to March 1978. The combined result of the monetary and fiscal measures which were implemented was a very marked turnaround in the external situation. Limits on domestic lending in lire encouraged recourse to banks' for foreign currency loans, and banks foreign indebtedness tended to rise. Similarly, domestic companies were encouraged to borrow abroad directly, leading to large capital inflows. The current account position improved, moving to a substantial surplus in 1978, and the exchange rate was held at a relatively stable level right up until the inception of the EMS.

b)   *The period since the inception of the EMS*

Italy joined the EMS in March 1979, having negotiated a wider (6 per cent) intervention threshold about central rates. This reflected the belief that convergence to similar economic performance could only be extremely gradual. Official policy has aimed to maintain the lira in a "defensible" position well within the intervention limits[4]. While intervention is carried out to "smooth and brake" the market to limit daily oscillations, changes in respect to the dollar are largely accepted.

In the period prior to membership of the EMS, Italy had a strong current account and a favourable competitive position, as reflected by a real exchange rate that was low by historical standards. This was further enhanced by a small devaluation immediately prior to joining. The authorities actually had to intervene in the spring of 1979 to prevent an appreciation towards the upper limit. However, in 1978 the general government borrowing requirement had risen from about 11 to over 15 per cent of GDP, increasing public demand for credit at a time when the economy had begun to recover. Additional domestic liquidity was created, facilitating a rapid acceleration of the growth of TDC. Largely as a consequence of this, domestic inflation began to accelerate, again leading to a deteriorating differential with other countries. But while it seemed desirable to raise interest rates to dampen inflation, it was feared that such action would be likely to trigger further capital inflows which would push the lira even higher. In the event, this dilemma was resolved in favour of keeping short rates low in relation to foreign rates, and the inflation differential continued to widen.

Pressures within the EMS tended to build up later in the year as the US dollar shifted from strength to weakness against European currencies. At the same time the Bundesbank raised its interest rates, further increasing strains, and central rates were realigned in September and November 1979, the Deutschemark being revalued against other currencies. Pressure on the lira began to build up from September, as a consequence of the adverse interest rate differential. The authorities had to intervene to prevent depreciation, and monetary policy was moved towards restriction. In October credit ceilings were tightened and the discount rate was raised to 12.5 per cent, with a further 3 points rise in December. As the interest rate differential moved significantly in Italy's favour, pressure on the lira temporarily subsided in early 1980.

The sudden fall in US rates in the second quarter of 1980 led to further pressures on the lira in June, as the Deutschemark temporarily strengthened vis-a-vis the dollar. The authorities intervened by running down dollar reserves to buy lire. Substantial monetary measures were avoided, however, because:

i) the authorities hoped to avoid increased interest rates as the period of rapid growth in the Italian economy came to an end by the middle of the year, and

ii) the subsequent turnaround in US interest rates and renewed strength of the dollar vis-a-vis the Deutschemark reduced pressures on the lira in the third quarter.

However, from the end of 1979 and throughout 1980 the current account deteriorated markedly. This was associated with the rise in the budget deficit in 1979, which contributed to internal demand pressure; the deterioration of competitiveness through increased unit labour costs; and the adverse effects of the second oil price rise.

Pressure on the lira again reasserted itself in the autumn of 1980 and resulted in further restrictive monetary measures. In particular, the discount rate was raised to 16.5 per cent. The rate of growth of the broad money supply (M2) decelerated from around 20 per cent to about 12 per cent per annum (Chart 2), and the growth of TDC also declined. In January 1981 the authorities reinforced their ability to control domestic money and credit aggregates by announcing that, as of March, banks could not raise foreign currency loans for financing imports. However, as the US dollar became stronger, the continued weakness of the Deutschemark (in light of a sizeable current deficit) led to a further rise in German interest rates[5], adding to the difficulties of the lira, which drifted downwards within the EMS and was soon perceived as being in fundamental disequilibrium. The EMS parities were again realigned on 22nd March, the central rate for the lira being devalued by 6 per cent. The Italian authorities also moved to tighten monetary policy further: the ceiling on bank lending was set at 16 per cent to December 1981; all foreign currency lending was frozen at its December 1980 level; an upper limit was placed on bank acceptances; the discount rate was raised to 19 per cent; and the marginal reserve requirement on bank deposits was raised from 15.75 to 20 per cent.

During 1981 the public sector borrowing requirement again increased substantially, and has been difficult to reconcile with the very tight stance of monetary policy. The current account has remained in deficit and, with very high Italian interest rates, has been associated with private capital inflow and public sector borrowing abroad. In light of the new restrictions on foreign currency lending, the net external position of banks has changed very little. There were some further losses against the dollar in the second quarter of 1981, and the exchange rate was again devalued in the EMS re-alignment of October. In June 1982 and March 1983 the lira was further devalued by small amounts within the EMS. By the end of 1983 its depreciation since the inception of EMS amounted to about 25 per cent in effective terms and nearly 50 per cent against the dollar.

CONCLUDING REMARKS

A number of features stand out in the case of Italy:

- Periods of major exchange rate pressures have tended to be preceded by increases in public sector deficits and deteriorations on current account.

- Considerable priority has been accorded to stabilizing the exchange rate, partly because of the importance of wage indexation which tends to amplify the domestic cost effects of exchange rate changes.

- Emphasis has been placed upon the control of domestic credit expansion, particularly the private sector component, rather than the money supply, because the Italian authorities believe this to be a more efficient means for influencing short-term capital flows and the exchange rate. However, during the 1970s such an orientation of policy was generally followed well after destabilizing pressures had been permitted to build up.

- It should be recalled that the inflation differential has tended to deteriorate, and the resulting upward pressure on the real exchange rate has been offset by a series of devaluations. Monetary policy has been constrained in effectively countering these pressures throughout most of the 1970s as a consequence of excessively large budget deficits.

NOTES

1. In 1982 exports and imports of goods and services represented roughly 27 per cent and 28 per cent of GDP, respectively.

2. This has been discussed in some detail in OECD (1979, 1982).

3. This type of behaviour is consistent with the simulation properties of the Bank of Italy's econometric model. Depreciations are quickly passed on in export prices and slightly more slowly in consumer prices. The initial favourable effects on profits quickly tail off, however, as wages respond to rising consumer prices. It should be noted, however, that these simulations were conducted without any feedback effects from a monetary sector, which amounts to assuming constant interest rates or accommodating monetary policy.

4. Experience suggests that speculation tends to build up after 4½ per cent, and "band-wagon" effects become important.

5. See the note on Germany.

CANADA

For most of the decade until 1970, the Canadian dollar was fixed at a par value of US$0.925. In May of that year the Government of Canada announced that it would no longer intervene in the exchange market to maintain that parity or any other pre-announced exchange rate. Since then, the Canadian dollar has been allowed to float more or less freely (see Chart 1). The Bank of Canada has been prepared to conduct smoothing operations in the exchange market and to resist any apparently unjustified pressures in either direction; however, its basic philosophy of not relying solely on intervention to influence the exchange rate, as well as its comparative lack of reserves, has led it to limit such operations.

When foreign exchange market intervention occurs, the balance sheet of the Bank of Canada is not directly affected. Foreign reserves are owned by the Federal Government through the Exchange Fund Account, on behalf of which the central bank intervenes in the foreign exchange market. Acquisitions of foreign currency assets by the Exchange Fund Account constitute government outlays and, consequently, increase the Federal Government's financing requirement. In the short term this influences the government's cash balances, which are usually sufficient to allow debt management to be isolated from the Government's day-to-day financing needs. The impact of intervention is transferred to Government balances at the chartered banks and, eventually, to the public debt, by the device of shifting the Government's balances between the chartered banks and the Bank of Canada. Despite the fact that, as measured by net official monetary movements in the balance of payments statistics, official intervention has at times been substantial compared to the increase in the monetary base (see Chart 2), it has had no actual effect on the base. While discretionary shifts of Government deposits between the Bank of Canada and the chartered banks have been important in day-to-day adjustments of bank reserves, deposits at the central bank have been fairly stable over longer periods. Purchases of marketable debt instruments, often at the time of issue, have been the dominant influence on the monetary base[1] over the medium term.

An important feature of the Canadian economy is its very close ties with the US economy. Roughly 20 per cent of Canadian output is exported to the United States and financial markets of the two countries are highly integrated. A second important feature, which distinguishes Canada from most other industrialised countries, is the importance of the primary sector. Since primary goods account for a large share of exports, Canada tends to experience favourable terms of trade during commodity booms such as 1973-74, and adverse terms of trade when commodity prices slump.

OVERVIEW OF THE BEHAVIOUR OF THE EXCHANGE RATE SINCE THE EARLY 1970s

After the float of the Canadian dollar in May 1970, the nominal exchange rate appreciated quickly and from then until late 1976 traded within a very narrow range against the United States' dollar (see Chart 1). Its somewhat wider fluctuations on an effective basis

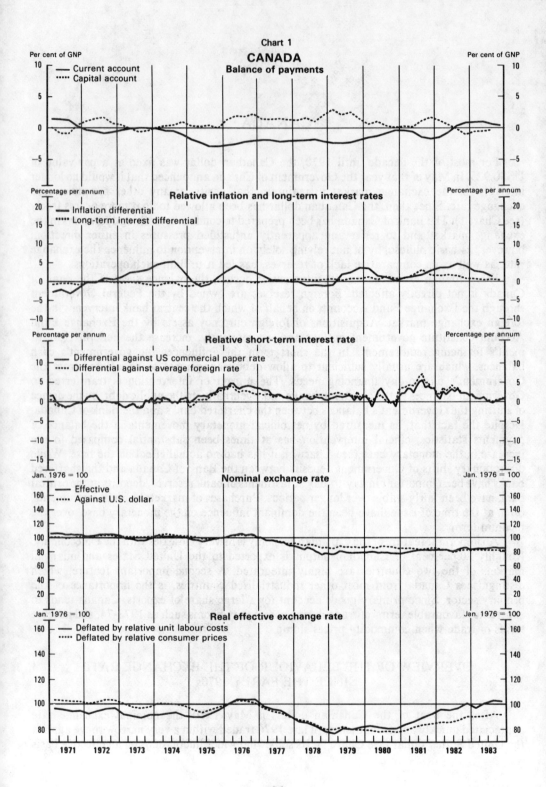

Chart 1
CANADA

Balance of payments

Per cent of GNP (left and right axes)
- —— Current account
- ····· Capital account

Relative inflation and long-term interest rates

Percentage per annum
- —— Inflation differential
- ····· Long-term interest differential

Relative short-term interest rate

Percentage per annum
- —— Differential against US commercial paper rate
- ····· Differential against average foreign rate

Nominal exchange rate

Jan. 1976 = 100
- —— Effective
- ····· Against U.S. dollar

Real effective exchange rate

Jan. 1976 = 100
- —— Deflated by relative unit labour costs
- ····· Deflated by relative consumer prices

1971 1972 1973 1974 1975 1976 1977 1978 1979 1980 1981 1982 1983

84

mainly reflected variations in the overall strength of the US currency. In real terms, as measured by unit labour costs in manufacturing, this implied relative stability until mid-1975 and, as the adverse inflation differential increased, appreciation thereafter. The weakening of the nominal exchange rate from late-1976 can be seen as a corrective adjustment which by 1978 had restored the competitive position vis-a-vis the United States to what it had been during the early 1970s, and in terms of all countries generally may have gone beyond this. Since 1978 the effective exchange rate has tended to rise in real terms. This partly reflects a policy of avoiding sharp movements in the exchange rate vis-a-vis the US dollar (which has strengthened markedly since 1980) as well as the relatively rapid inflation in Canada for most of this period. The strength of the exchange rate in 1976 and the weakness in 1977-78 mark the only wide swings in the real exchange rate, with the latter effectively reversing the former. The forces working to stabilize the real exchange rate, particularly vis-a-vis the United States, appear to work strongly in Canada.

The current account was, atypically, roughly in balance from late 1971 until 1974. Since then, it has been persistently and heavily in deficit. The largest deficits occurred during 1975-76, but the influence of these on the exchange rate was more than offset by an interest differential that increased throughout 1975 and remained substantially favourable during 1976. As capital flows, particularly to and from the United States, are very sensitive to interest differentials[2], the exchange rate during this period was stronger in both real and nominal terms, than at any time during the period under review. The subsequent weakness of the Canadian dollar occurred against a background of the near-disappearance of this differential, as the current deficit became the dominant influence. Similarly, during 1980, when interest rates in the United States were extremely volatile, there was a clear tendency for the exchange rate to respond to any lags in the adjustment of Canadian interest rates to movements in US rates. In 1981, the emergence of a large favourable interest differential against the US dollar allowed stability to be maintained while the exchange rate appreciated against other currencies in general, particulary in real terms. The relationship between interest rates and the exchange rate was not as strong as in 1980, however, reflecting the importance of other factors, notably the faster rate of inflation in Canada than in the United States.

The main additional factor influencing the exchange rate in 1981 was the adverse impact of the adoption, late in 1980, of policies designed to reduce the degree of foreign control of the energy sector in Canadian industry. This adversely influenced perceptions of Canada as an attractive place to invest, resulting in both reduced inflows from abroad and outward transfers of funds from Canada. To offset this capital outflow, while preventing the exchange rate from falling too far, it became necessary to maintain a substantially higher interest differential than might otherwise have been warranted. On one other occasion, unquantifiable considerations related to risk may also have influenced portfolio preferences in a manner adverse to the Canadian dollar. In 1976 uncertainties resulted in the aftermath of the elections in Quebec which gave rise to concern about the stability of Canada's federal structure and may have contributed to the exchange rate's subsequent decline.

EXCHANGE RATE MANAGEMENT AND THE CONDUCT OF MONETARY POLICY

a) The early period of floating

During the early 1970s, the authorities' main concern was the existence of a high level of under-utilised resources, a consequence of restrictive policies in 1969. From early 1970 until early 1973, the main objective of monetary policy was to bring about a relatively low level of

Chart 2

CANADA

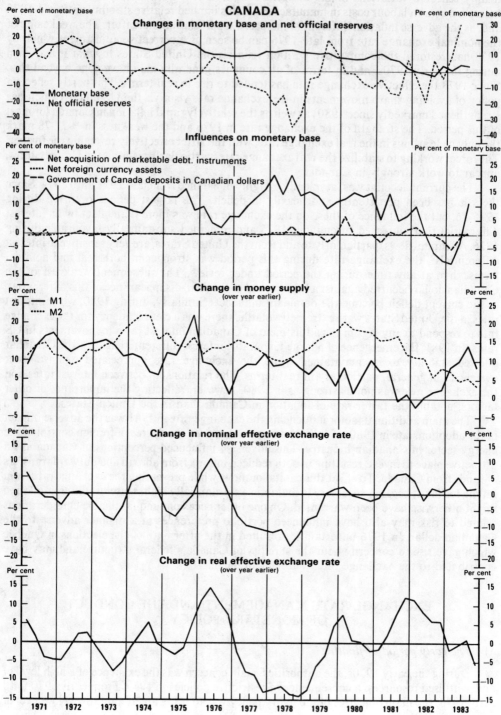

interest rates. It was hoped that this would prevent a sharp appreciation of the exchange rate which would reduce competitiveness and put an unnecessary obstacle in the path to recovery. Although the Bank of Canada was concerned about the acceleration of monetary expansion resulting from this policy stance, it did not take immediate action to contain it. By early 1973, inflationary pressures started to build up and the monetary authorities offered increasingly strong resistance to the very rapid growth of aggregate spending. Provision of reserves to the banks became more restrictive and interest rates were allowed to rise. By late-1974, against the background of a downturn in the United States, the restrictive stance had proved effective and aggregate spending slowed down, inflation began to recede, and the real economy moved into a mild recession. In view of these tendencies the stance of policy was eased. As these shifts were broadly in phase with developments in the United States, they did not result in strong pressures on the exchange rate vis-à-vis the US dollar.

The moderation of inflation late in 1974, however, proved to be short-lived. By mid-1975 the growth of nominal spending, wage settlements, and inflation was again becoming high. Since demand and economic activity did not weaken in Canada as much as they did elsewhere during 1974-75, a very large current payments deficit emerged. Furthermore, price inflation in the United States was slowing rapidly while wage trends were stable. Thus, at this stage, Canada found its economic performance diverging sharply from other countries in general and from its main trading partner in particular. In this circumstance, the focus of policy shifted back in late-1975 toward inflation control. One element of this shift was the implementation by the government of a wage and price control programme. A second element was the move toward monetary targeting which implied that interest rates and the exchange rate stood to fluctuate more over the short run than had been the case in the past.

b) *The shift to monetary targets*

The Bank of Canada took the view that a reduction in monetary growth would help to lower the rate of expansion of aggregate spending in the economy, and, consequently, inflation. It therefore appeared desirable to reduce the growth of the money supply "to a rate approximately in line with the sustainable real growth of the economy"[3]. However the gap between actual and desirable rates was considered to have been too large to be eliminated very quickly, since the consequences for the economy of such a sharp and immediate reduction in the growth of the money supply would have been too adverse. Rather than follow such a drastic policy, the central bank announced that it would lower monetary growth gradually over time. To this end a target range for M1 was selected, as this narrow monetary aggregate exhibited a more stable relationship to total spending than did the broader aggregates. Month-to-month variations in M1 were not to be suppressed where they reflected essentially short-run disturbances. Instead the Bank of Canada announced that it would take a broader view and look more at the underlying trend of M1.

The immediate effect of the more restrictive monetary policy pursued by the Bank of Canada was to prevent interest rates from following US interest rates down, attracting capital to Canada. This kept the Canadian dollar around its 1971-1974 value despite the high domestic inflation rate and the significant deterioration of the current account. By late 1976 the apparent over-valuation of the currency resulted in expectations that current account deficits would remain large while, at the same time, political uncertainties associated with the situation in Quebec emerged. In this climate of weakened confidence the Canadian dollar depreciated sharply, and, following a temporary turnaround in December, fell almost continuously throughout 1977. This downward adjustment was accepted by the central bank as necessary to restore Canada's competitiveness in world trade. But as the pressures continued well into 1978, the central bank started to resist them. It felt that by late 1977 the depreciation had already gone a long way to compensate for differential inflation and that the pace of the depreciation, which showed no signs of slowing down, was threatening to aggravate domestic inflation without any lasting benefit to competitiveness.

c) *The return to exchange rates as a key intermediate target*

Since 1978, the exchange rate against the United States dollar has been accorded more importance than previously and interest rates have been adjusted to influence its behaviour. Targets for M1 continued to be announced, however, until late 1982 when, in view of the apparent shift in the demand for money due to financial innovations, the practice was discontinued. Until the significance of the behaviour of M1 came into question, monetary targets proved to be broadly compatible with exchange rate objectives. From mid-1981, however, interest rate changes necessary to moderate the depreciation of the exchange rate resulted in growth of M1 well below the lower limit of the 4-8 per cent target range. Such undershooting was tolerated because of the distortions associated with financial innovations noted above[4]. Thus, the Bank of Canada did not perceive its problem in 1981-82 as one of conflicts in objectives. Moreover, the Bank of Canada considered at the time that without interest rate adjustment, or official intervention in the foreign exchange market, a band-wagon effect might tend to push the exchange rate well below its equilibrium value. The immediate effect of such a sharp depreciation, in the Bank's view, would be a substantial acceleration of domestic inflation[5] and a misallocation of real resources. The authorities felt that it would be necessary to raise interest rates eventually to suppress this surge of imported inflation and to bring the exchange rate back to its equilibrium value. However the interest rate rise in such a situation would be considerably larger than that required to defend the exchange rate in the first place. As inflationary expectations would also be adversely affected by depreciation, the real costs of raising interest rates quickly to stabilise the exchange rate are smaller than those which would arise in the future under a policy of no exchange rate defense despite the temporary low growth of M1.

After the relative calm of 1979, the central bank had to contend with the extremely high volatility of interest rates in the United States in 1980. In order to moderate the impact of the large swings in US interest rates on the Canadian exchange rate, interest rates in Canada were permitted to move sympathetically with those in the United States although neither as far nor as fast. Large changes in the short-term interest rate differentials nevertheless occurred, and, despite the current account improvement during 1980, these were reflected in the exchange rate.

There was some concern that, in view of the interest rate fluctuations that did occur, public perceptions of the stance of monetary policy would become unclear, particularly as variability of monetary growth increased simultaneously. Signs emerged that the public was focusing on interest rates rather than the money supply as a short-run indicator of monetary policy. This meant that when interest rates declined sharply, as in the spring of 1980, it might appear that policy was easing even in the face of falling monetary growth. By contributing to a feeling that restrictive phases of policy may quickly be reversed such falls in interest rates might have reduced the credibility, and delayed the impact, of later restrictive phases.

During 1981 and early 1982, the conjunction of continued strong inflationary pressures in Canada, the rapid fall of the inflation rate in the United States and the adoption of policies apparently favouring Canadian owned enterprises at the expense of foreign owned competitors required a record high short-term interest rate differential to moderate movements in the exchange rate. Despite good performance in achieving targets for M1 until

1981, and the slower rate of depreciation of the exchange rate since 1978, inflation continued at a rapid rate until late 1982, reflecting the persistence of inflationary expectations. This has led the monetary authorities to maintain a policy of restraint. As a result, during 1983, inflation has come down sharply.

CONCLUDING REMARKS

The openness of the Canadian economy and its strong economic and financial links with the United States have forced policy makers, and more particularly the monetary authorities, to pay a great deal of attention to developments in the exchange market. The adverse impact on expectations of inflation induced by depreciation have persuaded the authorities, since 1978, to make stabilisation of the exchange rate vis-à-vis the US dollar an important objective of monetary policy. In so doing, the authorities have sought to prevent an acceleration of inflationary pressures due to a depreciation of the exchange rate. This has been consistent with the Bank of Canada's view that sole reliance on monetary aggregates in judging the appropriate degree of monetary expansion is not warranted.

At the operational level adjustment of interest rates to developments in the United States is usually sufficient to moderate movements in the exchange rate against the US dollar. When M1 targets were in effect this sometimes resulted in deviations from the target range, but until 1981 such occasions proved temporary. The persistent undershooting of the target which occurred after mid-1981 owed much to financial innovations, but the priority given to exchange rate objectives probably also contributed to such development through policy-induced upward movements in interest rates.

NOTES

1. As Chart 2 indicates, the other items, changes in government balances at the Bank and changes in the Bank's net foreign currency position, reflecting mainly swaps with the Exchange Fund Account, have been small.

2. Econometric work at the Bank of Canada, as incorporated in the RDX2 model, suggests that an increase of 100 basis points in short-term interest rates will raise the exchange rate against the US dollar by about 1 per cent after one year and nearly 4 per cent after 5 years. See Rose and Sheikh (1980).

3. Bank of Canada (1975).

4. Indeed, predictions for M1 deriving from econometric work were within the target range for much of the period after mid-1981.

5. Simulations with the RDXF model suggest that a 10 per cent depreciation of the exchange rate leads to an increase of 0.8 per cent in the GNE deflator after one year and 4.9 per cent after five years. The Bank, however, believes the effects to be considerably greater than this.

BELGIUM

Since Belgium has a very open economy[1], the stability of the Belgian franc's exchange rate against the currencies of its main trading partners has always been one of the monetary authorities' main preoccupations. With the abandonment of fixed parities in the early 1970s, this concern for exchange rate stability resulted, as from 1973, in Belgium's participation in the European Monetary Agreements (the "snake", then EMS) and the maintenance of close links with the Dutch guilder up until 1976. The other objectives of Belgian monetary policy in the 1970s were to stabilize the domestic economy and to ensure the financing of the growing central government borrowing requirement. Unlike in other OECD countries, the monetary authorities did not adopt any growth targets for monetary aggregates, but relied instead on the growth of credit to the private sector, the level and change in interest rates as well as foreign capital movements to determine what type of policy to apply[2].

Priority has been given to exchange rate stability due to the authorities' concern to protect the Belgian economy from the possible effects of a change in parity. In the first place the authorities take the view that a change in the exchange rate caused by capital movements can result in changes which are not necessarily justified by the allocation of resources within the country. Secondly, the size of the external sector and the almost general indexation of incomes in Belgium mean that any depreciation would soon trigger domestic inflationary pressures. Appreciation, on the other hand, would have little effect on price and cost levels in view of their downward rigidity. Whereas from 1970 to 1973 exchange rate policy was aimed at averting any appreciation of the Belgian franc, from 1974 the main objective was to counter downward pressure on the franc.

OVERVIEW OF THE BEHAVIOUR OF THE EXCHANGE RATE

a) *Exchange rate developments since the early 1970s*

In accordance with the authorities' objectives, the exchange rate has fluctuated very little over the last 12 years (see Chart 1). In effective terms the franc appreciated slightly from 1976 to 1980, after having remained almost unchanged from 1971 to 1976. This trend was reversed in mid-1980, and the Belgian franc then tended to depreciate until the currency realignment within the EMS in February 1982. It was then devalued by 8.5 per cent, and accompanying measures were put into effect to restore equilibrium in the foreign balance, to reduce the public sector deficit and to contain the growth of unemployment. However, when currencies were again realigned within the EMS in March 1983, the franc was revalued by 1.5 per cent in order to limit the impact of revaluations by Germany and the Netherlands, which are Belgium's main supplier countries.

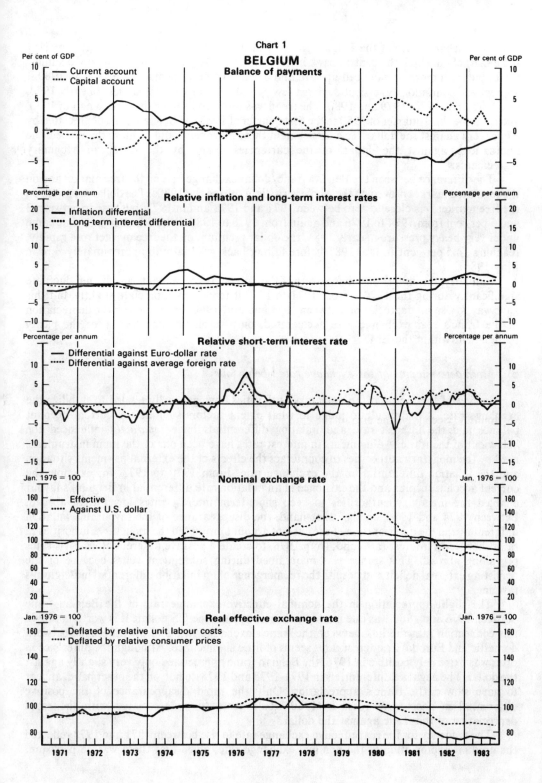

Chart 1

BELGIUM

Per cent of GDP

Balance of payments

Per cent of GDP

— Current account
····· Capital account

Relative inflation and long-term interest rates

Percentage per annum

— Inflation differential
····· Long-term interest differential

Relative short-term interest rate

Percentage per annum

— Differential against Euro-dollar rate
····· Differential against average foreign rate

Jan. 1976 = 100

Nominal exchange rate

Jan. 1976 = 100

— Effective
····· Against U.S. dollar

Jan. 1976 = 100

Real effective exchange rate

Jan. 1976 = 100

— Deflated by relative unit labour costs
····· Deflated by relative consumer prices

1971 1972 1973 1974 1975 1976 1977 1978 1979 1980 1981 1982 1983

The exchange rate of the Belgian franc against the US dollar on the regulated market – the market on which the central bank intervenes regularly (see below) – followed a similar trend, but with more pronounced upward and downward movements. From 1971 to 1980 it appreciated continuously, except during a few periods of temporary weakness in early 1974, late 1975, mid-1978, 1979 and 1980. The trend was reversed as from the second half of 1970, and from the third quarter of 1980 to the first quarter of 1983 the Belgian franc depreciated by 67 per cent against the dollar. To a large extent these movements did no more than reflect the fluctuations, against the dollar, of the currencies linked by the European Monetary Agreements.

The difference between the Belgian franc/dollar exchange rate on the free market and on the regulated market proved on the whole very slight during the 1970s. The dollar premium on the free market was close to zero between 1971 and 1973 and in 1977, but rose to between 3 and 5 per cent from 1974 to 1976 and again from 1978 to 1980. When the Belgian franc came under very heavy pressure in early 1981, the dollar premium on the free market rose rapidly, reaching 14.5 per cent in late 1981 before falling back gradually to approximately zero in May 1983.

Similarly, the effective exchange rate of the Belgian franc in real terms did not fluctuate significantly during the 1970s. From 1971 to 1978 it tended to appreciate slightly, but this gave way to a small depreciation between 1978 and mid-1980. From then on the depreciation in the franc's real exchange rate accelerated, only stabilizing in 1982 after the parity realignment within the EMS.

b) *Main determinants of the exchange rate's behaviour*

In view of the fact that the monetary authorities have generally tended to stabilize the exchange rate, it is difficult to judge to what extent factors such as the current account balance and the interest rate and inflation differentials have *separately* influenced the behaviour of the franc. Adjustments in interest rates have been one of the main instruments used by the monetary authorities to counteract the effects of the external payments situation and the inflation differential on the exchange rate. From 1970 to 1973, for example the current account surplus and the existence of an inflation rate differential in Belgium's favour enabled the monetary authorities to keep short-term interest rates lower than abroad. Between 1974 and 1976, on the other hand, the disappearance of the favourable inflation differential and the deterioration of the current account prompted the monetary authorities to raise short-term interest rates and, from 1976, to create a positive differential vis-à-vis rates prevailing abroad. This stance was maintained during subsequent years because of the persisting external deficit and despite the reemergence of an inflation differential in Belgium's favour.

The slight appreciation in the nominal effective exchange rate of the Belgian franc between 1976 and 1980 was due mainly to its rise against the US dollar. It is worth noting in this connection that the link between the franc's exchange rate and the difference between domestic and Eurodollar interest rates seems of little significance. Although the difference in rates was extremely positive in 1976, the Belgian franc appreciated only very slightly against the dollar. The negative differentials in 1971-1973 and 1978 do not, on the other hand, appear to have slowed the franc's appreciation. Only the rapid disappearance of the positive differential in short-term rates in 1980 would seem to be associated with the rapid depreciation of the franc against the dollar.

The tendency for the real effective exchange rate to rise between 1971 and 1978 reflected the gradual appreciation of the nominal exchange rate, given that there was no persistent inflation differential. During 1978-79 a substantial favourable inflation differential emerged which offset the continued rise in the nominal exchange rate, stabilizing the real rate. Since then, the favourable performance with respect to inflation has been reinforced by nominal depreciation; as a result the real exchange rate has fallen rapidly, thus improving the competitiveness of the Belgian industry.

EXCHANGE RATE MANAGEMENT AND THE CONDUCT OF MONETARY POLICY

Three main instruments have been used to stabilize the Belgian franc's exchange rate: exchange controls based on a two-tier market, interest rate adjustment and official intervention on the foreign exchange market.

a) *Exchange controls*

Since 1955 the Belgian monetary authorities have taken measures to liberalize exchange control regulations; however, in order to protect the economy from external disturbances, they have at the same time, maintained a two-tier market for the franc. This separates current transactions (except transfers), which go through the regulated market, from capital transactions, which go through the free market, the central bank only intervening on the regulated market in order to maintain the franc's parity against the other European currencies. In spite of this segmentation of the foreign exchange market, speculative pressures can arise particularly by way of changes in leads and lags associated with current external transactions[3]. At times of crisis on the foreign exchange market the Belgian monetary authorities have furthermore taken specific measures to control these movements of capital through the regulated market. Thus, from 1971 to 1973, in order to restrict capital flows, the Belgo-Luxembourg Foreign Exchange Institute (IBLC) set strict limits on banks' operations in foreign currency and convertible francs. In addition, in 1971 the IBLC prohibited the payment of preferential interest on foreign convertible franc accounts and, in 1973, imposed a special levy of 0.25 per cent on any increase in deposits in such accounts. In spite of these provisions the official reserves grew substantially during those three years and the increase in the banking system's net foreign assets was an important factor in swelling domestic liquidity[4], although the general stance of monetary policy was rather restrictive at that time.

From 1974 to the beginning of 1983 the Belgian monetary authorities took measures to relieve the downward pressures on the franc. In 1974 the ban on the payment of interest on banks' convertible foreign currency accounts was lifted and the IBLC made banks subject, individually, to limits on their foreign currency operations in the regulated market. From 1976 to 1981, whenever speculative outflows of capital occurred, the monetary authorities sought to restrict lending to the company sector in order to prevent firms from rebuilding their cash positions, as movements in these positions facilitated speculation. Among the measures adopted were a reduction in facilities available to financial intermediaries for refinancing with the central bank and a dual requirement that these institutions hold a minimum amount of government securities and that they increase such holdings in proportion to any extension of their short-term credit to businesses or households. In March 1983 additional measures were taken to speed up the conversion of export earnings into Belgian francs and to limit increases in holdings of foreign financial assets. These provisions were compatible with the general thrust

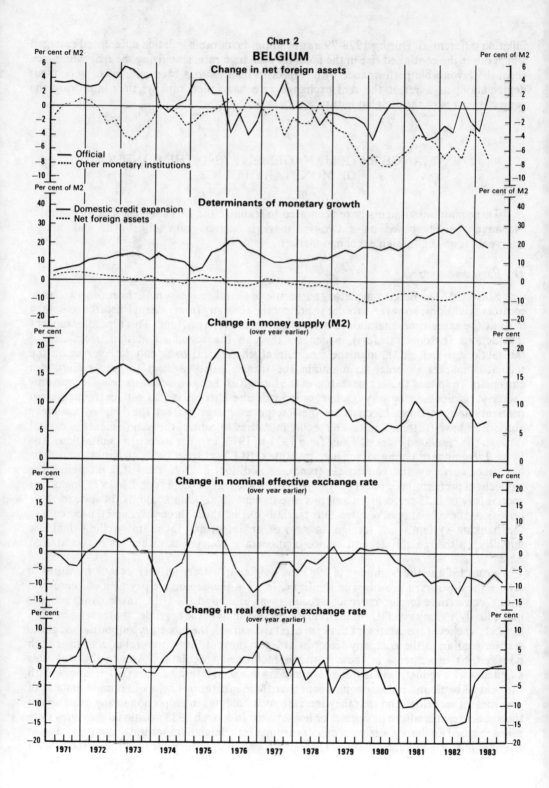

Chart 2
BELGIUM

Change in net foreign assets

Per cent of M2

— Official
⋯⋯ Other monetary institutions

Determinants of monetary growth

Per cent of M2

— Domestic credit expansion
⋯⋯ Net foreign assets

Change in money supply (M2)
(over year earlier)

Per cent

Change in nominal effective exchange rate
(over year earlier)

Per cent

Change in real effective exchange rate
(over year earlier)

Per cent

1971 1972 1973 1974 1975 1976 1977 1978 1979 1980 1981 1982 1983

of monetary policy throughout this period. Indeed, the objective was to help increase the liquidity of financial intermediaries in order to offset the restrictive monetary impact due to the disappearance of the current account surplus and to support economic activity, while taking care not to fuel speculation against the Belgian franc.

Insofar as the existence of a two-tier foreign exchange market made it possible to protect the economy from temporary exchange rate fluctuations due to speculative capital movements, it had a stabilizing effect and helped to prevent the spread of inflationary pressures. However, since this segmentation of the foreign exchange market did not make it possible to stabilize the franc completely in the face of external disruptions, other instruments such as interest rate adjustment and direct intervention on the exchange market by the central bank proved to be necessary; the first in order to reinforce the effect of the different measures on capital flows going through the regulated market and the second to offset the impact of the current account deficit.

b) *Interest rate adjustment*

As noted above, the monetary authorities have adjusted interest rates to influence capital movements since the early 1970s. In 1971 and 1972 the central bank's rates (the discount rate and rate on advances) were lower to discourage inflows. However, at the end of 1972 they were raised again to prevent an acceleration in inflation due to excessive growth of domestic demand. During periods of heavy downward pressures on the exchange rate between 1976 and the beginning of 1983, the monetary authorities permitted short-term domestic rates to increase steeply in relation to short-term rates abroad. However, in many instances this situation was only temporary and the central banks's interest rates were soon lowered to be consistent with the stance of monetary policy which was then one of supporting economic activity.

c) *Official intervention on the foreign exchange market*

Judging from the change in official reserves (see Chart 2), the scale of central bank intervention to stabilize the exchange rate was considerable during the period under review. From 1971 to 1978 the impact of such interventin on money creation was rather small, primarily because holdings of foreign assets by the other financial intermediaries regularly moved in the opposite direction. The same was true from 1978 to 1982 (except during 1979) but this time the effects did not fully cancel out since the destruction of liquidity due to the central bank's intervention outweighed the creation of money due to the growth of net foreign assets held by the other financial intermediaries. It should be noted that this destruction of liquidity would have been far greater had the authorities not borrowed abroad in order to bolster the central banks's foreign currency reserves[5]. The main purpose of borrowing abroad was to finance the public sector deficit because since 1975 household saving has not been sufficient to meet the borrowing requirements of both firms and government.

CONCLUDING REMARKS

Specific features of the Belgian economy (its high exposure to foreign trade and the indexation of virtually all incomes) have led the monetary authorities to adopt an objective of exchange rate stability, which has taken precedence over internal objectives whenever the Belgian franc has come under pressure on the foreign exchange market. Between 1971 and 1973, as part of this policy, measures were taken to discourage capital inflows; however, they did not prevent an accumulation of net foreign assets by the banking system (central bank and financial intermediaries) which contributed to the rapid increase in domestic liquidity. From 1974 on the Belgian authorities primarily tended to prevent a depreciation of the exchange rate. In spite of the deterioration of the current balance, this course has been justified because of the danger of reviving inflation inherent in a devaluation of the franc, given the characteristics of the Belgian economy stressed above. In the monetary authorities' view, the balance-of-payments deficit reflects structural maladjustment in the economy and, because of this, necessitates using instruments other than exchange rate manipulation (in particular, industrial policy and incomes policy). In this connection, by relying primarily on interest rate adjustment and by intervening on the foreign exchange market, the monetary authorities succeeded in stabilizing the Belgian franc until early 1982, when a devaluation took place. Raising the central bank's rates during the foreign exchange crises that occurred between 1975 and 1982 ran counter to the general stance of monetary policy, which was to support economic activity, but the rises were always temporary and, on the whole, the differentials between Belgian and foreign short-term rates were fairly narrow.

The real conflict between the objectives of Belgian monetary policy was more at the domestic level. On the one hand, the monetary authorities did not wish to raise interest rates, the object being to support economic activity, but, on the other hand, private saving needed to be stimulated so that the public sector deficit could be financed. In practice, this conflict was resolved by keeping interest rates at a relatively low level with the result that, from 1975 on, household saving was insufficient to meet the borrowing requirements of private enterprises and the public sector and that the private sector showed a preference for foreign financial assets with a higher return. This is why the authorities had to resort increasingly to financing the budget deficit by monetary means and by borrowing abroad.

NOTES

1. In 1982, Belgian exports of goods and services were equal to 70 per cent of GNP, while the share of imports was 73 per cent.

2. For the motivation of this choice, see OECD (1979), pp. 90-92.

3. The monetary authorities estimate that a lag of only one day in the average settlement periods for exports and imports can generate a net inflow or outflow of capital of the order of FF 10 billion.

4. During these three years the increase in the banking system's net foreign assets accounted for one-quarter of the total increase in the money stock (M1) and quasi-money. It was for this reason that in 1972 and 1973 measures were taken to sterilize partially banks' foreign liabilities by introducing reserve requirements against these or by imposing minimum levels for holdings of government securities.

5. From 1975 to 1981, when the current account was almost continuously in deficit, net cumulative borrowing abroad by the public sector (excluding financial institutions) totalled some BF 500 billion. At the same time the non-bank private sector increased its net foreign financial assets by BF 278 billion while financial intermediaries reduced their net foreign liabilities by BF 261 billion.

NETHERLANDS

The Netherlands has a very open economy, with exports and imports of goods and services each amounting to more than 50 per cent of national income. The immediate influence of the exchange rate on prices has led the authorities to attach a high priority to maintaining a stable exchange rate. That they have been so successful in this is partly attributable to the Netherlands' large natural gas reserves, which have largely insulated the Dutch economy from the oil price increases of the past decade. More important, however, has been the willingness of the authorities promptly to adjust money market conditions in the light of exchange market developments.

As stable anti-inflationary policies have prevailed in Germany during the past decade, and in view of the high degree of dependence of the Dutch economy on that of Germany[1], orienting the guilder towards the Deutschemark has been a natural way for the authorities to conduct their policies in order to achieve price stability. Thus, since April 1972 the Netherlands has taken part in the European exchange rate arrangements (the "snake" and, since March 1979, the European Monetary System). Until 1976 the Benelux arrangement also called for fluctuations between the guilder and the Belgian franc to be confined within narrower margins than those between currencies of other participants. The result has been short-term exchange rate stability against the currencies of the Netherlands' main trading partners despite erratic fluctuations in major countries' exchange rates since the shift to generalised floating.

Although priority has been given to the exchange rate the authorities attach importance to the money supply (M2), as they view monetary growth as an important determinant of inflation in the long run. Their objective, which is aimed essentially at the medium term, is formulated quantitatively in terms of a "liquidity ratio", i.e. the ratio between the money supply and national income. To achieve this objective the authorities rely mainly on restraining the two main sources of domestic creation of money: short-term financing of the public sector's borrowing requirement and "money creation" by banks[2]. Direct methods are used to regulate bank lending, which severs the link between domestic money creation and short-term interest rate developments.

OVERVIEW OF THE BEHAVIOUR OF THE EXCHANGE RATE

a) *Exchange rate developments since the early 1970s*

1970-76. Since 1969 the authorities have attempted almost continuously to restrain the expansion of the money supply in order to reduce inflationary pressures. The guilder was regarded as a strong currency during the early 1970s, however, and speculative considerations against a background of a disorderly international monetary situation resulted in very high capital inflows. These made it difficult for the authorities to make their policies effective and

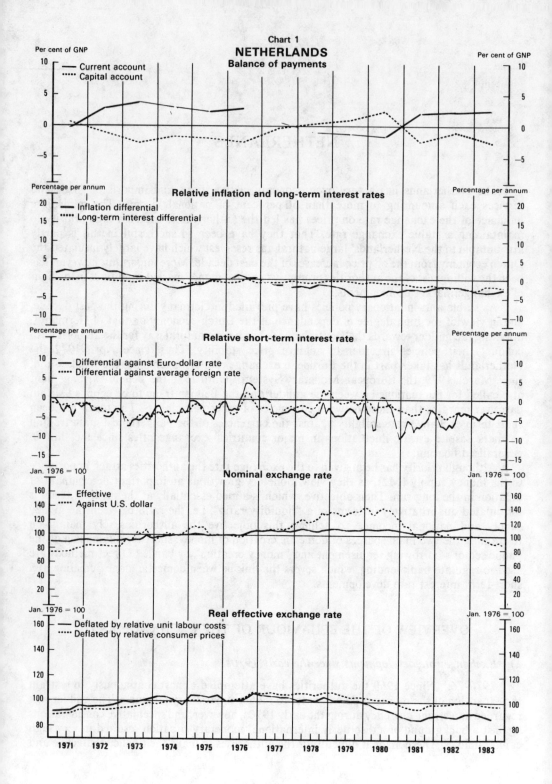

Chart 1
NETHERLANDS

Balance of payments

Per cent of GNP

— Current account
⋯⋯ Capital account

Relative inflation and long-term interest rates

Percentage per annum

— Inflation differential
⋯⋯ Long-term interest differential

Relative short-term interest rate

Percentage per annum

— Differential against Euro-dollar rate
⋯⋯ Differential against average foreign rate

Nominal exchange rate

Jan. 1976 = 100

— Effective
⋯⋯ Against U.S. dollar

Real effective exchange rate

Jan. 1976 = 100

— Deflated by relative unit labour costs
⋯⋯ Deflated by relative consumer prices

1971 1972 1973 1974 1975 1976 1977 1978 1979 1980 1981 1982 1983

in May 1971 the guilder was permitted to float at the same time as the Deutschemark. A fixed exchange rate was re-established with the Smithsonian agreement in December 1971; but early in 1973 the new parity alignments came under heavy pressure, and, from March, the European "snake" floated without any commitments to parities against currencies of non-participants.

Although this gave greater autonomy to monetary policy, the Dutch authorities continued to be constrained by exchange market developments in the context of the "snake". The rising production of natural gas contributed to substantial current account surpluses throughout the period (Chart 1). Despite both the revaluation of the guilder in September 1973, which matched an earlier revaluation of the Deutschemark, and efforts to keep interest rates below international levels, partly by abstaining from restrictions on bank lending, persistent inflows of foreign exchange resulted. These inflows made it very difficult to contain monetary growth, particularly after conditions eased in Germany in 1975. When, in addition, rapid creation of money by banks occurred during 1976, feeding a sudden acceleration of inflation, monetary growth exceeded 20 per cent (Chart 2). Restrictions on bank lending were reimposed in early 1977.

During March 1976 international sentiment about the guilder began to shift when the market learned that a revaluation of the Deutschemark would not be followed by the guilder. As a result the guilder weakened during the spring. For a few months the central bank intervened heavily while offsetting most of the monetary impact in the money markets. In August, however, as renewed speculation of a Deutschemark revaluation developed, the pressure on the guilder required an immediate adjustment in monetary conditions if the exchange rate was to be maintained. Consequently short-term interest rates were permitted to rise markedly. The guilder recovered strongly when this occurred, but calm only returned to the exchange markets when the Deutschemark was revalued in October. The guilder indeed did not follow the Deutschemark on this occasion.

The result of the adherence to the hard currency option throughout this period was that the guilder appreciated steadily against other currencies in general. As the authorities proved unable to make an anti-inflationary stance effective, either by restraining monetary growth or through other policies, there was little difference between inflation in the Netherlands and that in other countries. The nominal appreciation of the exchange rate was therefore reflected in a rise in the real exchange rate (Chart 1). This contributed to a persistent squeeze on corporate profits, and hence investment, which temporarily received insufficient attention because of the rapidly rising proceeds from natural gas. By the end of the period, however, this came to be recognised as a serious problem.

1977-80. As gas production levelled off and export performance in non-energy sectors deterioriated, the current account surplus disappeared and a deficit emerged during 1978-80. The monetary impact of the overall balance of payments turned negative, relaxing the external constraint on implementing a restrictive monetary stance. In this circumstance the authorities were able to respond effectively to the uncomfortably high liquidity ratio which had resulted from the rapid monetary expansion during 1976. Policy was framed within a medium-term approach which sought a gradual reduction in the liquidity ratio of 1 per cent per year, on average. Given the balance of payments deficit, money market policies aimed at stabilizing the exchange rate were more in accordance with a broadly non-accommodating monetary stance than had been the case until 1977. Although the authorities did not feel justified in bringing about a significant reduction in the liquidity ratio, partly because of an unexpected weakness of output, monetary growth came down sharply (Chart 2).

The combination of a strong exchange rate and the reduction in monetary expansion, together with restrictive income policies, resulted in a sharp reduction in inflation, both in

Chart 2

NETHERLANDS

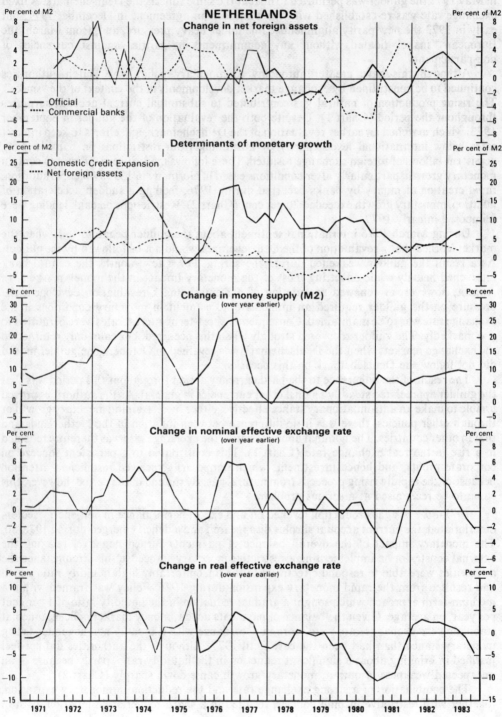

Change in net foreign assets

Per cent of M2

— Official
···· Commercial banks

Determinants of monetary growth

Per cent of M2

— Domestic Credit Expansion
···· Net foreign assets

Change in money supply (M2)
(over year earlier)

Per cent

Change in nominal effective exchange rate
(over year earlier)

Per cent

Change in real effective exchange rate
(over year earlier)

Per cent

1971 1972 1973 1974 1975 1976 1977 1978 1979 1980 1981 1982 1983

absolute terms and relative to other countries. During 1977-78 the combination of nominal appreciation and a favourable inflation differential resulted in little change in the real exchange rate. When the Deutschemark weakened, vis-a-vis the dollar, after 1979, however, the real exchange rate depreciated substantially. In spite of this improvement in competitiveness, the depressed level of activity, related to the restrictive policies and the second oil price shock, prevented corporate profits from taking advantage of this development.

1981-1983. In 1981 the current account shifted back into surplus and, in spite of the maintenance of a substantial adverse interest differential, encouraging capital outflow, the balance of payments has once more led to a steady creation of liquidity. This has again led to a situation in which complications in monetary management can arise, particularly since a large government budget deficit emerged after 1979. The authorities have broadly succeeded, however, in limiting monetary financing of this deficit by borrowing in the capital market. Since bank lending to the private sector during 1981 was moderate, the authorities were able to hold monetary expansion to a relatively low rate. Controls on bank lending were suspended by the end of the year. During 1982 there were some signs of a monetary acceleration, but this was not inconsistent with the authorities' intention of relaxing their policy stance for a time. In view of the sharp recession and the substantial progress in reducing inflation, they suspended temporarily their objective of reducing the liquidity ratio, although they have been careful not to tolerate excessive ease in monetary conditions.

During the period 1981-83 the fundamental disequilibria among countries participating in the EMS became evident. The inflation differential was increasing in favour of the Netherlands and Germany. Furthermore, with the German current account recovering, the Deutschemark regained its strength within the EMS. Consequently, realignments raising the value of the guilder and the Deutschemark in terms of other participating currencies within EMS were necessary on four occasions (October 1981, February 1982, June 1982 and March 1983[3]). Thus, despite the strength of the dollar since late 1980, the guilder has appreciated slightly on a trade-weighted basis. The relatively low inflation rate, however, has permitted a consolidation of the gains in competitiveness that were made during 1979-80, and by 1982 the real exchange rate had returned to the levels prevailing at the beginning of the 1970s.

b) *Main determinants of the exchange rate's behaviour*

The preceding review of exchange market developments underlines several points:

– The main factor determining the guilder's value has been the Deutschemark's behaviour, given the priority which has been attached to exchange rate stability within the context of various institutional arrangements dominated by the German currency. Except for some very small Deutschemark revaluations within the snake and EMS, which the Netherlands followed only partially or not at all, there has been virtually no change in the relationship between the two currencies.

– Money market conditions have usually been permitted to respond quickly to developments in the exchange market in order to ensure the stability of the guilder. Interest rate differentials have therefore largely mirrored current account developments, favouring foreign financial centres by a substantial margin during periods of surplus (until 1976 and again from late 1980 until the present), and more or less disappearing when the current account moved into deficit at the end of the decade.

– The policy of attaching the guilder to the Deutschemark has meant that over the medium term Dutch inflation could not diverge significantly from German inflation. This has indeed been the case, and has been reflected in the persistent tendency since

101

1976 for the Netherlands to be a "low inflation" country. In the Dutch context an important influence has also been the production of natural gas, which rose steadily until 1976 and then, particularly from 1980, began to decline. This gas, being either exported or substituted for imports of energy, can provide more real resources to the economy only by serving as payment for an increase in net imports of other goods. Thus, it is likely that the real exchange rate has been influenced by the profile of gas production. This suggests that, in the context of a fixed exchange rate, inflation has been somewhat higher than it would have been had the gas reserves not existed.

EXCHANGE RATE MANAGEMENT AND THE CONDUCT OF MONETARY POLICY

The primary instrument used to maintain stability of the exchange rate within the EMS, at least vis-a-vis the Deutschemark, is the regulation of money market interest rates. Adjustment of these is usually sufficient in this respect, even though it may create temporary disturbances in the money market. A supplementary instrument is direct intervention in the foreign exchange market. Restrictions on capital movements are also used at times to influence exchange market conditions in order to facilitate monetary control. These are discussed below.

a) *The regulation of money market rates*

The money market structure in the Netherlands is such that the banks are virtually in permanent need of additional cash. This forces the commercial banks to have recourse to the central bank, which in turn allows the authorities to make their interest rate policy effective. They regulate both the amount and the price of the credit which they are prepared to extend to banks. The bulk of each bank's likely need for cash is provided by a quota which fixes the amount of credit it may obtain over a three month period at official rates, the most important of which is the Lombard rate. If a bank exceeds its limits a surcharge is applicable. On a proportion of the excess borrowing the surcharge is variable, i.e. adjustable on a daily basis, which makes it possible for the central bank to ensure that excessive borrowing is always at a penalty rate. Since the central bank credit policy is designed to be a quantitative one, such interest rate surcharges are intended as supporting measures. Additional cash may be provided through "special" loans and dollar swaps.

The instruments for providing additional cash are mainly used to help control developments in the foreign exchange market. When exchange market conditions are stable additional cash is provided at a rate which makes the total availability of cash grow in line with the forecast need during each three month period. If interest rate adjustments are needed to maintain orderly conditions in the exchange market the central bank provides somewhat more (or less) cash to influence money market rates. When major adjustments are required it changes its own rates.

b) *Intervention in the foreign exchange market*

Direct intervention in the foreign exchange market is usually kept modest except during periods of currency unrest. At times its negative impact on bank liquidity may be offset by allowing recourse to the bank on comparatively easy terms. When the authorities wish, however, it serves to transmit pressure immediately to the money market, which in turn leads to developments tending the stabilize the situation.

c) *Restrictions on capital movements*

On occasion measures have been introduced to restrict capital movements. These are usually aimed at discouraging inflows in order to prevent excessive liquidity creation from interfering with monetary objectives. Most importantly, from 1971-1974 sales of guilder-denominated bonds had to be met by repurchases of such bonds from other non-residents. For a time this reduced the excessive capital inflows that had hitherto been occurring through this channel, but eventually the market found ways to circumvent the measure and it was abandoned. Another measure aimed at discouraging inflows was the prohibition, applied to non-banks, on taking up financial credits abroad for use in the Netherlands. This was used to support restrictions on bank lending to the private sector. While controls of this type do not normally play a major role in monetary management in the Netherlands, they are at times necessary to make credit ceilings an effective means of restraining monetary growth.

CONCLUDING REMARKS

The Netherlands is unusual among the countries considered in the survey in the extent to which the authorities have been prepared to adjust their monetary policy to that of Germany in order to gain the benefits of the hard currency option. Leaving aside several small adjustments, the guilder has been closely tied to the Deutschemark almost continuously since 1970. Its stability vis-à-vis the German currency has been achieved, despite the international monetary disturbances during this period, because the Dutch authorities have generally allowed exchange market pressure to be transmitted quickly to the money market. This has been sufficient to generate immediate adjustment in the short term, albeit at the cost of occasional disturbances in the money market, while in the medium term the authorities have made it clear that their commitment to the exchange rate takes precedence over other considerations.

This policy has had important benefits in the form of a stable exchange rate environment vis-à-vis main trading partners and a low rate of inflation. It has, however, at times entailed costs. In particular, the early tendencies for the real exchange rate to rise and for inflation to be faster than in Germany, even if only slightly, have long contributed to the problem of low corporate profitability and investment. More recently, the emergence of large budget deficits has aggravated the financial difficulties of other sectors, mainly industry. The policy of avoiding monetary financing of such deficits aims at minimising these difficulties by contributing to control of the money supply and maintenance of confidence in the guilder. The authorities take the view that the problem of upward pressure on interest rates from the large deficits themselves must be attacked at its source, notably by restraining the growth of public expenditure and reducing the structural component of the budget deficit.

NOTES

1. In 1982 29.5 per cent of Dutch exports went to Germany, while 21.1 per cent of Dutch imports came from Germany.
2. This corresponds to lending to the private sector plus long-term lending to the public sector minus long-term liabilities.
3. On the last occasion the revaluation of the guilder did not fully match that of the Deutschemark.

SWEDEN

During the past decade, Sweden has changed its exchange rate regime twice, while adhering throughout to the principle of exchange rate stability. Until 1973, the authorities were committed to maintaining a fixed parity against the dollar. When the major countries moved to a more generalised managed floating of their currencies in 1973, Sweden joined the European intervention arrangement (the "snake"). This association came under increasing strain in 1976/77 and was discontinued from the autumn of 1977, when the krona was devalued and pegged to a weighted average of a representative currency basket. The aim was to stabilise the external value of the krona in relation to the most important trading partners. Specifically, this option appeared more realistic than trying to maintain a formal relationship with a single dominant currency (such as the Deutschemark) influenced by policies which were often inappropriate for the "smaller" country.

Several considerations have led the authorities to adhere to exchange rate stability. First, it has been considered desirable to avoid fluctuations in internationally traded goods prices as the economy is very open with exports and imports each accounting for about 30 per cent of GNP. Second, the maintenance of a fixed exchange rate has been seen as a means of limiting the rate of inflation in the long run. Indeed the authorities have felt that, in a floating exchange rate regime, a small open economy such as Sweden may have only limited scope for preventing exogenous shocks from generating "vicious" inflation-depreciation circles.

OVERVIEW OF THE BEHAVIOUR OF THE EXCHANGE RATE

a) *Exchange rate developments since the early 1970s*

Exchange rate policy has played an important role in domestic stabilisation efforts and on seven occasions since the early 1970s discretionary changes in the krona's exchange rate have been made (see table below). The result has been a step-wise depreciation of the effective exchange rate, interrupted only by a temporary appreciation between early 1974 and the end of 1976 when the strength of the Deutschemark pulled the currencies in the "snake" arrangement up with it. By the autumn of 1983, the effective exchange rate was 30 per cent lower than at the beginning of the 1970s. The following paragraphs review the policy measures and macro-economic developments which have been associated with exchange rate adjustments.

Discretionary changes in the Krona exchange rate

Date	Devaluation %	Reference
December 1971	1	Against gold
February 1973	5	Against gold
October 1976	1	Within the "snake"
April 1977	6	Within the "snake"
August 1977	10	Against the currency basket
September 1981	10	Against the currency basket
October 1982	16	Against the currency basket

1971-1975.   In the years to the mid-1970s, the Swedish krona appreciated in effective terms (7½ per cent beween 1973 and 1976), largely as a result of the upward pull of the Deutschemark within the "snake" arrangement, and despite a policy aimed at keeping the Swedish economy out of phase with developments elsewhere in the area. A relatively moderate current account deficit in the boom year 1970 was followed by a restrictive policy stance which contributed to the recession of 1971. With the external account improving, unemployment rising and inflation moderating, policies became more expansionary. At the same time the authorities chose the "hard currency option" associating the krona with the "European Snake" in early 1973. The economy picked up, but the upturn gathered momentum only during the final phase of the strongly overheated international boom of 1973. In contrast to many OECD countries, Sweden suffered very little adverse movement of the terms of trade at the time, as prices of many important export goods such as timber and steel rose dramatically, cushioning the Swedish economy, at least initially, from the effects of the first oil price rise. Consequently, despite the tightening of policies abroad, it was felt that Sweden was in a relatively good position to retain an accommodative stance in view of its favourable current account situation. Foreign exchange outflow in the spring of 1974 led to a tightening of monetary policy to encourage private capital inflow, but apart from this demand management policies continued to be expansionary right up to 1976 in a conscious attempt to ride out the world recession, which was expected to be brief, and with the hope that it would subsequently be supported by a renewed upswing abroad. Therefore, unlike most other countries, Sweden did not effect the real adjustment demanded by the terms of trade losses due to the first oil shock. This led to a strong deterioration of the external position which was exacerbated by the weakness of the international recovery in 1976-77.

1976-1977.   By late 1975, weaker than expected demand trends (notably for export industries) led to an easing of monetary policy to support employment. During the summer of 1976, domestic interest rates below international levels and relatively ample liquidity within the business sector led to considerable capital outflows, which were exacerbated by expectations of revaluation of the Deutschemark. These outflows started slowly during the summer but they accelerated sharply from mid-September. The Riksbank intervened heavily to defend the krona, but, as the situation became clearly unsustainable, monetary policy was sharply tightened at the beginning of October. The subsequent realignment of parities within the "snake" in mid-October 1976 eliminated exchange market pressures in the near term, and the unwinding of speculative positions strengthened the krona. The tighter monetary policy stance was maintained during early 1977 and the exchange markets remained relatively calm, necessitating minimal intervention. However, concern about its international competitiveness led Sweden to request a new currency realignment, which took place in early April 1977. The Swedish krona was devalued by 6 per cent against the Deutschemark, the guilder and the Belgian franc and by 3 per cent against the Danish and Norwegian kroner.

Renewed speculative pressures built up against the krona by mid-1977, as it became evident that a strong recovery of Swedish exports could not be counted on, and that the relative cost-position of Swedish firms had deteriorated markedly. Furthermore, actual and expected inflation differentials between Sweden and several other snake countries, notably Germany, appeared to imply the need for periodic exchange realignments. Expectations of a devaluation of the krona led to leads and lags in commercial payments, with a strongly increased net demand for foreign currency as a result[1]. By the end of August 1977, and after heavy official intervention, made possible by government borrowing abroad, the krona was taken out of the "European snake", and devalued by 10 per cent. At the same time it was pegged to a representative currency basket[2].

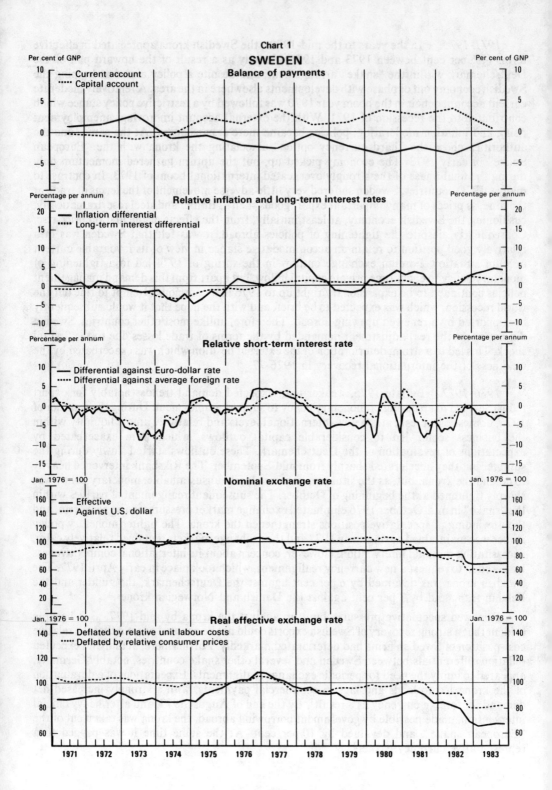

Chart 1

SWEDEN

Per cent of GNP

Balance of payments

Per cent of GNP

- Current account
- Capital account

Percentage per annum

Relative inflation and long-term interest rates

Percentage per annum

- Inflation differential
- Long-term interest differential

Percentage per annum

Relative short-term interest rate

Percentage per annum

- Differential against Euro-dollar rate
- Differential against average foreign rate

Jan. 1976 = 100

Nominal exchange rate

Jan. 1976 = 100

- Effective
- Against U.S. dollar

Jan. 1976 = 100

Real effective exchange rate

Jan. 1976 = 100

- Deflated by relative unit labour costs
- Deflated by relative consumer prices

1971 1972 1973 1974 1975 1976 1977 1978 1979 1980 1981 1982 1983

1978-1980. A pronounced weakness of domestic demand during 1977 combined with very moderate wage settlements to produce a rapid improvement in the external balance and a better outlook for inflation. This permitted more expansionary policies, aimed at combatting unemployment[3], to be implemented in 1978-79. It quickly became obvious, however, that this expansion of aggregate demand was excessive. Inflationary pressures reasserted themselves and the trade account again deteriorated under the impact of excessive domestic demand and the oil price hikes of 1979-80. Though the internal employment objectives were not achieved, monetary restraint was enforced from mid-1979. However, the authorities were unwilling to see interest rates rise by enough to prevent considerable monetisation of the budget deficit, and liquidity in the economy remained ample. Against a background of high and rising world interest rates this led to considerable currency outflows, requiring almost continuous support for the krona by direct intervention in exchange markets, financed by public sector borrowing abroad.

1981-1983. In early 1981, capital outflows and speculative pressures on the krona again gathered momentum. To some extent this was a response to budget proposals in January 1981 which had no obvious solutions to Sweden's structural problems and pointed to little resolve to achieve a better budget balance. The Riksbank intervened heavily, monetary policy was tightened, and a new fiscal package emphasising expenditure cuts was presented at the beginning of February. When, in addition, a new programme of wage restraint was agreed with the trade unions speculative pressures on the krona quickly abated. As capital flows reversed, some relaxation of monetary policy became possible. During this period the dollar appreciated sharply against the currencies of some of Sweden's most important trading partners, so although the krona remained stable against the "basket" currencies as a group, it rose strongly against European currencies such as the German mark. This created difficulties for Swedish firms, and in September 1981 the krona was again devalued by 10 per cent.

The trend towards easier domestic financial conditions continued into early 1982. However renewed capital outflows, considered excessive in relation to developments in the current account, caused increasing concern. Moreover, monetary growth accelerated relatively sharply in the first half of the year, so the authorities moved in mid-summer to a somewhat tighter stance. Although the 1981 devaluation had brought relative unit labour costs back to their 1970 levels, this was felt to be inadequate to correct what was considered to be a major structural imbalance. With domestic demand weaker than in the rest of Europe, the new administration, which came into office in October 1982, felt that there was no alternative to another devaluation. Thus, the krona was devalued by a further 16 per cent, which enabled the authorities to allow some easing of financial conditions in late 1982 and 1983, following international trends.

b) *Main determinants of the exchange rate's behaviour*

The review above has underlined several interrelated factors which lie behind the exchange rate development: (see Chart 1):

- The current account was comfortably in surplus in the early part of the 1970s, helping to maintain the strength of the krona until mid-1976. Since then, the deterioration of the current account has been substantial and apparently largely structural. The lack of success in reducing the external imbalance has on several occasions, notably 1976-1977 and again after 1980, fostered mistrust in the currency and prompted the authorities to devalue the krona.

107

- Changes in the inflation differential have had, at times, important effects on exchange rate developments. During the early 1970s, both the nominal and real effective exchange rates remained relatively stable, reflecting an inflation rate in Sweden close to that abroad. On the other hand, in 1975-76 and again, to some extent, in 1980-81, the real effective exchange rate (as measured by relative unit labour costs) appreciated steadily as a result of an adverse inflation differential caused by rapid increases in wage costs. In both cases, considerations of competitiveness led the authorities to devalue the currency.

- Short-term interest rates have only occasionally moved in favour of Sweden. Against a background of rising current account surpluses in the early 1970s the authorities were able to permit a substantial adverse interest differential to emerge. Conversely, when the inflation differential moved strongly against Sweden and the current account went into heavy deficit around 1976-77 the authorities effected a large favourable interest differential. Since early 1978 domestic interest rates have normally been kept below foreign rates despite the weak current account position. It is likely that this has undermined incentives, which derive from quantitative restrictions on domestic credit expansion, to borrow abroad.

EXCHANGE RATE MANAGEMENT AND THE CONDUCT OF MONETARY POLICY

While there is recognition that excessive monetary creation may tend to aggravate internal as well as external disequilibria, the authorities have refrained from the explicit adoption of monetary targets. Rather, monetary policy has, through the use of selective credit and interest rate controls, generally aimed at fostering financial conditions conducive to high employment. Moreover, monetary expansion has been seen to influence inflationary developments only indirectly, the latter being largely the result of labour market conditions, wage-behaviour and world inflation. However, as reviewed above, this domestically orientated monetary policy stance has repeatedly been adjusted to cope with the mounting external imbalances which have developed since the mid-1970s. This has led the authorities increasingly to direct their monetary policies towards protecting the foreign exchange reserves and achieving better external balance. The most important ways of managing the exchange rate have been general demand management policies, and in particular *(a)* interest rate policy; *(b)* intervention in foreign exchange markets; *(c)* compensatory borrowing; and *(d)* foreign exchange controls.

a) *Interest rate policy*

The general aim of the authorities since the 1960s has been to shield domestic interest rates from international developments in order to reserve this instrument for domestic stabilisation purposes. Thus, during the early part of the 1970s, when Sweden enjoyed a rising current account surplus and an international inflation differential moving increasingly in its favour, an important gap developed between Swedish and foreign interest rates. This was again the case after the 1977 devaluation when the current account improved markedly and was felt to give some leeway to pursue a more domestically orientated policy. On the other hand, during periods of exchange rate disturbances, interest rates have been increased sharply and maintained above international levels for extended periods, despite difficulties in achieving major policy objectives such as full employment. Particularly steep increases took place in 1976-77, in 1979-80, in 1981 and in the summer of 1982 when domestic interest rates had lagged considerably behind international trends, encouraging capital outflows. The higher degree of internationalisation of Swedish interest rate policies has mainly been triggered by the growing imbalance on the external accounts and an inflation differential which has moved against Sweden. As a result a much higher correlation existed between Swedish and international interest rates during the latter part of the decade.

b) *Intervention in foreign exchange markets*

The obligation to maintain a fixed exchange rate implies that the authorities must be willing to offset any excess demand for or supply of foreign currency that might arise out of either external commercial or financial transactions. Intervention in foreign exchange markets have been frequent and, in times of currency unrest, of considerable size. For example, during the 1976 crisis, Riksbank intervention reached SKr 4 billion in just two months (equivalent to a third of its foreign exchange reserves), while in the months before the 1977 devaluation sales of foreign currency amounted to almost SKr 9 billion. Also, in the autumn of 1979, in early 1981, and again in 1982, counterspeculative interventions were necessary on a large scale.

There is little evidence that the authorities have systematically attempted to sterilise the monetary impact of external currency flows (Chart 2). The latter added on average 1½ percentage points per annum to the growth of money supply in the period 1971-73, when the purpose was to stimulate economic activity. They were about neutral in their monetary impact from 1974-77, when monetary policy in general was tight. Since then, the net effect has been a drain of liquidity amounting an annual average to 4½ per cent of the money supply. In none of these periods was there any apparent offsetting movement in the liquidity creation by the central bank. Indeed, during the latter period, the Riksbank has markedly increased its liquidity absorbing open market operations. This must be seen against the rapidly growing impact of the budget deficit on domestic monetary developments since 1978, coinciding with the worsening of the external deficit. Thus, the focus of the Riksbank has shifted towards achieving a reasonable domestic liquidity creation, by restraining bank lending to the private sector and allowing external transactions to have their liquidity absorbing impact fully reflected in the money supply.

c) *Compensatory borrowing*

In recent years, governments facing deficits on their budgets and in external transactions have had considerable recourse to official compensatory borrowing in order to avoid the severity of the credit restrictions which would otherwise have to be imposed on the private domestic sectors. Such borrowing has either taken place through state owned enterprises or by direct government borrowing. The latter option has been used to a considerable extent by the Swedish authorities. Thus, the first international loans were floated in 1977 and, since then, the government's external debt has increased at a rapid rate (from an annual average of 0.6 per cent of GNP in the 1974/77 period to 2.1 per cent from 1978 to 1981). This has enabled the authorities to resist downward pressures on the exchange rate in the face of persistant external deficits without exhausting official reserves.

d) *Foreign exchange controls*

The authorities have attempted to minimise the conflicts between internal and external objectives by the extensive use of foreign exchange controls. These regulations have not applied to direct investments abroad or to short-term transactions connected with foreign

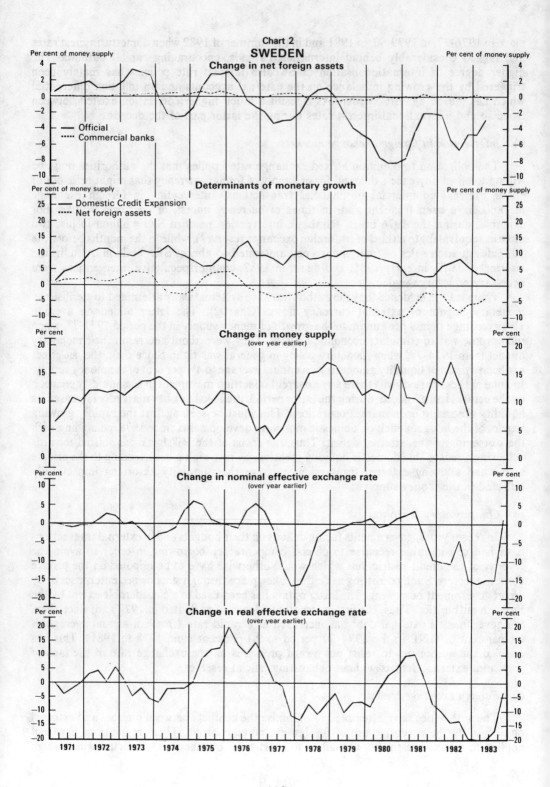

Chart 2
SWEDEN

Per cent of money supply

Change in net foreign assets

- —— Official
- ····· Commercial banks

Per cent of money supply

Determinants of monetary growth

- —— Domestic Credit Expansion
- ····· Net foreign assets

Per cent

Change in money supply
(over year earlier)

Per cent

Change in nominal effective exchange rate
(over year earlier)

Per cent

Change in real effective exchange rate
(over year earlier)

1971 1972 1973 1974 1975 1976 1977 1978 1979 1980 1981 1982 1983

trade. Given the existence of these and other unregulated types of transaction, the effectiveness of such controls has, in recent years, been increasingly called into question. Econometric evidence suggests that, despite controls, about 40 to 50 per cent of a domestic monetary shock is offset by capital flows[4]. Changes in leads and lags in payments connected with foreign trade are perhaps the most important way in which monetary impulses influence the exchange market[5]. The potential impact of these has increased in recent years as the scope for Swedish firms to choose between domestic and foreign financing has grown substantially.

CONCLUDING REMARKS

The lessons to be drawn from the Swedish experience underline the need for the general orientation of demand management policies to be consistent with those prevailing abroad, if the "hard currency option", i.e. fixing the exchange rate to a strong currency such as the Deutschemark, is to be successful. In 1974-76, while monetary policy was restrictive in order to promote private capital inflows, fiscal policy was firmly directed towards domestic objectives, i.e. the maintenance of a high employment level. This involved accommodating domestic cost pressures until they proved well out of line with those in Germany and in other members of the "European snake". As a result, a devaluation of the krona became inevitable. For some time afterwards, fiscal and monetary policies were directed towards restoring external balance, but in 1978/79 there was a return to an expansionary policy stance. This made it difficult to avoid the international acceleration of inflation accompanying the second oil shock, as the domestic cost pressures were exacerbated by a weak krona.

More recently, the chronically weak external balance has repeatedly forced the authorities to adjust monetary policy towards maintaining the exchange rate stability in the short run. However, in September 1981, the authorities chose to devalue rather than accept the deflation that would be required to force the domestic inflation rate in Sweden into line with that of its main trading partners. With the new administration in power from October 1982, the krona was again devalued as an important part of a comprehensive programme to stabilise the domestic economy. Overall, the Swedish experience confirms the traditional view that the scope for monetary independence is very limited in a small open economy.

NOTES

1. It has been estimated that from June to late August, devaluation expectations led to outflows between SKr 6 to 8½ billion. See Franzen and Uggla (1978), pp 86-96.

2. The basket consists of 15 currencies, weighted by their respective share in trade with Sweden. However, due to its importance in the total of trade payments, the weight of the US dollar has been doubled. The weights are revised every year so that they are always based on the trade-data in the five preceeding years.

3. The central government budget deficit tripled from SKr 18 billion in 1977 to SKr 54 billion in 1980.

4. Lybeck (1977).

5. An adverse shift in trade payments e.g. delaying the repatriation of export revenue and accelerating import payments by one week may entail a capital outflow of about SKr 3½ billion. C.f. Franzen and Uggla (1978).

SWITZERLAND

Switzerland is a small economy but an important financial centre, and has frequently been the recipient of large balance of payments inflows. The switch to floating exchange rates in January 1973 was seen as a prerequisite for effective monetary control. The domestic money markets are not well developed, and sterilization of official intervention through open market operations has tended not to be important. The main instruments of monetary policy have been changes in minimum reserve requirements, and the mopping up of excess liquidity by forcing banks that raise Swiss franc loans for non-residents to convert them into dollars at the Swiss National Bank[1]. Since 1979 franc-dollar swaps have served as a major instrument of control of bank liquidity. Emphasis on aggregates oriented policy was formalised in 1975 with the adoption of a target for the rate of growth of M1. This was temporarily abandoned in 1978 in favour of an exchange rate target, but from 1980 targets have been announced for the monetary base. Central government has a relatively limited role, and its budget deficits have always been relatively small, no important conflicts with monetary policy having arisen from this source.

Exports account for about 35 per cent of Swiss GNP, and extreme appreciations of the real exchange rate for the franc can be seriously damaging for domestic industry. Consequently, the authorities have not been able to ignore the exchange rate consequences of the stance of domestic monetary policy. A further complicating factor for exchange rate management is the growing role of the Swiss franc as a subsidiary international reserve currency. Approximately 4-5 per cent of the world's central bank reserves are estimated to be held in Swiss francs. In addition, Swiss banks have been heavily involved in Euro-currency transactions.

OVERVIEW OF THE BEHAVIOUR OF THE EXCHANGE RATE SINCE THE EARLY 1970s

The main presumed determinants of exchange rate movements in the case of Switzerland are shown in Chart 1. The inflation differential with the rest of the world was fairly steady up until 1973, but subsequently moved substantially in favour of the domestic economy, fluctuating within a range of 4 to 10 per cent. The nominal exchange rate appreciated from 1973 to 1978, a phenomenon which was particularly marked in this latter year. Subsequently, the rate depreciated until early 1979 and thereafter remained steady until 1981/82, when a small appreciation was followed by a similar depreciation. During 1983 the franc gradually appreciated. The behaviour of the real exchange rate has broadly been dominated by movements of the nominal rate, given the steady and favourable inflation differential. It appreciated substantially during 1978.

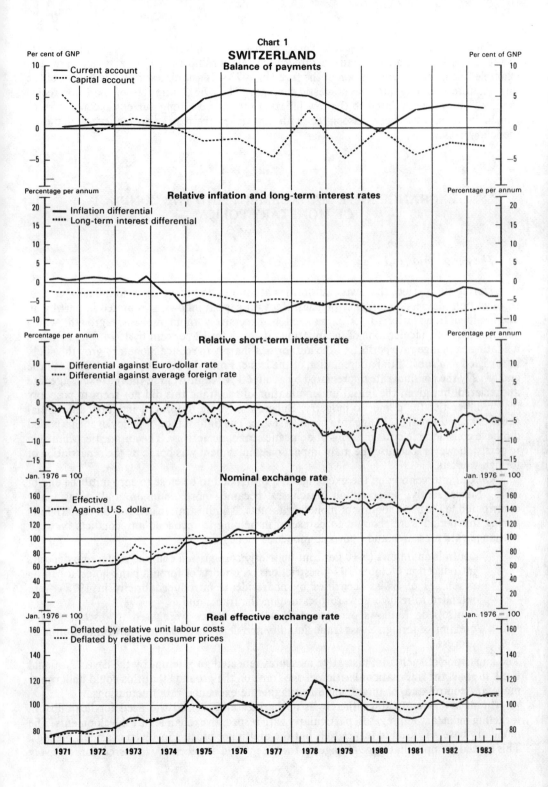

Chart 1

SWITZERLAND

Balance of payments

Per cent of GNP

- Current account
- Capital account

Relative inflation and long-term interest rates

Percentage per annum

- Inflation differential
- Long-term interest differential

Relative short-term interest rate

Percentage per annum

- Differential against Euro-dollar rate
- Differential against average foreign rate

Nominal exchange rate

Jan. 1976 = 100

- Effective
- Against U.S. dollar

Real effective exchange rate

Jan. 1976 = 100

- Deflated by relative unit labour costs
- Deflated by relative consumer prices

1971 1972 1973 1974 1975 1976 1977 1978 1979 1980 1981 1982 1983

For most of the period under consideration the interest differential has been unfavourable to the Swiss franc, and has had no discernible relationship with the exchange rate. For example, the marked appreciation of the franc in 1978 was associated with a widening of the interest differential against the domestic currency. The overall strength of the franc seems mainly to have been related to the low inflation rate and a strong current account surplus which, in turn, have been associated with the generally restrictive stance of domestic monetary policy.

EXCHANGE RATE MANAGEMENT AND THE CONDUCT OF MONETARY POLICY

a) *The period prior to 1978*

During this period, the Swiss authorities attempted to give priority to inflation control through tight domestic monetary policies. Buoyant capital inflows, stimulated in part by an undervalued franc prior to 1973, had led to excessively rapid monetary growth, which contributed to an acceleration of the inflation rate to about 12 per cent by 1974. The switch to a floating exchange rate permitted the authorities sharply to reduce monetary growth which, in turn, led to a substantial appreciation of the franc. From the first quarter of 1973 until the end of 1977 the nominal rate appreciated by about 60 per cent. At first, the real exchange rate appreciated, but given the initial undervaluation of the franc this did not seem to pose any major difficulties for domestic industry. Subsequently, the improved inflation differential acted to keep the real exchange rate broadly stable. The tight stance of policy over this period did have considerable costs in terms of domestic economic activity. The authorities were able to persist, however, because the main impact on employment was borne by the repatriation of foreign workers.

Official intervention on the exchange market tended to be close to zero until the end of 1975. Subsequently, intervention purchases became more common and occasionally contributed to the overshooting of monetary targets. Administrative controls on capital flows during this period were thought to be useful in helping to reconcile any conflicts between exchange rate pressures and domestic monetary policy:

- controls on inflows (a 10 per cent quarterly commission charged on foreign deposits introduced in October 1974; restrictions on imports of foreign bank notes; a ban on purchases of Swiss securities by nonresidents introduced briefly in 1978) were intended to reduce upward pressure on the franc; and
- controls on outflows denominated in Swiss francs were used to discourage the creation of foreign Swiss franc liquidity and deposits through a Eurofranc multiplier process.

The imposition of such administrative measures reflected an attempt by the Swiss National Bank to resist the internationalisation of the franc on the grounds that this could undermine monetary control and/or might serve to exaggerate exchange rate fluctuations.

From a very early stage the Swiss authorities emphasized the need for flexibility in targeting monetary aggregates, particularly with respect to exchange rate developments. The monetary base was used to target M1, but the multiplier process involved considerable lags. This tended to imply that large changes in the base would be necessary to correct for relatively minor deviations from targets, which might serve to disrupt the foreign exchange market. Consequently, minor deviations from targets were permitted during this period, but for the most part these were broadly achieved (see Table 1 below).

Table 1. **Growth of monetary aggregates, 1975-77**

		Percentage change over previous year		Multiplier[a]
		Monetary base	Money supply M1	
1975	Target	6.0	6.0	1.5
	Outturn	6.2	4.4	1.5
1976	Target	6.0	6.0	1.7
	Outturn	3.8	7.7	3.5
1977	Target	–	5.0	–
	Outturn	5.4	5.5	1.9

a) Ratio of absolute change in M1 to absolute change in monetary base.

b) *Experience with exchange rate targeting in 1978*

In the course of the 1970s the pursuance of non-inflationary monetary policies, together with Switzerland's traditional attraction for financial investments which provide security, led to considerable portfolio substitution into francs in spite of administrative controls. The weakening of the US dollar intensified this process in the course of the year. By October the exchange rate had appreciated 35 per cent in nominal terms, and by 30 per cent in real terms (Chart 2) over one year earlier. This latter development led to a significant overvaluation of the franc, implying potentially damaging effects on the domestic export sector. Consequently, a target was set for the franc/Deutschemark exchange rate of "well over" 80. The bilateral rate against the Deutschemark was selected because the policy objectives of the Bundesbank were regarded as being very close to those of the Swiss National Bank. An explicit exchange rate target became necessary because the smallness of the Swiss economy in relation to currency movements had caused it to be disproportionately affected.

To achieve their objective for the exchange rate, the Swiss authorities intervened heavily, buying US dollars in order to manipulate the appropriate cross rate with the Deutschemark. This was believed to be necessary in order to avoid tensions within the "European snake" arrangements. Additional measures to ward off capital inflows were also taken. In particular, a tax was levied on non-resident franc deposits. The sluggishness of the money multiplier process had, in earlier years, created considerable scope for intervention policies provided that these were quickly reversed. However, at this time the authorities came to realise that if long-term priorities remained committed to monetary targets, markets would tend to anticipate the reversal and exchange rates would not be greatly affected in the short run. In the face of portfolio diversification on the scale which occurred in 1978, a significant deviation from the monetary target had to be permitted. The rate of growth of M1 exceeded 17 per cent during 1978, compared to the previously set target of 5 per cent. This policy, together with the recovery of the US dollar in early 1979, caused the nominal and real exchange rates to depreciate to more "normal" levels.

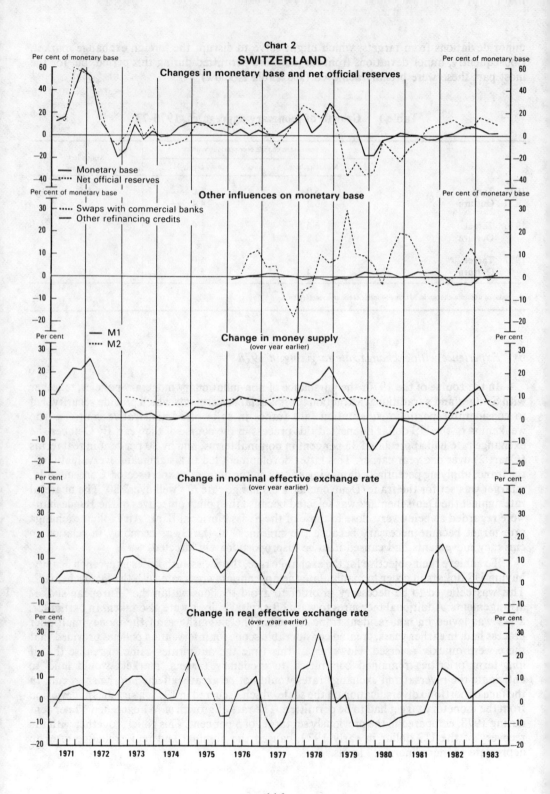

Chart 2

SWITZERLAND

Changes in monetary base and net official reserves

Per cent of monetary base

— Monetary base
······ Net official reserves

Other influences on monetary base

Per cent of monetary base

······ Swaps with commercial banks
— Other refinancing credits

Change in money supply
(over year earlier)

Per cent

— M1
······ M2

Change in nominal effective exchange rate
(over year earlier)

Per cent

Change in real effective exchange rate
(over year earlier)

Per cent

1971 1972 1973 1974 1975 1976 1977 1978 1979 1980 1981 1982 1983

c) The period since 1979

By the spring of 1979 the Swiss authorities returned to a policy of tight monetary control, and by 1980 were in a position to set formal targets for the monetary base. This was regarded as indispensable for signalling to markets that monetary policy was again to be directed primarily towards inflation control. The main reason for the switch away from an M1 target was the influence of the exchange rate expectations on the demand for money, which made the multiplier difficult to forecast[2]. This endogeneity of the multiplier tends automatically to permit the money supply to adjust according to shifts in money demand in the short run. One problem in this respect is that asset demand shifts may be induced by changes in exchange rate expectations or by an acceleration of inflation. Automatic flexibility of the money supply in response to a shift in currency preferences is desirable, while the accommodation of inflation is not. However, in this respect, the Swiss authorities believe that if the monetary base target is "credible" over the medium term, then short-run fluctuations in the money supply are unlikely to be important. The base itself is not targeted in a rigid manner, because the short-run situation frequently requires flexibility in the implimentation of policy. This has been reflected in an undershooting of the target, particularly in 1980 and 1981 (see Table 2).

The monetary target for 1980 was undershot largely because the authorities intervened to support the weakening position of the Swiss franc. Attempts to sterilize the negative impact on monetary growth by offering swaps to commercial banks (Chart 2) proved to be insufficient to achieve the target. This was partly a consequence of the reintegration into bank deposits of bank notes which had been held in vaults during the period of restrictions and disincentives on non-resident deposits. In 1981, policy was more deliberately restrictive. This was because the acceleration of inflation, which began as a consequence of the previous excessive monetary expansion, had continued with oil price developments and the more rapid growth of the broad money supply. The tightening of policy led to some short-run upward pressure on the exchange rate. But the Swiss authorities have chosen more and more to ignore such developments, believing that if market perceptions of the medium-term stance of policy tend to be unchanged, attempts at fine-tuning the exchange rate and/or the money supply will, in general, be largely ineffective. A flexible approach to targeting the monetary base, while permitting short term fluctuations in the money supply and the exchange rate, is believed to reduce possibly more damaging uncertainty about the long-run stance of monetary policy[3].

Table 2. Growth of the monetary base, 1980-83

Percentage change over previous year

	1980	1981	1982	1983
Target	4	3	3	3
Outturn	1.5	1.4	2.6	3.6

Another interesting aspect of the Swiss experience during the 1970s was the largely ineffective nature of controls to ward off capital inflows and to prevent the internationalisation of the franc. Most of these measures have been dismantled since 1979. This has reflected a view that such developments cannot be stopped, and that removal of the controls would:

- give the authorities more information on the size and magnitude of the transactions involved; and
- help to bring such transactions back to Switzerland, where at least some measure of control could be exercised.

CONCLUDING REMARKS

Swiss monetary policy has, with the temporary exception of 1978, been oriented mainly towards domestic inflation control. This has gradually evolved into a flexible system of targeting the monetary base over a medium-term horizon. The endogeneity of the money multiplier, related to the sensitivity of asset demands to exchange rate expectations, has permitted M1 to respond in the short run to fluctuations in currency preferences. But, in general, any attempt to fine tune the money supply or the exchange rate has been regarded as undesirable. However, the exceptional period of 1978 illustrates the potential importance of conflicts between money and exchange rate objectives in a small open economy.

The Swiss experience is also of considerable interest when examining the efficacy of what is referred to earlier in this study as exchange rate management without monetary adjustment:

- Sterilization of capital inflows has not always been feasible and/or desirable. In 1973 and 1978, it was not possible to sterilize very large inflows in order to achieve monetary control. In any case, given the nature of speculative inflows which took place at the time (notably in 1978), sterilized intervention would not have permitted the exchange rate pressures to be alleviated.
- Administrative controls on capital flows tended largely to be ineffective.

The Swiss case suggests that exchange rate management will normally require monetary adjustment, and exchange rate developments have generally been dominated by the overall stance of domestic monetary policy vis-à-vis the rest of the world.

Notwithstanding 1978, which was affected by special circumstances, Switzerland, unlike most small open economies, has been able to orient domestic monetary policy towards inflation control, without running into serious conflicts with the exchange rate. Two factors stand out in explaining this phenomenon. In the first place, there have been no major conflicts with other aspects of domestic economic policy. In particular, monetary policy is not complicated by any requirement to coordinate with fiscal policy, given that the latter is not used as an active tool of demand management in Switzerland. Second, and perhaps more importantly, Switzerland's major trading partner is Germany. While no formal exchange rate target has been set, the pursuance of similar objectives in both countries have led to a de facto coordination of monetary policies which have generally permitted exchange rate conflicts to be avoided.

NOTES

1. For more details see OECD (1979), Annex I.
2. See Roth (1981) and Johnson (1982).
3. See Schiltknecht (1981).

DATA SOURCES AND METHODS

Chart 1

This chart presents figures relating to exchange rate developments and the main factors which are thought to influence them. It is uniform for all countries (the United States excepted) and is based on the OECD Secretariat's data. The *first panel* shows a four quarter sum of current and capital accounts, respectively, expressed as a percentage of nominal GNP/GDP similarly constructed, except for Sweden, Switzerland and the Netherlands where only annual data is available. The *second panel* shows relative inflation as the annual rate of change in the GDP deflator for the United States and Canada minus the trade-weighted sum of changes in GDP deflators in the other six major OECD economies. For all other countries the annual rate of change of the consumer price index minus the trade-weighted sum of the other ten countries' rate of change in CPI is used. The long-term interest differential, a proxy for differential inflation expectations, is constructed as the domestic rate minus the trade-weighted average of the rates in other countries. These are rates on long-term government or public corporation bonds, with the exception of Italy, where private sector bonds are used.

The *third panel* shows the short-term interest differential as the domestic rate minus the trade-weighted sum of rates in the other countries. The rates used are for the United States: 6 month commercial bills; Japan: call money; Germany: 3 month commercial loans; France: call money; United Kingdom: 3 month treasury bills; Italy: interbank deposits; Canada: 90 day finance company paper; Switzerland: Eurocurrency Swiss franc deposits in London; Sweden: 3 month treasury bills; Netherlands: 3 month treasury paper; Belgium: 3 month treasury bills. The differential against the Eurodollar rate is the domestic rate minus the 3 month deposit rate for US dollars in London. Nominal exchange rates in the *fourth panel* are indices (1976 = 100) of foreign currency per unit of domestic currency for dollars and a trade-weighted basket of currencies, respectively. The *fifth panel* shows real effective exchange rates. These are the nominal effective rate deflated by relative unit labour costs, to provide some measure of trade competitiveness, and relative consumer price indices, which reflect relative purchasing power parity.

Chart 2

This chart shows data relating to net official reserves and the money supply process. The series presented differ between countries, depending on the importance of the monetary base in the conduct of monetary policy, and are extracted from various sources listed below. In the United States and Canada the monetary base is shown with net official reserves in the *first panel*. However, in these countries official reserves are held by the treasury and not by the cental bank, so that changes in the latter do not have a direct impact on the monetary base. The *second panel* shows the main counterparts to the monetary base, including the net foreign assets of the central bank, which differs substantially from the official net reserves shown in the first panel. For Germany and Switzerland official reserves are held by the central bank, and this series is shown with the monetary base in the first panel, the second panel shows influences on the monetary base other than net official reserves. For countries where policy operates mainly to control the demand for credit from the banking system as a whole, which includes all of the other countries covered by the survey, an alternative set of data is presented. The first panel shows the net foreign assets of the central bank and the commercial banks. The second panel shows the main counterparts of the broad money supply as domestic credit expansion and the net foreign assets of the banking system as whole.

The rate of growth of the broad money supply (usually M2 or M3) is shown in the *third panel* for all countries. In some countries narrow monetary aggregates are (or have been) targeted by the authorities. In these cases the rate of growth of M1 is also shown. For Sweden the money supply is defined as currency plus all bank deposits plus bank certificates held by non-banks. Non-resident deposits are included in the definition of money in the cases of the United States, Canada, (if Can.$), Sweden and France. Foreign currency deposits are included in the definition of money in the cases of Germany, France, Italy, the Netherlands, Switzerland and Belgium. The *fourth and fifth* panels show changes in the nominal effective exchange rate and the real effective exchange rate (deflated by relative unit labour costs), respectively, in order to indicate major turning points in the levels series presented in Chart 1.

DATA SOURCES

All countries: *OECD Balance of Payments and Exchange Rate Statistics.*

United States: Federal Reserve System *Monthly Bulletin; OECD Main Economic Indicators.*

Japan: Bank of Japan, *Economic Statistics Monthly; OECD Main Economic Indicators.*

Germany: *Monthly Report of the Deutsche Bundesbank.*

France: *Bulletin Trimestriel de la Banque de France; Rapport annuel du Conseil National du Crédit; OECD Main Economic Indicators.*

United Kingdom: *Bank of England Quarterly Bulletin; OECD Main Economic Indicators.*

Italy: Bank of Italy, *Annual Report* and *Bollettino; International Financial Statistics (IMF).*

Canada: Bank of Canada *Review* and *Annual Reports; OECD Main Economic Indicators.*

Belgium: *Bulletin de la Banque Nationale de Belgique.*

Netherlands: *Annual Report* of the Netherlands Bank; *OECD Main Economic Indicators.*

Sweden: Sveriges Riksbank; *OECD Main Economic Indicators.*

Switzerland: Swiss National Bank *Monthly Bulletin; OECD Main Economic Indicators.*

Annex II

THE DETERMINANTS OF EXCHANGE RATE MOVEMENTS

121

A. INTRODUCTION

Exchange rates are relative prices of national currencies, and under a floating rate regime they may naturally be viewed as being determined by the interplay of supply and demand in foreign exchange markets. This proposition is uncontroversial, but it provides no more than a starting point for understanding exchange rate determination and its relationship to other macroeconomic variables and to policy. Supply and demand in currency markets are dependent on conditions in other markets, real and financial, which are affected in turn by exchange rates themselves. In fact any analysis which attempted to be general would describe exchange rates as being determined in a complex process of interaction simultaneously with all other variables in the international macro-economy. Such an approach would prove too cumbersome to be helpful empirically. Simplifying assumptions have therefore been used in most standard models to provide explanations which are in varying degrees partial. Each model has its own specific insights emphasising particular linkages, for example with trade and relative price developments, or with conditions in money and financial markets more generally.

The experience of floating exchange rates since 1971-73 has led to a radical reconsideration of how exchange rate determination may best be understood. The dust has yet to settle on many issues, but a broad consensus was reached at an early stage on the fundamental proposition that the determination of exchange rates is best viewed as being akin to the determination of the prices of financial assets. The basis and implications of this "asset-market" approach are discussed in Parts B.1 and B.2, where it is first compared with the earlier "balance of payments" view. A conceptual framework for the empirical analysis of exchange rate movements is then derived in Part B.3 which is a general implication of the asset-market view. The special assumptions which have been used to obtain some of the best-known theoretical and econometric results are described briefly in Part A.4; and the apparent failure of econometric exchange rate models to explain much of recent experience is discussed.

The subsequent analysis then considers how exchange rate movements in the floating rate period appear to have been related to the main suggested determining variables: relative price levels in Part C.1; interest rates in Part C.2; money supplies in Part C.3; portfolio preferences and asset supplies in Part C.4; and current account developments in Part C.5. With robust econometric evidence generally absent, much of the empirical discussion is necessarily speculative; it is based largely on the notes describing the experience of individual countries and currencies. A summary is provided in Part D. More technical aspects of the preceding discussion of exchange rate determination are presented in an Appendix to the Annex.

B. GENERAL OVERVIEW OF EXCHANGE RATE DETERMINATION

1. *Exchange rates determined by balance of payments flows*

Early analyses of the impact of monetary and fiscal policy on exchange rates had been conditioned by the nature of the international financial system, and the policy pre-occupations of earlier post-war years[1]. Under the Bretton Woods regime, exchange rates were viewed as "adjustable pegs", to be used for the correction of "fundamental disequilibria" in the balance of payments, which were usually to be identified by persistent imbalances on current account. The economic analysis of exchange rates correspondingly focused on their influence on current account flows, and on the mechanism which parity adjustment could thereby provide for the correction of payments imbalances.

The equilibrating role which might be played by transactions on capital account received less attention: apart from a structural element net capital flows were usually assumed to be dependent on the difference between domestic and foreign interest rates, but to be independent of the exchange rate because expectations of currency movements, which might otherwise have formed a link, were usually taken as fixed[2]. When these assumptions about the balance of payments were appended to the conventional "Keynesian" analysis of the determination of output and interest rates in a closed economy, a framework was provided in which the impact of monetary and fiscal policy on a floating exchange rate could be examined. The main object of the exercise, however, was to examine the relative efficacy of fiscal and monetary stabilisation policies under fixed and floating exchange rate regimes. This, together with the usual adoption of an assumption of fixed domestic production costs, reflected the policy pre-occupations of the time.

Consider, for example, the implications of *an increase in the domestic money supply*. It is assumed that the economy is initially in internal and external equilibrium, but that output is not supply-constrained. The excess supply of money puts downward pressure on interest rates: this has internal and external effects. Internally, interest-sensitive expenditure increases, and output expands towards a new equilibrium where the increased money stock is willingly held, owing partly to higher incomes and partly to lower interest rates. Externally, lower domestic interest rates cause the capital account to deteriorate; and there is, in addition, a deterioration in the current account owing to an increase in imports stemming from the rise in income. Without official intervention in the foreign exchange market, this incipient deterioration in the overall balance of payments will cause the exchange rate to fall[3] to the point where the competitiveness of domestic goods and services, and hence the current account balance, are sufficiently improved for overall external balance to be restored in spite of the sustained deterioration on capital account. In the final equilibrium the current account balance must therefore be more favourable than in the initial position; and hence the expansionary effect on output of the increase in the money supply must be greater than if the authorities had intervened to prevent the depreciation.

The proposition that the effectiveness of monetary policy is enhanced by exchange rate flexibility, through the associated reponse of the current account, was one of the most significant implications of this analysis[4]. From the viewpoint of the issue of exchange rate determination this proposition is less pertinent, and the import of the analysis may be summarised as follows. *The exchange rate is viewed as being determined by the equilibration of balance of payments flows, with the responsiveness of the current account to variations in competitiveness providing the crucial mechanism.* Domestic monetary expansion is predicted to lead to depreciation of the domestic currency in order to maintain, *via* the current account, external balance with whatever mix of lower interest rates and higher output is required to restore internal equilibrium.

2. *From flow-equilibrium to asset-market views of exchange rates*

A number of features of the above analysis became increasingly inadequate in the light of more recent experience. One is the assumption of fixed domestic production costs, invariant in particular to both monetary conditions and the exchange rate. On this assumption, movements in the exchange rate entail equal changes in competitiveness (or the real exchange rate) which lead to the effects described on the current account and output. The "purchasing power parity" (PPP) view of exchange rate determination (considered in Part C.2 below), which holds that exchange rate movements tend to offset changes in relative price levels so that real exchange rates tend to be stable, clearly has no role. This suggests that the analysis is concerned mainly with the short-term determination of exchange rates, and the short-term effects of monetary and fiscal policy in an open economy before prices have had time to adjust.

The second problem with the above analysis, however, contradicts this interpretation. This is that it is essentially static and ignores the lags with which output and trade volumes are likely to respond to exogenous disturbances. In reality, exchange rates and interest rates, being determined in "flexprice" markets, will tend to respond quickly to shocks which disturb supply and demand. On the other hand expenditures, income, output and trade (and also goods prices set in "sticky-price" markets) are likely to respond more slowly as plans are changed and contracts re-drawn. These observations carry two important implications:

- The changes in interest rates and exchange rates which may be required in the short run to maintain equilibrium in foreign exchange and other financial markets may exceed the changes required when sufficient time has elapsed for the more sluggish variables in the real economy to adapt and bear the burden of adjustment. This question of "overshooting" will be examined in the Appendix.
- Second, and more fundamentally, delays in the response of trade volumes to exchange rate changes mean that the current account cannot, in the short run, play the equilibrating role in the foreign exchange market described above.

Traded manufactured goods are usually invoiced in the currency of the exporter and primary products in dollars[5]. Since the prices of the latter, in dollars, respond quickly to changes in that currency's exchange rate, it is a fair generalisation that when the currency of an industrialised country (including the United States) depreciates, the domestic-currency prices of its exports will (at least in the short run) remain unchanged, while those of its imports will rise. This deterioration in its terms of trade will cause the current account balance to worsen until export and import volumes have responded sufficiently to offset the unfavourable change in relative prices. The current balance will thus tend to follow a "J-curve" path, and may well not show an improvement from its initial position until a year or more has passed[6]. This means that *the role of equilibrator of the foreign exchange market in the short run must pass to the capital account,* otherwise the market would be unstable. The capital account can take on this role if it is assumed that capital flows depend on the exchange rate (as well as the interest differential), which will be the case if they depend on expected exchange rate movements, provided the latter are not unstable. In the example considered above of an increase in the money supply, the implication is that the domestic currency must depreciate in the short run to the point where expectations of its future appreciation are sufficiently

124

optimistic to generate a capital inflow large enough, despite the fall in the domestic interest rate, to offset the current account deterioration[7].

Finally, the assumption that capital flows are related to interest rate levels implies that a change in the differential between domestic and foreign interest rates will have a permanent effect on the capital account. This may be considered an apt description of a world where capital is relatively immobile internationally, and where it is mainly new wealth which is being allocated each period among assets denominated in different currencies. For the immediate post-war decade or so, when private capital flows were, to a large extent, discouraged by exchange controls, and international financial markets were relatively undeveloped, such a treatment may have been appropriate. But following the subsequent relaxations of capital controls, and the development of international capital markets encouraged by, in particular, the growth of multi-national corporations and the recycling of OPEC surpluses, it seems more reasonable to regard capital flows as adjustments of the composition of stocks of assets and liabilities, at least for the countries and currencies with which this study is primarily concerned. On this view, the effect of a change in interest differentials (or exchange rate expectations) will be to revise the preferred currency composition of portfolios[8].

The last two arguments – that transactions on capital account bear most of the burden of adjustment towards short-run equilibrium in the foreign exchange market, and that capital flows represent responses to imbalances between actual and desired portfolios – form the basis of the *asset-market* view of exchange rates which is represented in most of the recent theoretical and empirical work in this area. On this view, while it is acknowledged that exchange rates, in the absence of official intervention, maintain equilibrium between balance of payments flows, the nature of the process is considered to be such that they are better regarded as asset prices, as being determined by the willingness to hold available stocks. The relevant stocks in this case are those of financial assets denominated in different currencies; and the implication is that a freely determined exchange rate will tend in any period towards a value where the stocks of assets denominated in the two currencies concerned are willingly held. This view may provide useful insights because the behaviour of exchange rates typically resembles that of other asset prices in such respects as volatility (in relation to their presumed underlying determinants) and the absence or weakness of correlation between their changes in successive periods[9].

This equilibrium condition, common to all versions of the asset market approach, implies a direct influence of the current account through its effect on asset supplies. In the short run the exchange rate is likely to be dominated by factors affecting asset demands – simply because the potential scale of portfolio adjustments may exceed the relatively inert current balance. However, over longer horizons, once factors affecting demands have have time to adjust, the growth of asset supplies (and hence the current account) may dominate the broader swings of the exchange rate. Moreover, the current account itself can be expected to adjust to previous exchange rate movements over the medium-term. Finally, the current account may also play a significant role in the short run if it affects exchange rate expectations. These considerations will be expanded upon below, as the implications of asset market equilibrium are explored.

3. *Asset-market equilibrium: a general interpretation*

The stocks of assets denominated in two currencies will be willingly held if their expected yields give wealth-holders no incentive to switch out of one currency into the other. This will be the case when the expected nominal interest differential in favour of any foreign asset in relation to a comparable domestic asset, net of any risk premium which wealth-holders may require to persuade them to hold the outstanding stock of foreign-currency assets, is equal to the market's expected rate of appreciation of the domestic currency over a time-horizon which matches the term of the interest-bearing assets[10]. This is to say that expected yields on domestic and foreign assets, when expressed in terms of a common currency, must be equalised apart from a risk premium. The latter measures the differential preference of wealth-holders for one currency or the other relative to the respective supplies of assets denominated in each, and which reflects the risks of capital gains and losses arising from uncertainty about the future course of the exchange rate[11].

This statement about relative asset yields may now be re-interpreted as a condition which the current exchange rate must satisfy in asset-market equilibrium. Since the expected appreciation of the domestic currency is the proportional difference between the expected future exchange rate and its current value, the statement implies that the current exchange rate must be related in a particular way to its expected value, the interest differential, and the risk premium. More specifically, the domestic currency will tend to appreciate from one period to the next if its expected future value increases; if domestic interest rates rise in relation to foreign rates; or if the risk premium on foreign currency rises owing to a change in preferences in favour of the domestic currency or a relative increase in the supply of foreign currency assets. Now the expected future nominal exchange rate may be regarded as comprising an expected future real exchange rate and the expected future relationship between foreign and domestic price levels; and the latter expected price ratio may be further decomposed into the corresponding current price ratio and the difference between expected foreign and domestic inflation rates.

This leads to an interpretation of the asset-market equilibrium condition which identifies *five components of, or contributors to, exchange rate movements:* it indicates that *the value of a currency will tend to rise in any period if:*

i) foreign prices are currently rising faster than domestic prices;
ii) expectations of domestic interest rates are being revised upwards in relation to expectations of foreign interest rates;
iii) expectations of domestic inflation are being revised downwards in relation to expectations of foreign inflation;
iv) expectations of the future real exchange rate are being revised upwards; and
v) there is an increase in the risk premium on foreign currency.

This decomposition is a general implication of the asset-market approach: it assumes nothing more than the equilibrium condition posited above[12]. It retains what may be regarded as the central insight of the asset-market approach, that exchange rates, like the prices of all durable (or financial) assets which are purchased and held with a view to resale, are crucially dependent on *expectations,* so that changes in them may be very largely a reflection of revisions to expectations resulting from "news" or "surprises"[13]. The difficulty of formally describing or modelling the formation of expectations must, to some extent, explain the widespread failure of econometric work in this area which will be referred to below. The inherent unpredictability of new information explains much of the difficulty of forecasting exchange rate changes.

The decomposition may also be regarded as helpful in providing a general accounting framework for the analysis of observed exchange rate movements[14]. But its use as such is fraught with difficulties, not only because of the general problem of identifying expectations, but also because the component influences will tend to be interrelated. Thus faster domestic growth may raise expectations of domestic inflation *(iii),* but this effect may be outweighed by expectations that domestic interest rates will be raised as a policy response *(ii).* Furthermore,

126

any change in relative interest rates which is not matched by a change in the expected movement of the exchange rate must imply a change in the risk premium *(v)*. The latter will also tend to vary with shocks to the current account, because these affect the rate of accumulation of foreign assets which may, in turn, also bring about revisions to expectations about the real exchange rate *(iv)*. These possibilities illustrate the fact that the general framework provided by the above classification acquires operational significance only when special assumptions are adopted which endow it with more precise structural content.

4. *Exchange rate models and econometric evidence*

Three models comprising different special assumptions within the asset-market framework may be distinguished[15]:

i) The flexible-price monetary (or "monetarist") model;
ii) The sticky-price monetary (or "Dornbusch") model;
iii) The portfolio-balance model with static or stable exchange rate expectations.

These may be regarded as representative of most models which have been applied in econometric work on the determinants of exchange rate movements in the period of floating. The list is in increasing order of generality of the assumptions adopted. Models *(i)* and *(ii)* are called "monetary" because money is the only asset whose supply and demand play any role. Other assets denominated in different currencies are assumed to be perfect substitutes in demand: there are assumed to be no risk premia or portfolio preferences, and expected returns are always equalised irrespective of asset supplies.

Model *(i)* also assumes that PPP rules: the real exchange rate is constant and expected to remain so. This, together with the assumption of no risk premium, carries the further implication that the differential between domestic and foreign interest rates is given by the difference between expected rates of inflation. Model *(i)* thus eliminates influences *(ii)-(v)* of the above framework and concentrates on the influence of relative price levels *via* PPP. The model assumes finally that prices are sufficiently flexible to hold the supply and demand for money in equilibrium. The relationship between the supplies of domestic and foreign money, relative to the demands for them, therefore determines the exchange rate.

Model *(ii)* resembles model *(i)* in its description of how exchange rates are determined in the long run. But its predictions about short-run behaviour are significantly different because of its assumption that prices are sticky, responding only gradually to excess demand and supply in the goods market. It is interest rates which maintain money-market equilibrium in the short run. The differential between domestic and foreign interest rates may in the short run deviate from the differential between expected inflation rates; and such deviations are mirrored in expected and actual movements in the real exchange rate. Models *(i)* and *(ii)* thus carry starkly contrasting predictions about the influence of interest rates and interest differentials on exchange rates. Given the supply of money, the flexible-price model predicts that a relative increase in domestic interest rates will be associated with a depreciation of the domestic currency on the grounds that it signifies a relative increase in expected domestic inflation and implies a relative contraction in the demand for money[16]. The sticky-price version predicts the opposite, on the grounds that an increase in domestic interest rates (which arises from an excess demand for money) must be offset, for equilibrium in international capital markets, by a lower expected rate of appreciation, which will be brought about by a rise in the current exchange rate in relation to its long-run equilibrium. Because both models assume no risk premium, the interest differential in favour of domestic assets is in both cases always matched by expected depreciation. But whereas in model *(i)* the latter is given by the difference between expected inflation rates at home and abroad (because PPP is assumed), in

127

model *(ii)* it depends on the gap between the current exchange rate and its long-run equilibrium. A further characteristic of model *(ii)*, which is particularly well-known, is that when responding to monetary disturbances, the exchange rate will in the short run *"overshoot"* its new long-run equilibrium.

Model *(iii)* differs from *(i)* and *(ii)* in assuming that assets other than moneys denominated in different currencies are imperfect substitutes. Thus a role in exchange rate determination is attributed to changes in non-monetary asset supplies such as those arising from bond-financed fiscal deficits, sterilised intervention in the foreign exchange market, and current account imbalances. Changes in portfolio preferences also have a potential role, although this has been neglected in most econometric applications. Drastically simplifying assumptions have also usually been adopted about exchange rate expectations: in fact the assumption most commonly adopted is the static one that the exchange rate is not expected to change. Recent work in which this assumption has been modified will be referred to below.

The monetary models have been more widely estimated than the portfolio balance model, partly because of the ready availability of the required data (for money stocks, real incomes, and interest rates), and partly because of the apparent success with which model *(i)*, in particular, was applied in early investigations. The portfolio balance model, which is more general but which correspondingly carries less straightforward prior implications for the parameters to be estimated, and whose requirements are more problematical because of the paucity of data for asset stocks in the form needed, has been less commonly applied.

The Appendix describes how, following initial results for all three models which seemed favourable, all three broke down under later scrutiny – in particular when they were confronted with the task of explaining important exchange rate developments after 1976. Most prominently, they failed to explain the depreciation of the US dollar in 1977-78. More recent research has failed to resurrect them. Tables 1 and 2 of the Appendix, which summarise the econometric results, tell similar stories of unfulfilled promise. It would be an overstatement to say that the models described have been shown to be devoid of any empirical explanatory power: some studies of the monetary models have shown certain exchange rate movements to have been closely related to relative movements in money stocks and interest rates, while some estimates of the portfolio balance model have appeared to confirm the influence of current account developments. But such relationships have been shown to be unreliable – in the case of relative interest rates even the direction of their influence has been shown to be uncertain – and there have been important developments which none of the above models have succeeded in explaining.

There are a number of possible explanations for the empirical failure of these asset-market models. The possibility which has received most attention in recent research is that the role played in the determination of exchange rates by expectations is inadequately accounted for in all the econometric work which has been referred to. This may be considered a deficiency stemming from the failure of theoretical models to convey what are the clear implications of the asset-market approach set out in the general framework of Part B.3. There have, in particular, been a number of attempts to take fuller account of the role of changes in *expectations about real exchange rates* – item *(iv)* of that framework – and of the way in which such changes may occur in response to fresh information or "news" about the current account. This recent work has been partly a response to the observation that certain notable exchange rate movements have been closely associated with current account developments in a way which cannot be explained by the portfolio balance model considered earlier. This applies most notably to the problematical case of the weakness of the US dollar through 1977-78 and its subsequent recovery.

Encouraging econometric results have been obtained along these lines (for example, Hooper and Morton (1982)), and are discussed in the Appendix. They suggest that the behaviour of exchange rates in the last decade can be understood only in terms of an approach which is more general than the models described earlier and which, in particular, takes seriously the question of how expectations are formed about inflation and real exchange rates, and which does not neglect the current account – a factor which the earlier flow approach had of course emphasised. These new results have, however, been put in some perspective by Meese and Rogoff (1981), who re-estimated the new model constructed by Hooper and Morton, together with the flexible-price and sticky-price monetary models for four dollar exchange rates (against the Deutschemark, sterling, yen, and a trade-weighted average index) over two periods, March 1973-November 1976 and March 1973-November 1978, and examined their subsequent out-of-sample forecasting performance, using actual data for the explanatory variables. They found that although the Hooper-Morton model out-performed the forecasts of the other two structural models over the longer forecast period – the sticky-price monetary model did better over the shorter period – the forecasts of each of the structural models were consistently less accurate than those provided by a random walk model, i.e. a model which simply takes the current exchange rate to be the best predictor of its future value.

Meese and Rogoff interpret the apparent failure of what may be regarded as the current "best-practice" economic models to provide exchange rate forecasts superior to – or even as good as – the simplest univariate time-series model as evidence of serious instability in the economic structure. They mention, in particular, the two oil shocks, changes in policy rules, and technological change. Such instabilities may obviously be important; but a greater part of the explanation may still well lie in the problem of expectations. The econometric models may well have failed to identify the determinants of exchange rate expectations, and to distinguish between anticipated and unanticipated movements of the explanatory variables. This may also be true of the Hooper-Morton model, even though it does attempt more seriously to address the issue.

C. MAJOR SOURCES OF EXCHANGE RATE PRESSURE

1. *Relative price levels, real exchange rates and purchasing power parity.*

There are essentially two ways in which exchange rates may be affected by relative price developments in domestic and foreign economies. First, an autonomous increase in domestic costs and prices which is not accommodated by monetary policy may cause the domestic currency to *appreciate* because it will tend to tighten domestic monetary conditions and put upward pressure on interest rates while expectations of future inflation may be unaffected and even reduced. Thus some have suggested that increases in indirect taxes and wages in the United Kingdom in 1979, while the declared stance of monetary policy was being tightened, contributed to the appreciation of sterling. But this is essentially a short-term phenomenon.

Over longer periods, and when price movements are accommodated by monetary policy, inflation in one economy in relation to the rest of the world may be expected to cause a compensating depreciation, for competitiveness to be maintained at a level consistent with a sustainable current balance and an acceptable rate of domestic economic activity. The remainder of this section is essentially concerned to examine the basis and empirical validity of the theory or "Law" of Purchasing Power Parity (PPP), which is usually interpreted as stating that competition in trade will tend to ensure that movements in exchange rates will be such as to compensate for differences in national inflation rates. The relative price competitiveness of any country's goods – or international differences in the price of any bundle of goods when expressed in a common currency – will then be constant: in other words exchange rates will be constant in real terms[17].

There are a number of reasons why the rigid formulation of PPP may fail to hold, both in the short run and over longer periods. Some have already been referred to in the discussion of the asset-market approach. The movements of exchange rates over *short periods* are unlikely to be dictated by current trade flows or the balancing of the current account; and furthermore, the consequences for the current balance of substitution in response to relative price disparities are unlikely to materialise without long lags. More fundamentally, exchange rates and goods prices are determined in different kinds of markets. The prices of most goods and services, apart from primary commodities, are determined in "sticky-price" markets where demand usually exerts a weaker influence in the short run and expectations play a much smaller role than in "flexprice" foreign exchange markets. This implies first, that even if real exchange rates tend not to change in the long run in response to some kinds of disturbance, they will change in the short run simply because exchange rates respond faster than prices. A second implication is that since changes in expectations will tend to affect exchange rates but not prices, "...in periods which are dominated by 'news' which alters expectations, exchange rates are likely to be more volatile, and departures from purchasing power parity are likely to be the rule rather than the exception" (Frenkel, 1981a, p.667).

Even over *longer periods,* when current account considerations may indeed dominate, there are a number of reasons why PPP may not hold in a rigid sense. It was already noted in the main text on policy issues that real exchange rates are difficult to define. There may be significant swings or trends in the relative non-price advantages offered by different countries' traded goods; there may be changes in administered trade barriers; and observed changes in real exchange rates will depend upon the price indices used, and problems such as productivity bias may be important[18]. Another obstacle to PPP in the long run is that the restoration of current account balance following any disturbance to it is unlikely to require the exact restoration of the original real exchange rate, because the change in net investment income arising from the intervening current account imbalances will imply a different long-run imbalance on the trade account[19]. This third objection (Isard 1978) is the single argument which has been raised against the proposition that real exchange rates will tend to remain constant in the long run in the wake of purely monetary disturbances.

Three kinds of evidence may be referred to. First, a number of studies of the "Law of One Price" – the micro analogue of PPP – have shown significant and persistent disparities between countries in the common-currency prices of individual goods other than primary commodities. For example, Isard (1977, p.942), in a study of US, German, Canadian, and Japanese industrial prices, found that "exchange rate changes substantially alter the relative dollar-equivalent prices of the most narrowly defined domestic and foreign manufactured goods for which prices can readily be matched. Moreover, these relative price effects seem to persist for at least several years and cannot be shrugged off as transitory." A number of studies by Kravis and Lipsey (e.g. 1978) have also cast serious doubt on the validity of any assumption that competition in trade is such that PPP will be maintained. Secondly, there have been a number of econometric studies of PPP. The results, summarised in the Appendix, are mixed, finding support for the proposition in data for the hyper-inflations of the 1920s but persistent deviations from PPP in the 1970s. The third set of evidence is provided by the data on real exchange rates and relative unit labour costs shown in Chart 1.

Chart 1

REAL EXCHANGE RATES AND RELATIVE UNIT LABOUR COSTS

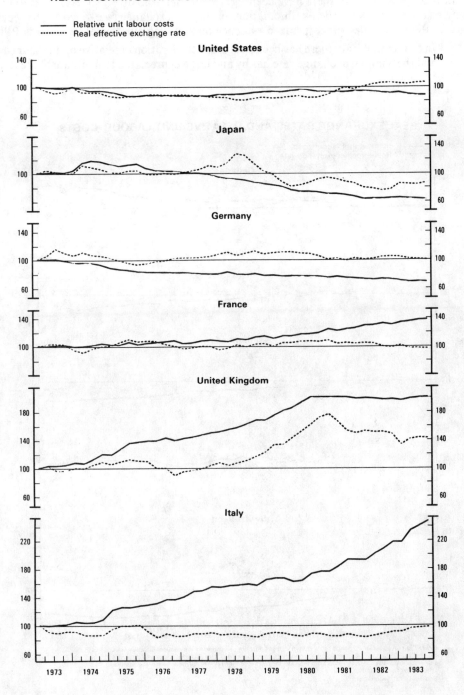

——— Relative unit labour costs
·········· Real effective exchange rate

United States

Japan

Germany

France

United Kingdom

Italy

1973 1974 1975 1976 1977 1978 1979 1980 1981 1982 1983

131

This shows the quarterly movements of the real effective exchange rate and relative unit labour costs for the 11 countries covered in the survey over the period 1973-1982[20]. A number of features stand out. First, there have been significant short-run divergences from PPP in all countries, reflected in year-to-year fluctuations of the real exchange rate. Second, the secular trends in these variables suggest mixed evidence on any long-run tendency towards PPP.

- In France and Italy there has been a secular deterioration in relative unit labour costs, and the nominal exchange rate has by and large depreciated to maintain the real rate

Chart 1 *(cont'd)*

REAL EXCHANGE RATES AND RELATIVE UNIT LABOUR COSTS

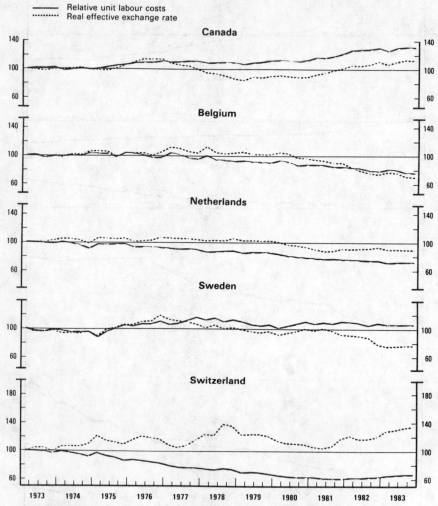

Note: The real effective exchange rates shown in this Chart are calculated as the nominal effective rates deflated by relative unit labour costs for the countries covered by the survey. Relative unit labour costs are also presented in the chart. The difference between the two series then reflects the movement of the nominal effective exchange rate.

Source: OECD Secretariat.

constant, as would be predicted by PPP. In Germany, Japan and Switzerland the secular decline in relative unit labour costs has largely been offset by appreciations of their respective nominal exchange rates. In Switzerland and Japan there have, nevertheless, been some very large year to year swings in the real exchange rate.
- In the United Kingdom PPP held reasonably well until 1978, but subsequently the real appreciation of sterling has been particularly marked.
- In the United States relative unit labour costs and the real exchange rate declined around 1975, while in Canada they increased. Subsequently, there have been no secular movements in either country. In Canada a sustained period of depreciation from 1976 to 1978 has led to a prolonged departure from PPP. In the United States the depreciation of 1978 actually exacerbated the earlier divergence from PPP. However, it is of some interest to note that the marked appreciation of the dollar during the 1980s has almost exactly restored the real exchange rate to its 1973 level.
- Amongst the smaller economies relative unit labour costs have declined in Belgium and the Netherlands for most of the period. Until the end of the 1970s, consistent with PPP, their real exchange rates remained fairly constant. Subsequently, however, fixed nominal exchange rates and/or their depreciation, has led to a declining real exchange rate in both countries. In Sweden the real exchange rate has by and large followed relative unit labour costs and, if anything, movements in the nominal rate have acted to exacerbate divergences from PPP.

To summarize, since PPP hypothesizes a relationship between two variables which are endogenous it cannot even in principle provide a complete understanding of exchange rate determination. It has been used, rather, as a component of some exchange rate theories – most notably the monetary model. There are good reasons why PPP should not be expected to hold in the short run; and all the evidence is that it does not. PPP is more likely to be valid over longer periods, but real exchange rates are still unlikely to be stable in the presence of such disturbances as changes in trade barriers and structural changes in the real economy. There is evidence that there was a tendency towards PPP in the 1920s, possibly owing in part to the dominance of monetary disturbances. The current period of floating has exhibited mixed evidence on PPP as a long-run tendency. There have been large and persistent swings in the real exchange rate, which indicate that PPP is an unreliable "law". In looser terms, however, there may be real competitive forces which assert themselves in determining relative prices across national borders over longer periods. Moreover, the insight that real exchange rates will be largely independent of nominal magnitudes in the long run may have some implications for the conduct of monetary policy.

2. *Relative interest rates*

It has already been indicated that there is a crucial distinction to be drawn between changes in relative (nominal) interest rates which directly represent changes in the relative yields on assets denominated in different currencies, and changes which merely reflect and offset changes in expectations about future exchange rate movements. In the former case, domestic interest rates may rise with a tightening of domestic monetary policy, and the exchange rate may be expected to appreciate owing simply to the increased attractiveness of domestic currency assets. Secondary supporting effects may also flow from expectations of slower domestic inflation (owing to slower prospective monetary growth) or an improved current account (due to lower domestic activity)[21]. In the latter case, however, domestic interest rates may be pushed upwards by higher inflation expectations (perhaps on account of faster monetary growth), and since these should be associated with correspondingly more pessimistic exchange rate expectations, there is no direct inference to be drawn about the relative attractivenes of domestic and foreign assets. The domestic demand for money may, however, be reduced; and this could cause the exchange rate to fall, not rise. The former positive direction of association between movements in the interest differential in favour of the domestic currency and the exchange rate may be expected to apply in the short run, and where interest rates are dominated by domestically-oriented monetary policy; the latter negative association may be expected to be more prevalent over longer periods, and where interest rates are determined primarily by the external policy objective of exchange rate stability.

Econometric evidence summarized in the Appendix shows that both correlations have been in evidence, and that the positive association – which is the more pertinent to many policy considerations – has been difficult to disentangle and quantify. In fact it is fair to say that the negative association has been more in evidence in econometric results, particularly (as would be expected) when long-term interest rates have been used. But this may well be because inflation or exchange rate expectations have not been separately identified in an adequate way, or because the simultaneous dependence of domestic interest rate policy on exchange rate pressure has not been adequately taken into account.

3. *Money supplies*

It is a unanimous prediction of all exchange rate theories that relative expansion of the domestic money supply will cause the domestic currency to depreciate; only transmission mechanisms differ. On some views the link is provided by the response of prices and then PPP. Other views would emphasise the mechanism provided by the response of interest rates, as described in Part C.3. A third possible link is provided by the response of price expectations to monetary shocks, or of inflation expectations to monetary shocks, or of inflation expectations to changes in monetary growth. It is of course possible to combine all three linkages; and the Dornbusch model does so in a particularly vivid way (see Appendix), obtaining the prediction of overshooting; i.e. that on account of the stickiness of goods prices, the response of exchange rates to monetary shocks will be greater in the short run than in the long run.

In contrast with the unanimity of theory, the econometric evidence of money supply effects on exchange rates is mixed, problematical, and inconclusive, as is shown in the Appendix. One problem which may be worth mentioning here is the simultaneous dependence of the external counterpart of monetary expansion on the exchange rate itself. If there is official intervention in the foreign exchange market seeking to stabilise the exchange rate, then the external counterpart will tend on this account to be positively correlated with the value of the domestic currency. If this intervention is not then sterilised, any negative impact of monetary expansion on the exchange rate may be difficult to discern. The same simultaneity problem has also hampered all attempts to quantify the exchange rate effects of intervention.

This simultaneity problem stands out from country experiences. For example, exchange rates have often weakened during periods of excessively permissive monetary growth. This was the case in the United Kingdom, Italy and France on a number of occasions during the 1970s. Loose monetary policy was also associated with the weakness of the Canadian dollar from 1976 to 1978, as it was with the US dollar in 1978. However, there have also been periods when the attempt to stabilize a previously strong currency has led to faster than desired monetary growth. This was the case, for instance, in Germany and Japan in 1973 and in Germany and Switzerland during 1978.

4. *Portfolio preferences and asset supplies*

Any difference there may be between the interest differential in favour of foreign currency and the expected rate of appreciation of the domestic currency was referred to in Part B.3 as the risk premium on foreign currency. It is the premium required by wealth-holders for assets in both currencies to be willingly held, given the supplies of assets denominated in the two currencies and the preferences of wealth-holders. In Part B.4 models were described where the risk premium was assumed to be zero – where assets were assumed to be perfect substitutes – so that preferences and the supplies of interest-bearing assets play no role. But a portfolio balance model was also discussed where a risk premium was assumed to exist, and where the effects of changes in asset supplies – arising from current account imbalances, bond-financed fiscal deficits, and sterilised intervention – can be traced. The mixed econometric success of this approach was also referred to.

This section is concerned mainly with an examination of further evidence on the issue of the risk premium: are assets denominated in different currencies perfect substitutes, or, owing to exchange rate uncertainty, do risk premia exist which may provide a role in exchange rate determination for asset supplies and portfolio preferences? The potential influences of asset supplies have already been alluded to. Two examples of the potential influence of *portfolio preferences* are worth mentioning. First, Dornbusch (1980) has argued that the real appreciation of the DM in relation to the dollar in the 1970s may have been partly the result of portfolio diversification by dollar holders as they became increasingly aware, while gaining experience of floating exchange rates, of the different characteristics of the returns on assets denominated in different currencies. Secondly, Hacche and Townend (1981b), on the basis of some evidence that the currency preferences of OPEC countries differ from those of industrial and non-oil LDCs, have drawn attention to the possible implications for currency values of the large shifts in wealth entailed in OPEC current account surpluses. The problem with the empirical verification of such arguments, of course, is that neither expected yields nor preferences are directly observable: actual yields and currency shares in portfolios are measurable (the latter with some difficulty), but are not necessarily any indication of expected or preferred values.

For similar reasons – more specifically, because the expected exchange rate and its expected movements are not directly observable – tests of the existence of a risk premium require assumptions to be made about how expectations are formed. As a result, they become tests of a joint hypothesis concerning both the characteristics of equilibrium expected returns (the risk premium question), and the nature of the expectations formation process. Most of these have in fact been joint tests of the existence of a risk premium and the efficiency of the foreign exchange market.

An asset market is said to be *efficient* if the prices formed in it fully reflect available information, so that systematic profit opportunities are unavailable to investors. An implication of efficiency in the foreign exchange market is that since covered interest arbitrage is necessarily free of exchange risk, covered returns on assets denominated in different currencies will be equalised, apart from a margin of indeterminacy dependent on transactions costs, unless there are exchange controls or non-exchange ("political") risks. Aside from these qualifications, the nominal or uncovered interest differential in favour of foreign currency assets should be matched by the forward premium on domestic currency, or the proportional difference between the forward and spot exchange rates. The covered interest differential will then be zero: domestic and foreign interest rates will be in *covered parity*. The empirical evidence, summarised in the Appendix, overwhelmingly supports the view that efficiency in this sense holds in international capital markets. With covered parity holding, a rather more convenient definition for the risk premium suggests itself: it may be regarded as the difference between the forward premium on domestic currency and its expected rate of appreciation which, in logarithmic terms, is simply the difference between the forward exchange rate and the expected future spot rate[22].

A second implication of efficiency relates to speculative rather than covered arbitrage activity. This is that in an efficient foreign exchange market forecasting errors should be serially uncorrelated, or "white noise". Otherwise, if successive differences between the actual spot rate and its previously expected value were serially correlated, then investors would be forming their forecasts irrationally and there would be information in the time-series of the exchange rate which could be exploited for profit[23]. Now speculative efficiency and the absence of a risk premium together form a joint hypothesis which is testable against the data: if there is no risk premium, the forward rate measures the expected future spot rate, so that efficiency then implies that successive differences between the logarithmic values of the actual spot rate and its corresponding previous forward value should be serially uncorre-lated[24]. In other words, the forward rate should be an unbiased predictor of the future spot rate. If there is a risk premium, however, this implication does not follow from the efficiency hypothesis, since the risk premium may well, in particular, be serially correlated.

It is therefore clear that the numerous studies which have been made of the forecasting performance of the forward rate form tests of the joint hypothesis that the exchange market is efficient and that there is no risk premium. Most writers have in fact, however, preferred to relate their results to one hypothesis or the other. The results are mixed and ambiguous; but they seem to be tending towards rejection of the joint hypothesis and hence on one interpretation, towards acknowledgement of the existence of risk premia[25].

It is worth referring finally to an implication of exchange rate data, following from the hypothesis that currencies are perfect substitutes, which has been noted by many writers. This is that expected exchange rate changes, which on the hypothesis of no risk premium are measured by forward premia or interest rate differentials, invariably account for a minor proportion of subsequent actual changes. In other words, the greater proportion of exchange rate movements are unexpected, representing responses to unforeseen shocks. Mussa (1979) suggests the "general empirical regularity" that "over 90 per cent of month-to-month or quarter-to-quarter changes in exchange rates are attributable to unexpected exchange rate changes". Hacche and Townend (1981b), in their study of quarterly movements in eight effective exchange rates between 1972 and 1980 calculated that this proportion, on average, ranged from 48 per cent in the case of the dollar to 177 per cent for the DM. Dooley and Isard (1979) arrived at similar conclusions for the DM-dollar rate over the period 1973-78, after attempting to take account of variations in the risk premium.

5. Current account developments

Even in the asset-market approach, current account developments can affect exchange rates through a number of mechanisms. First, current account imbalances may impact on domestic demands for goods and assets by affecting domestic income and wealth. Second, a deficit in a country's current account implies a shift in private sector wealth from domestic to overseas residents; and since the desired proportion of domestic currency assets in portfolios is likely to be larger for domestic than for foreign residents, this is likely to cause a depreciation of the domestic currency. Third, the value of a currency may be affected by the current account imbalances of other countries between which wealth is thereby being redistributed if agents have different preferences for the currency concerned. Fourth, shifts in current accounts may be interpreted as signifying the need for changes in real exchange rates, if market participants expect the latter to move in a way which prevents indefinite transfers of wealth through current account imbalances.

Hooper and Morton have made the most serious attempt thus far to provide an econometric model which explicitly identifies a role for the current account through:

- unanticipated developments affecting expectations of the real exchange rate; and
- the cumulated current account plus intervention affecting asset supplies and the exchange rate through the risk premium.

In none of the equations did the risk premium coefficients have either the expected sign or a value significantly different from zero. However, in their preferred results (which excluded the risk premium variable) they found that a $1 billion increase in the cumulative US current account (proxying an increase in the stock of net foreign currency assets) would lead to a 0.4 per cent appreciation of the weighted average dollar rate, via the expectations mechanism. Dornbusch (1980) adopted a different approach, by assuming that contemporary forecasts published by the OECD were representative of market expectations, so that deviations of the outturn from them could be used to measure unanticipated current account "shocks". He found that these deviations contributed significantly to an explanation of movements in the dollar effective rate and the $-yen rate, but not to the $-DM rate, between 1973 and 1979.

D. SUMMARY

The points which stand out would seem to include the following:

a) There are strong links from monetary policy to exchange rates in any theoretical framework. The main transmission mechanisms were seen to be:

    i)   interest rate differentials;
    ii) relative prices and inflation expectations;
    iii) domestic demand and the current account.

b) It was also noted that there are strong theoretical arguments that exchange rates may overshoot in response to monetary policy. Expansionary monetary policy will tend to improve competitiveness in the short run (and vice versa) but not necessarily the current account.

c) The empirical evidence on PPP indicates that changes in nominal exchange rates are associated with relatively long-lived changes in real exchange rates, and that there are large variations in the latter, even over periods of a number of years, which have to be explained.

d) There are important theoretical reasons (but less evidence) which suggest that shifts in portfolio preferences, and shifts in wealth between countries with different preferences, may play a role in affecting exchange rates.

e) Econometric work has been hampered by the problem of non-observable variables, such as exchange rate expectations, risk premia and the like. More successful results may have to await accumulation of sufficient data for a long enough period to be examined for expectations to "wash out".

f) The importance (at least in the short term) of expectations implies that the stability of exchange rates (if an objective) may also require the stability of expectations. This may have particular relevance for the way in which monetary policy is conducted with respect to domestic and external objectives.

Appendix

TECHNICAL ASPECTS OF MODELS AND ECONOMETRIC EVIDENCE

a) *The asset-market approach: three special cases*

At least until relatively recently, most econometric work on the determinants of exchange rate movements in the period of floating has been based on one or other of three theoretical models. These may be regarded as representative of an extensive and rather more diverse literature. They are summarised here in increasing order of generality.

i) *The flexible-price monetary model*

In what is also sometimes referred to simply as the "monetary" or "monetarist" model, three radically simplifying assumptions are adopted[26]. First, there is assumed to be *no risk premium*. This requires either that wealth-holders are indifferent to exchange risk or, if they are risk averse, that exchange risks faced by creditors and debtors are usually offsetting and diversified away. Then, irrespective of relative asset supplies, the interest differential between foreign and domestic assets always equals the expected rate of appreciation of the domestic currency: uncovered interest parity holds. Comparable interest-bearing assets denominated in different currencies are thus perfect substitutes, and both portfolio preferences and such influences on the supplies of interest-bearing assets as bond-financed fiscal policy, sterilised intervention in the foreign exchange market, and current account imbalances lose an influence they might otherwise exert. The fifth of the components listed in B.3 is therefore eliminated. Three of the four components remaining are then eliminated by the second assumption that *purchasing power parity (PPP)* holds and is expected to continue to do so. This means that the real exchange rate is expected to remain unchanged – so that component *(iv)* of the sources of exchange rate variation is eliminated – and this in turn implies that the interest differential between foreign and domestic assets must equal the difference between expected foreign and domestic inflation rates, so that components *(ii)* and *(iii)* eliminate each other. What then remains is the PPP condition that the exchange rate, apart from a constant, is equal to the ratio of foreign to domestic price levels. The third assumption is that *prices are flexible,* sufficiently so as to ensure the maintenance of money-market equilibrium. The ratio between foreign and domestic price levels, and hence the exchange rate, may then be expressed in terms of foreign and domestic money supplies and the variables (other than prices) and parameters which enter the respective demand functions for foreign and domestic money. Interest rates then reappear as determinants of the exchange rate; but the direction of their influence is different, as will be seen.

In this model, any money-market disequilibrium is eliminated by an adjustment of demand in response to a movement in prices. The other determinants of the demand for money are determined outside the model – real income implicitly by the productive technology, and interest rates by inflation expectations[27]. Any such movement in prices then requires a compensating movement in the exchange rate for the real exchange rate to be held constant and PPP to be maintained. For given values of the foreign variables, the exchange rate is therefore in effect the variable which "clears' the domestic money market *via* the domestic price level: this may be seen as the analogue for a small open economy of the closed-economy quantity theory of money.

If, then, starting from equilibrium there is *an increase in the domestic money supply,* this model implies, assuming that the price-elasticity of demand for money is unity, that the price level must rise and the exchange rate depreciate in the same proportion. If there is *an increase in domestic interest rates,* the domestic currency must again depreciate, because higher interest rates imply a lower demand for, and an excess supply of money: for equilibrium to be restored, prices must rise, and this requires the exchange rate to fall. This *unequivocal implication that the value of the domestic currency will be negatively associated with the interest differential in its favour* is a distinctive feature of the monetary model. Its sense is clear when it is recalled that changes in interest rates in this model do not represent changes in relative yields: by the assumption of no risk premia, yields are always equalised, and changes in the interest differential occur in order to offset changes in inflation and exchange rate expectations which would otherwise give rise to disparities in expected yields. Interest rates then affect exchange rates only indirectly, *via* the demand for money. Finally, *an increase in domestic real income* (perhaps owing to a resource discovery or a more favourable *current account* balance) should cause the exchange rate to appreciate through an increase in the demand for money.

The implications for the exchange rate of changes in the corresponding foreign variables follow in the same way from the assumed maintenance of equilibrium in the foreign money market by the foreign price level. In sum, exchange rates in the flexible-price monetary model are determined by domestic and foreign monetary conditions: factors which do not affect the supply or demand for money at home or abroad do not affect the external value of the domestic currency.

ii) *The sticky-price monetary model*

The second set of special assumptions to be considered is based on the model developed by Dornbusch (1976), by whose name it is sometimes known; it has subsequently been extended by many authors[28]. It shares with the first model the assumption of no risk premium (or perfect asset substitutability) but it does not assume for the short run either than prices are sufficiently flexible to maintain money-market equilibrium or that the exchange rate is tethered by PPP.

The domestic interest rate takes on the role of equilibrator of the domestic money market; and the exchange rate maintains equilibrium in the currency market by always moving instantaneously to the point at which, for given expectations of its future level, the uncovered interest parity condition is satisfied. With prices given in the short run, the exchange rate determined in this way in turn determines competiveness; and competiveness, together with the interest rate which clears the money market, helps to determine the demand for domestically produced goods. In the version of the model which assumed fixed output, domestic prices then respond to the excess demand or supply of goods; and this movement in prices feeds back to competitiveness, and also to the interest rate via the demand for money. The economy thus moves towards a long-run equilibrium where the supply and demand for goods are in balance and the real exchange rate is not expected to change. The latter condition means that, in the long run, the domestic interest rate is fixed by the foreign rate and the differential between domestic and foreign inflation rates: as in the previous model, the domestic price level must then be the variable which ensures equilibrium in the money market. The former condition determines the long-run equilibrium real exchange rate as that which, at the given rate of interest, generates a demand for goods equal to supply. This real exchange rate, which will clear the goods market in the long run, provides the anchor for expectations at each point in time: exchange rate expectations are thus assumed to be *"rational"* or consistent with the model.

With this new set of assumptions, a once-for-all *increase in the domestic money supply* will, in the long run, have consequences similar to those predicted by the flexible-price model: domestic prices will be proportionately higher, because this is the only way the demand for money can expand to match the new supply, and the exchange rate must be proportionately lower so that the real exchange rate is restored to the level at which net exports are consistent with goods-market equilibrium. The short-run implications, however, are significantly different. Expectations of the long-run price level and exchange rate immediately adjust to their actual future values; but because prices are sticky, the domestic interest rate has to fall for the larger money stock to be willingly held. For the foreign exchange market to be held in equilibrium, the expected rate of appreciation of the domestic currency therefore has to rise; hence the exchange rate has to fall by more than its expected future (and long-run equilibrium) level. This is the well-known result that with sticky prices the exchange rate will need to *overshoot* its lower long-run equilibrium for asset-market equilibrium to be continuously maintained in the wake of a monetary expansion.

Although the instantaneous responses of the interest rate and exchange rate hold the money market and foreign exchange markets in balance, they disturb equilibrium in the goods market by raising aggregate demand through a reduction in the cost of finance and an improvement in competitiveness. It is this excess demand which sets off the rise in the price level towards its new long-run equilibrium. As the inflation proceeds, the transactions demand for money expands, putting upward pressure on the interest rate which thus begins to return to its original level; and as the interest rate increases, the exchange rate rises towards its long-run equilibrium. The exchange rate and domestic interest rate, it will be noted, are positively associated throughout. In contrast with the monetary model, interest rates are determined independently of exchange rate expectations, and changes in them imply incipient changes in relative yields on different currencies which have to be offset, for uncovered parity to be maintained, by movements in currency values.

iii) *The portfolio balance model with static or stable exchange rate expectations*

The third example of the asset-market approach is the portfolio balance model exemplified by Branson (1977, 1979). Unlike the two previous models, this does not assume that currencies are perfect substitutes: it assumes rather than in response to exchange risk wealth-holders seek to diversify their portfolios, being prepared to hold interest-bearing assets in different currencies in non-zero amounts which depend on the configuration of their relative yields. Asset-market equilibrium does not then require the equalisation of expected yields (uncovered parity); and *risk premia* provide a conceptual measure of divergences among them arising from different asset supply and demand conditions. The supplies of interest-bearing assets, as well as domestic and foreign money, therefore have to be brought into the analysis. Thus suppose there are four assets – domestic and foreign (non-interest-bearing) money, and domestic and foreign bonds. Neither of the two moneys is held by residents of the other

140

country, so that domestic residents hold domestic money and domestic bonds, both of which are public sector liabilities (and therefore "outside assets" of the private sector), and foreign bonds. It is also assumed that foreign bonds are the only tradeable asset: foreign residents do not hold domestic bonds, and any increase in domestic liabilities to overseas residents arising from a current account deficit will entail a fall in domestic holdings of foreign bonds, which are denominated in the foreign currency. This assumption facilitates the analysis of exchange rate dynamics[29]; domestic holdings of foreign bonds represent net foreign assets, and they are assumed to be positive.

The proportion of their wealth which domestic residents wish to hold in each asset then depends on their relative expected common-currency yields, and hence on the interest rates on domestic and foreign bonds and the expected movement of the exchange rate. The current exchange rate impinges on these demands in two ways. First, movements in the exchange rate will tend to affect expectations about its future rate of change; and the assumption is adopted here that expectations of its future level are relatively stable, so that actual appreciation tends to reduce expected future appreciation and hence the relative expected yield on domestic assets[30]. Secondly, exchange rate changes entail revaluation, in terms of domestic currency, of foreign assets which are denominated in foreign currency; and, since domestic residents are assumed to be in a net credit position abroad, domestic wealth will fall when the exchange rate rises, but by a smaller proportion than its foreign-assets components. Each of these influences implies that a rise in the exchange rate will switch demand from domestic to foreign assets, owing first to a change in relative expected yields and second to the involuntary reduction in the proportion of domestic wealth held in foreign assets which appreciation entails.

The exchange rate is then viewed as being determined in the short run (when asset supplies are given) simultaneously with the two interest rates by the equilibration of asset markets. But the exchange rate which thus emerges may go on to disturb asset supplies, because it will affect the current balance and hence (assuming no official intervention) the net acquisition of foreign assets by domestic residents. As in the flow model of B.1, the current account is assumed to respond favourably to depreciation and unfavourably to appreciation: a rise in the exchange rate thus reduces the supply of foreign assets to the domestic economy. In contrast with the flow model, however, the portfolio balance model – like the Dornbusch model – draws an explicit distinction between the flexibility of interest rates and exchange rates on the one hand and the stickiness of real variables on the other, and between the short-run responses of exchange rates as they help to equilibrate asset markets and their longer-run responses after the adjustments of real variables – including asset supplies – have run their course. The long run is therefore in this context defined naturally as the period in which asset supplies again become stationary; and this requires, as a condition of long-run equilibrium, that the current account should be in balance[31].

Now consider the implications of the disturbance of such an equilibrium by *an increase in the domestic money supply*. This may be due to a money-financed fiscal deficit (in which case there is an increase in private sector wealth), domestic open-market operations (where there is also a reduction in the supply of domestic bonds), or non-sterilized intervention in the foreign exchange market (where there is also a reduction in the supply of foreign bonds). These distinctions were irrelevant in models *(i)* and *(ii)* because neither wealth nor bond supplies played any role. In fact, however, the three possibilities have consequences which are qualitatively similar, although quantitatively different. In each case, an excess supply of money and an excess demand for both domestic and foreign bonds emerge at the original interest and exchange rate; and both a decline in the domestic interest rate (which switches demand from domestic bonds to money and foreign bonds) and a depreciation of the domestic currency (which switches demand from foreign bonds to money and domestic bonds) are

141

required to restore asset equilibrium. As in the Dornbusch model, the exchange rate and domestic interest rate are positively associated, although there is now no clear chain of causation from the latter to the former.

In the new asset equilibrium, with goods prices unchanged, the domestic currency has depreciated in real terms: by assumption the current account will now move into surplus and foreign assets begin to grow. There thus develops an excess supply of foreign bonds which requires the exchange rate to rise for portfolio balance to be maintained. One consequence of the improvement in the current account is therefore a partial reversal of the original depreciation; and this, by reducing net exports, will tend to bring the growth in foreign assets to a halt. Meanwhile, however, the increase in foreign assets will also have been raising investment income from abroad, thereby tending to push the current account further into surplus. For stability, it has to be assumed that trade elasticities are sufficiently large for the latter effect to be outweighed by the former, so that the current account surplus resulting from the initial depreciation is eventually eliminated and full equilibirum restored.

The exchange rate in this final long-run equilibrium will clearly be higher than in the temporary asset equilibrium – another case of *overshooting,* accounted for now by lags in the response of trade to the exchange rate, rather than lags in the response of prices to money. Moreover, the real exchange rate in the final equilibrium should be higher than it was initially, because, although the current account is in balance in both positions, investment income must be higher after the effects of the monetary expansion have worked through, so that the trade balance must have deteriorated. This implies, unless there have been effects on activity, that competitiveness has deteriorated: if the domestic price level has risen in proportion to the money supply, the proportionate depreciation must have been smaller. In the portfolio balance model, therefore, PPP need not hold even in the weak sense in which it held in model *(ii): purely monetary disturbances may change real exchange rates, even in the long run.*

Three further disturbances may now be considered more briefly with attention restricted to short-term effects. An *exogenous improvement in the current acount* will cause an immediate appreciation as portfolios are rebalanced in the face of an increased supply of foreign currency assets; no change in interest rates is required. A *bond-financed fiscal deficit* will entail an excess supply of domestic bonds and excess demands for money and foreign bonds. A rise in the domestic interest rate is unambiguously required for asset equilibrium, but the exchange rate may rise or fall depending on the substitutability of assets in demand: if foreign bonds are a closer substitute than money for domestic bonds, the exchange rate will tend to rise, and conversely. Finally, *sterilised intervention* in support of the domestic currency will entail an increase in the supply of foreign assets and an equal reduction in the supply of domestic bonds. Again the consequences are ambiguous, depending upon substitutability conditions: substitution between domestic bonds and money should lead to a lower interest rate, and this may offset the appreciation implied by substitution between domestic and foreign bonds. In the last two cases considered, it will be noted that the exchange rate may be either positively or negatively associated with the domestic interest rate.

b) *Survey of econometric evidence*

i) *The flexible and sticky price monetary models*

Some representative results for both the flexible-price and sticky-price monetary models are summarised in Table 1. Some relatively successful results were obtained for the former model by Frenkel for the 1920s, and by Bilson for the period 1970 to 1977. However, the early optimism about the explanatory power of the flexible-price model has been tempered by the observation (by e.g. Frankel, and Hacche and Townend) of data which contradict its distinctive prediction about the relationship between exchange rates and interest rates. Moreover, there may be an inherent mis-specification in the usual assumption that the money supply (particularly its external counterpart) and interest rates are exogenous to the exchange rate. Frankel similarly found some early support for the sticky price monetary model over the period 1974-78, but subsequent econometric support for this model has also been relatively scarce.

Furthermore, the empirical validity of both versions of the monetary approach has been questioned more radically as a result of increasing doubts about the reliability of PPP, even in the long run, and also because of their failure, in econometric investigations, to explain some of the most important exchange rate developments of recent years (see Table 1). Thus Dornbusch (1978) found that the depreciation of the dollar in 1977-78 could not be explained in terms of Frankel's monetary model and that it had occurred in spite of relatively slow monetary growth in the United States. Dornbusch (1980) found that the same model did not fit the data for the DM-$ rate, 1973-79, at all well. Similarly poor results were obtained by Hacche and Townend (1981) when they attempted to explain the movements in sterling, 1972-80, in terms of a number of variants of the monetary model; and Beenstock, Budd, and Warburton (1981) also failed, using the monetary approach, to quantify the influences which had resulted in sterling's appreciation between 1976 and 1980. Frankel (1981) describes the failure of his model to fit 1974-81 data for most of the major currencies.

ii) *The portfolio balance model*

Some results obtained for the portfolio balance model described in the previous section of this Appendix are summarised in Table 2. These econometric applications have neglected the feedback mechanism entailed in the dependence on the exchange rate of the current account and the accumulation of foreign-currency assets, and have been more concerned to investigate the short-run dependence of exchange rates on asset supplies. The explanatory variables are then, in principle, the supplies of domestic and foreign money, the supplies of domestic and foreign government interesting-bearing debt, and the net supply of foreign assets to the domestic private sector. The two studies by Branson and others ommitted the supplies of interest-bearing assets and proxied the net bi-lateral supplies of foreign assets by the cumulated aggregate current-account surpluses (from some bench-mark) of the two countries concerned in each case. Martin and Masson, more correctly, included variables representing bond stocks, and used bi-lateral current account data for their proxies for net foreign asset supplies. Both Branson, Halttunen and Masson, and Martin and Masson adjusted the cumulated current account surpluses for cumulated official intervention, and in estimation attempted to allow for simultaneous determination of intervention policy.

The initial results obtained by Branson and Halttunen may be seen to have been mixed, but they were regarded as "mildly encouraging". Those subsequently obtained by Branson, Halttunen and Masson for the DM-$ rate appeared more satisfactory: after allowance for the simultaneous determination of intervention, the coefficients estimates were in all cases right-signed and significant, and the model seemed to fit the data well. The later results of Martin and Masson were, however, much worse: the only consistently significant influence on the three exchange rates examined was found to be cumulated official intervention, and this with a perverse sign. Thus, as in the case of the monetary models, the optimism which had been encouraged by the early econometric applications of the portfolio balance model was soon disappointed.

iii) *Expectations and the current account*

Recent work has interpreted the failure of econometric attempts to identify exchange rate models as being a result of an inadequate treatment of expectations, and more

Table 1. Econometric results for the monetary models[a]

Authors	Currencies and Period	Special Features	Summary of results
1. Frenkel (1976).	DM : $, Feb. 1920-Nov. 1923	Interest differential represented by forward premium. Real income variables and US money omitted, on grounds that German hyper-inflation the dominant factor.	"Fully consistent with prior expectations" : $\ln S = -5.135+0.975 \ln M+0.591 \ln r$ (0.731) (0.050) (0.073) where S is DM per $, and r is forward premium on $ (Standard errors in brackets). $R^2 = .994$; See = .241 ; DW = 1.91
2. Bilson (1978).	DM : £, Apr. 1970-May 1977	Interest differential represented by forward premium ; lagged adjustment to equilibrium exchange rate ; mixed estimation procedure allowing imposition of priors ; inclusion of time trend.	Consistent with monetary model. In dynamic simulation, superior to a simple PPP model but inferior to a "sophisticated" PPP model including prices and interest rates but not money supplies or real incomes. "Rational expectations" version of the monetary model superior to an RE version of PPP.
3. Bilson (1979a).	DM : $, 1963 Q1-1978 Q3	Interest differential measured by forward premium ; polynomial lags on exogenous variables ; inclusion of time trend.	"Provide strong support for the monetary theory". The model "captures all of the major turning points" ; but most significant variable a quadratic time trend. Inclusion of prices "did not offer any support for the Dornbusch model".
4. Bilson (1979b).	33 currencies against $ 1954-74	Interest differentials proxied by inflation differentials ; generalised least squares estimation.	"Provide convincing evidence that the monetary approach leads to predictions of the actual exchange rate which are, on average, both less biased and less disperse than those based on" PPP.
5. Girton and Roper (1977).	Canadian $: US $ 1952-74	Dependent variable is "exchange market pressure" = sum of exchange rate change, and intervention/money ratio. Interest rates excluded.	Coefficients right-signed and significant ; high explanatory power.
6. Frankel (1979).	DM : $, July 1974-Feb. 1978	Short and long interest differentials included ; instrumental variable estimation to correct for shortcomings of long rates as proxies for expected inflation.	Coefficients right-signed ; in particular, different signs on long and short interest differentials. But significance levels weak after allowance for autocorrelation, until IV estimation used.
7. Driskill (1981).	SF : $, Mar 1973-Nov. 1977	Estimates reduced-form of Dornbusch model − interest rates absent − and compares this with the reduced-form of an amended model which allows for under-shooting and non...	After exclusion of real income variables, and addition of a dummy for the 1973-4 oil price shock, results for both models satisfactory, but more supportive of amended model. Results support long-...

	Data / period	Method	Findings
8. Dornbusch (1978).	DM : $, Mar. 1974-May 1978	money; short and long interest differentials included; coefficient of unity imposed on relative money supplies.	which includes lagged dependent variable; but real incomes and short interest differential not significant. "I take the evidence, theoretical and empirical, to reject the monetary approach".
9. Dornbusch (1980).	DM : $. 1973 Q2-1979 Q4	As for (8).	Coefficients of relative money supplies (when freely estimated) and relative real incomes not significant. When coefficient of unity imposed on relative money supplies and lagged dependent variable included, the latter was the only significant determinant. "... little doubt that the monetary approach is an unsatisfactory theory".
10. Hacche and Townend (1981).	£ effective rate, Feb. 1972-Feb. 1980	Partial adjustment allowed for in demand for money and exchange rate; instrumental variable estimation to allow for endogeneity of domestic interest rate and intervention.	In OLS estimates, no variables significant apart from domestic interest rate and intervention counterpart of change in money supply, the latter wrong-signed. In IV estimates, no determinants significant.
11. Frankel (1981).	DM, £, FF, Y and Can $ against US $, 1974-81, various monthly periods	Frankel 1979 re-estimated on more recent data, but with inflation expectations measured by actual inflation rather than long interest rates.	"Results discouraging" for the monetary models; some evidence suggested that the problems may lie in drifts in real exchange rates and demand for money functions.

a) Abbreviations used include: OLS : Ordinary least squares; IV : instrumental variables; RE : rational expectations; 2SLS : two stage least squares.

145

Table 2. Econometric results for the portfolio balance model[a]

Authors	Currencies and Period	Special Features	Summary of Results
1. Branson and Halttunen (1979).	DM and Yen against $; FF, IL, SF and £ against DM; July 1971-June 1976 and April 1973-June 1976.	For each exchange rate, explanatory variables are domestic and foreign money stocks, and domestic and foreign cumulated current account surpluses. N.B. i) supplies of interest-bearing assets omitted; ii) because of lack of bilateral data, domestic net claims on the foreign country represented by the two countries' respective net foreign assets, proxied by cumulated current account surpluses.	"As a whole", the results seem "mildly encouraging": after taking account of serial correlation of residuals, the following variables were right-signed and significant: $: DM — over full period, both German variables only; over short period, no variables; $: Yen — In both periods, the Jap. cum. current account only; DM : FF — Over full period, both money stocks only; in short period French cum. current account also; DM : IL — Money stocks only; DM : SF — German money stock only; DM : £ — In full period, UK money stock and German cum. current account; in short period, UK money stock only.
2. Branson, Halttunen, and Masson (1977).	$: DM, Aug 1971-Dec 1976.	As for (1), except that i) cumulated intervention netted from cumulated current account surpluses; ii) exchange rate equation estimated simultaneously with policy reaction functions for intervention and DCE, by 2-stage least squares.	"The estimates look reasonable and support the asset-market model". In OLS estimates, after allowing for auto-correlation all coefficients right-signed, but US money the only significant determinant. In 2SLS estimates, each coefficient significant and right-signed; $R^2 = 0.94$. (Policy reaction functions indicate a sterilisation coefficient not significantly different from unity, and intervention aimed at smoothing).
3. Martin and Masson (1979).	Can. $, Yen, and basket of 8 W. European currencies against $, Apr. 1973-Apr. 1978.	For each exchange rate, explanatory variables are domestic and US money and bond stocks and the bi-lateral net foreign asset position with the US. N.B. i) bond stocks proxied by public debt; ii) bi-lateral net foreign asset stocks calculated from bi-lateral current account data (vis-a-vis US); iii) bi-lateral net foreign asset stocks defined in some variants as excluding direct investment flows; iv) exchange rate equation estimated simultaneously with reaction function for intervention by two-stage least squares;	Results "very mediocre". In 2SLS estimates, the following variables were significant: Can. $: US$ — dummy for Quebec election of 1976; cumulated intervention (with perverse + sign); US money (with perverse - sign). Yen : US$ — US money (with perverse - sign); cumulated intervention (with perverse + sign). W. Eur. : US$ — cumulated intervention (with + sign). Thus "the empirical verdict on the utility of the portfolio balance model... must be judged unfavourable".

a) See Note to Table 1.

146

particularly a result of the neglect of the influence of the current account on expectations about the real exchange rate. This orientation of recent work has partly been a response to the observation that exchange rate movements have, in some important cases, been closely associated with current account developments – most notably the dollar's weakness through 1977-78 and its subsequent recovery. The current account has a specific role in the portfolio balance model. Its assumptions entail that the transfer of wealth from the foreign to the domestic private sector implied by a current account surplus takes the particular form, in the absence of intervention, of an increase in privately-held foreign government debt, denominated in foreign currency. For this to be willingly held, the exchange rate must rise. The domestic-currency value of the foreign bonds is thereby reduced, and their relative rate of return raised on account of more pessimistic expectations about the future movements of the domestic currency.

A number of doubts arise, however, as to whether the apparent influence of current account developments can be explained by portfolio re-balancing. First, the quantitative importance of such wealth effects is unlikely to be large in the short term because the current account imbalances of the industrialised countries are generally small, over short periods, in relation to the stocks of internationally mobile assets denominated in their currencies. Secondly, portfolio re-balancing cannot explain cases where intervention was sufficient to offset any effect which the transfer of wealth may have had on asset demands. In particular, Hooper and Morton (1980) note that while the cumulated US current deficit during 1977-78 was $28 billion, purchases of dollar assets by foreign central banks were more than double that amount in the same period. Even on the extreme assumption that the entire transfer of wealth from US to foreign residents was switched out of dollars into other currencies, portfolio re-balancing should have caused the dollar to appreciate rather than depreciate; and this is the effect which model *(iii)* would have predicted.

The current account acquires a role of its own, however, independent of intervention, if it is assumed to affect exchange rate expectations. The long-run equilibrium real exchange rate in model *(iii)* is determined by the condition that the current account be balanced. If expectations are assumed to be "rational" or consistent with the model, the expected future real exchange rate must then be determined by this condition and will respond to shocks which disturb current account conditions and prospects. This approach has been adopted in recent papers[32] which have argued that this injection of "rationality" into the expectations assumptions of the portfolio balance model provides a transmission mechanism for the current account which may be more important than its wealth effects. In reality, of course, current accounts need not balance even over long periods if there are persistent structural capital flows in one direction. But even for a country where this is the case[33], it is still true that there are limits outside which current account imbalances are unsustainable, and that non-transitory disturbances to the current account (and to structural capital flows) will usually imply a need for corrective real exchange rate adjustments which is likely to affect expectations.

An example of the application of this idea is provided by Hooper and Morton's attempt to explain the movements in a trade-weighted index of the dollar's value against ten other currencies between 1973 and 1978. They found that after elimination of the risk-premium variable, whose coefficient was persistently wrong-signed but insignificant, their model explained 80 per cent of the quarterly variations in the value of the dollar over the estimation period. All remaining coefficients were right-signed (the interest coefficients being signed as in the Frenkel model) and only that on the short interest differential was not significant. Their results imply that although the dollar's fluctuations over the period as a whole were caused in about equal part by monetary and real factors, about 45 of its depreciation through 1977 and

147

1978 had been due to a revision of expectations about the equilibrium real exchange rate caused by the current account deficit.

Hooper and Morton's representation of the formation of real exchange rate expectations is however *simpliste,* and it may be argued that their results merely re-state the known correlation between the value of the $ and the US current account. Dornbusch (1980) adopted a different approach, by assuming that contemporary forecasts published by the OECD were representative of market expectations, so that deviations of the outturn from them could be used to measure unanticipated current account "shocks". He found that these deviations contributed significantly to an explanation of movements in the dollar effective rate and the $-Yen rate, but not the $-DM rate, between 1973 and 1979.

The above account of the way in which the econometric modelling of exchange rates has evolved suggests that the exchange rate movements of the last decade cannot, in general, be satisfactorily explained on the basis of the special assumptions adopted in any of the three models described above. The relative generality of Hooper and Morton's model – especially its acknowledgement of the active role of exchange-rate expectations and their dependence on the information transmitted by the current account – may be considered a necessary advance; but it is possible to question both its particular assumptions about expectations formation (as seen above) and the significance of its apparently successful results (as Meese and Rogoff (1981) have shown).

iv) *Purchasing power parity*

Some representative results of econometric studies of the relationship between exchange rates and relative price levels are summarised in Table 3. The usual procedure has been to regress either the exchange rate on domestic and foreign price levels, or the rate of change of the exchange rate on domestic and foreign inflation rates, and to examine whether the estimated parameters support the hypothesis that the exchange rate responds proportionately to price disturbances, perhaps after allowance for lagged adjustment. A problem with this procedure is that since prices cannot generally be assumed to be exogenous to the exchange rate, coefficients obtained by OLS must be expected to provide biased estimates of the exchange rate's responses to price movements. Frenkel (1978), having obtained OLS estimates for three exchange rates in the 1920s which appeared to confirm long-run PPP, recognised the difficulty, and on the basis of "causality" tests which showed that exchange rate changes usually led rather than lagged behind price changes, inferred that it would be more proper to estimate the inverted regression, with relative price levels "explained" by exchange rates. These results again appeared to support the long-run validity of PPP. But Frenkel's alternative specification of course assumed that exchange rates had been exogenous to relative price levels, whereas both exchange rates and prices should in general be regarded as endogenous: exchange rates are likely to lead prices not because the former are exogenous to the latter, but because foreign exchange markets tend to respond faster to disturbances than goods markets. This implies that a simultaneous-equations estimation technique is more appropriate.

This was recognised by Krugman (1978) and Frenkel (1981) when they used instrumental variables to estimate equations for a number of exchange rates in the 1920s and 1970s. The results were mixed. For the 1920s they were consistent in both studies with long-run PPP. Krugman's estimates for 1973-6 also failed to reject PPP, although they were not less well-determined, markedly so in the case of the DM:$ rate. Frenkel's results for 1973-9 were much poorer for the exchange rates involving the dollar – with coefficients usually insignificant and sometimes even wrong-signed – but they were still reasonably satisfactory for the £-DM and FF-DM rates. Krugman qualified his relatively favourable

Table 3. Econometric results for purchasing power parity[a]

Authors	Currencies and Period	Special features	Summary of Results
1. Frenkel (1978).	$: £, FF : $, FF : £, Feb. 1921-May 1925.	i) 3 sets of prices indices : wholesale, raw material, food ; ii) Sims causality test used to test for exogeneity of prices.	i) Hypothesis that elasticities of rate of change of exchange rate with respect to domestic and foreign inflation rates are equal not rejected in each case ; ii) After allowing for lags in adjustment, elasticity with respect to differential inflation rate close to unity in long run, except in case of £ : $. Speeds of adjustment vary among price indices ; iii) Causality tests indicated that exchange rates "caused" prices rather than vice-versa. Equations therefore re-estimated with ratio of price levels the dependent variable. Long-run homogeneity not rejected in most cases.
2. Krugman (1978).	i) DM : $, Feb. 1920-Dec. 1923, £ : $, Feb. 1920-Dec. 1925, FF : $, Feb. 1920-Dec. 1926 ii) DM : $, IL : $, SF : $, £ : $, July 1973-Dec. 1976.	i) No allowance for lagged adjustment ; ii) Instrumental variable estimation used to take account of endogeneity of prices ; iii) Wholesale prices only.	i) In OLS estimates, after allowing for autocorrelation, only 2 of the 7 sets of data do not reject the hypothesis that the elasticity of the exchange rate with respect to relative price levels is unity in the short run, viz. IL : $ and £ : $ in 1970's ; ii) IV estimates more favourable : elasticity not significantly different from unity in any case ; but for DM : $ in 1970's, not significantly different from zero either ; iii) But variations in real exchange rates generally large, and substantially serially correlated in all cases.
3. Dornbusch (1978).	DM : $, March 1974-May 1978.	Regression of real exchange rate (defined using CPI's) on previous value.	"The real exchange rate depends to the extent of one third on its long-run value and two-thirds on its recent history" indicating "substantial and persistent deviations from PPP".
4. Frenkel (1981).	i) DM : £, Feb. 1921-Aug. 1923 ; FF : £, $: £, FF : $, Feb.1921-May 1925 ; ii) $: £, $: FF, $: DM, June 1973-July 1979 ; then £ : DM and FF : DM over same period.	i) Wholesale prices and CPI's ; ii) Instrumental variable estimation.	For the 1920's, the results support PPP ; but for the 1970's "the results (for all $ exchange rates) are extremely poor and the estimates are extremely imprecise" : coefficients on relative inflation rates all insignificant, and sometimes wrong-signed. But results better for £ : DM and FF : DM.

a) See note to Table 1.

results by observing that although the real exchange rates examined had, as predicted by PPP, usually been more stable than the corresponding nominal rates – with the notable exception of the DM-$ rate in the 1970s – there appeared to have been substantial serial correlation in the deviations of real exchange rates from their mean values. In other words, there appeared not to have been any strong tendency for purchasing power disparities to correct themselves. Dornbusch (1978) drew a similar inference from his own econometric investigation.

v) Covered interest parity

Table 4 summarises evidence on this question, referred to in C.5. It overwhelmingly supports the view that efficiency in this sense holds in international financial markets. In the Euro-markets, where exchange controls and political risk are absent, any apparent covered disparities may be accounted for entirely by transactions costs; disparities in onshore markets appear to be explicable usually by exchange controls.

vi) Efficiency and the risk premium: forward exchange rates as predictors of spot rates

Part C.5 refers to the implication of the joint hypothesis of speculative efficiency and the absence of a risk premium that the forward exchange rate will be an unbiased predictor of the future spot. Evidence on this issue is summarised in Table 5. On the joint hypothesis, if the spot rate is regressed on the lagged forward rate, then the constant should be zero, the coefficient should be unity, and there should be no serial correlation in the errors. If there is a risk premium, however, these implications do not follow from the efficiency hypothesis, since the risk premium may well, in particular, have a constant component and be serially correlated. Moreover, if there is a risk premium which is a component of the error term in the regression, the lagged forward rate will be correlated with the error term, so that OLS will not provide a consistent estimation procedure; the equation may, however, be estimated by instrumental variables.

Although Table 5 refers to tests of a joint hypothesis, Frenkel (1976, 1978) drew a strong inference about efficiency from his OLS regressions; these included the second lag of the forward rate as an additional explanatory variable to provide a more powerful test of the hypothesis that the first lag embodies all the relevant information for the systematic prediction of the spot. While Frenkel interpreted his results as evidence in favour of efficiency, the recent study by Cumby and Obstfeld (1980) preferred to assume efficiency and to conclude from their finding of significant serial correlation in the difference between the rate of change of the spot rate and the lagged interest differential (which is the same, under covered parity, as the logarithmic difference between spot and the lagged forward rate) that most exchange rates against the dollar displayed a risk premium. Frenkel (1979a), in a study of the DM-$ rate not included in Table 5 used the same dependent variable as Cumby and Obstfeld, but in a different way and with different results. Assuming efficiency, Frenkel interpreted the difference between actual appreciation and the lagged forward premium as being the same, apart from white noise, as the previous period's risk premium. He then investigated whether this ex post risk premium was correlated with relative asset supplies, as portfolio balance theory suggests for the ex ante premium. In over a hundred attempts using quarterly data, he failed to find a single specification where a significant asset-supply influence appeared. He concluded that "The evidence points in the direction of perfect substitutability of assets". But the difficulties involved in constructing asset stock data – to say nothing of the dubiousness of the necessary assumption that actual asset stocks measure asset preferences – together with the absence of clear confirmation in the other studies referred to, suggests that the evidence on this issue is more ambiguous.

Table 4. **Evidence on covered interest parity**

Authors	Interest rates and period	Special features	Summary of results
1. Frenkel and Levich (1975).	i) US and UK Treasury Bills ii) US and Canadian TBs iii) Euro-$ and Euro-£ deposits Jan. 1962 - Nov. 1967, weekly.	Estimation of transactions costs for calculation of "neutral band".	Very high proportion of observed disparities lie within the neutral band defined by transactions costs - 85 % for TBs, 99-100 % for euro-deposits.
2. Frenkel and Levich (1977).	As in (1), but 3 periods : i) Jan. 1962-Nov. 1967, the "tranquil peg". ii) Jan. 1968-Dec. 1969, the "turbulent peg". iii) July 1973-May 1975, the "managed float".	As in (1).	i) Transactions costs much higher in floating period, owing to wider bid-ask spreads ; ii) For 1962-7 and 1973-5, results as in (1) ; but proportion of disparities explained by transactions costs much lower in the 'turbulent peg' period in the TB comparison - only 30-40 %. Proportion still high, however, in the euro-deposit comparison. Results for 1968-9 explained by 'political risk' (more specifically financial uncertainty and reduced co-operation among central banks) rather than market inefficiency.
3. McCormick, (1979).	i) US and UK TBs ii) euro-$ and euro-£ deposits April-Oct. 1976, weekly.	As in (1), but based on refined (more closely aligned) data.	i) Transactions costs estimated to be much lower than data comparable to those used in (1) and (2) would suggest ; ii) Newly calculated neutral bands explain 100 % of disparities for euro-deposits, but only 20-30 % for TBs. Explained by UK exchange controls.
4. Dooley and Isard, (1980).	Euro-DM deposits and DM interbank deposits, Jan. 1970-Dec. 1974 monthly.	A portfolio balance model used to explain the differential between euro-DM and internal DM interest rates in the presence of controls on capital inflows.	Most of the change in the differential, from near zero in 1970 to 10 % in April 1973 then back to zero, explained by the effective tax imposed by actual controls, rather than by the risk of prospective controls.

151

Table 5. Evidence on forward rate as predictor of spot rate[a]

Authors	Currencies and period	Horizon	Techniques and special features	Summary of results
1. Frenkel (1976).	DM : £, Feb. 1921-Aug. 1923, monthly.	1 month.	OLS regression of S on F1 and F2.	Constant and coefficient of F2 not significant ; coefficient of F1 not significantly different from unity ; DW indicates absence of serial correlation. Efficiency inferred.
2. Cornell (1977).	$ against FF, July 1974-Jan. 1977 ; $ against £, Can $, DM, SF, DG and Yen, April 1973-Jan.1977; monthly.	1 month.	Examination of forecasting errors of lagged forward rate ; comparison with lagged spot (random walk).	Mean forecasting errors of lagged forward rate statistically insignificant in each case. Zero average risk premium inferred. But errors significantly auto-correlated in some cases, raising questions about efficiency. Results barely distinguishable from those for random walk.
3. Frenkel (1978).	DM : £, FF : £, FF : $, Feb. 1921-May 1925, monthly.	1 month.	As in (1).	As in (1).
4. Levich (1978).	$ against Can $, £, BF, FF, DM, IL, DG, SF, and Y, Jan. 1967-May 1975, weekly.	1, 3, and 6 months.	Examination of forecasting errors of lagged forward rate ; also tests of profitability of simple forecasting rules.	Mean forecasting errors of lagged forward rate statistically significant in most cases. Non-zero risk premia inferred. But errors not serially correlated ; efficiency inferred, and confirmed by unprofitability of forecasting rules.
5. Frenkel (1979a)	$ against DM, FF, £, IL, SF, DG, Jan. 1973-Apr. 1978, weekly.	1 month.	Regressions : i) (S-Ft) against constant ii) S on Ft and constant, with instrumental variables iii) S on Ft and (St-F2)	i) Constant not significant : i.e. zero mean forecast errors. i) Apart from £ and SF, constants differ significantly from zero, and coefficient of F1 differs significantly from unity. But results more consistent with efficiency and zero-risk premium when Jan 73-June 74 excluded. iii) Results mixed. In sum, results ambiguous except that DM : $ rate passes all tests for the period July 74-Apr 78.
6. Cumby and Obstfeld (1980).	$ against SF, DM, Can $, FF, DG, £, July 1974-June 1980, weekly.	1 week.	Tests for serial correlation in differences between (S-SI) and lagged interest differentials	Apart from £, all currencies showed significant serial correlation. Risk premium inferred.
7. Frenkel (1981a)	$ against £, FF, DM, June 1973-July 1979, monthly.	1 month.	OLS and IV estimates of regression of S on F1 and F2.	In all cases F2 not significant, and DW indicates absence of serial correlation. Joint hypothesis of zero constant and unit coefficient not rejected.

a) : In this table S and F refer to the logarithmic values of spot and forward rates ; F1 is the one-period lag of F, etc. For other abbreviations, see note to Table 1.

NOTES

1. The most influential work had been that of Fleming (1962) and Mundell (1963).
2. It will be seen that this treatment of the capital account contrasts sharply with that associated with the asset-market approach, and that the differences may be considered partly a reflection of differing perceptions about the degree of capital mobility in the international financial system.
3. Throughout this study, the "exchange rate" refers to the price of domestic in terms of foreign currency, so that a fall means depreciation of the domestic currency.
4. Another was the converse proposition that the effectiveness of bond-financed fiscal policy is likely to be reduced by exchange rate flexibility. This will be the case if the upward pressure on interest rates which results from, say, a fiscal expansion attracts capital inflows which outweigh any deterioration in the current account, so that the exchange rate rises and net exports consequently fall.
5. See Grassman (1973), Carse and Wood (1979), Page (1981).
6. This pattern of behaviour has been a typical empirical finding in large econometric models of major OECD countries.
7. From the viewpoint of the question of the effectiveness of monetary policy under different exchange rate regimes, the argument of this paragraph raises doubts about the short-term validity of the proposition mentioned earlier, namely that it is greater with exchange rate flexibility. This point was made by Niehans (1975).
8. McKinnon and Oates (1966), McKinnon (1969), and Branson (1969) were among the first to reject the Mundell-Fleming formulation and assume stock-adjustment responses in the capital account. The assumption that capital flows depend on interest rate levels continued, however, to be used by some writers, e.g. Niehans (1975).
9. The serial correlation question is examined in Part C.4.
10. For convenience of exposition it is assumed that expectations are uniform throughout the market.
11. The meaning of the risk premium is defined more precisely in Part C.5 and the Appendix.
12. The formal definition of the risk premium is such that the assumption of covered parity of interest rates is in fact also required: See Parts C.5 and Appendix.
13. Evidence that observed exchange rate changes are almost entirely unanticipated is referred to below in Part C.5.
14. See in particular Isard (1980, 1981).
15. These models and econometric results are summarized in the Appendix.
16. The interest rate elasticity of the supply of money may outweigh this effect so that in a larger simultaneous model the exchange rate may appreciate.
17. It was seen in Part B.4 that this proposition is a distinctive component of the monetary model of the exchange rate. There are other interpretations of PPP in the literature, of which one may be noted. This is the weaker proposition that real exchange rates are in the long run invariant to changes in money supplies, or that in the long run "the money supply affects the price of foreign exchange in the same way as other prices" (Niehans, 1980, p.256). Recall that this holds in the Dornbusch model of Part B.4, as well as in the monetary model, but is not usually imposed in this form in the portfolio balance model.
18. The "productivity bias" problem is associated with Balassa (1964).
19. See the discussion of the portfolio balance model in the Appendix.
20. Domestic unit labour costs relative to a trade weighted average of foreign unit labour costs.

21. A lower expected rate of return on real assets on account of lower activity levels may provide an offset.

22. See Appendix.

23. It may be noted that speculative efficiency and rationality of expectations are almost synonymous: in the absence of transactions costs, rational expectations imply speculative efficiency.

24. There is no implication, it should be noted, that successive differences between the current and previous logarithmic values of the spot rate itself should be serially uncorrelated. The frequently reported finding that the rate of change of the exchange rate is white noise – or that the exchange rate follows a *random walk* e.g. Mussa (1979), Frenkel (1981) – strictly speaking carries no efficiency implications. Even with efficiency and no risk premium the rate of change of the exchange rate may be serially correlated if interest differentials are serially correlated.

25. The efficiency of the foreign exchange market has also been tested by examination of the profitability of trading strategies based on the mechanical application of simple rules of thumb. The results usually suggest *ex post* that there were strategies which would have been profitable; but their implications for efficiency are again ambiguous.

26. See, for example Frenkel (1976), Bilson (1978, 1979).

27. It is perhaps surprising that inflation expectations, which are assumed to be represented by interest rates, are not assumed to be dependent on money supplies. This is, nevertheless, the case in most empirical applications of this model.

28. E.g. Buiter and Miller (1981), Eastwood and Venables (1980).

29. Its relaxation in discussed in Part B.

30. The assumption more usually adopted is that exchange rate expectations are static, i.e. that the exchange rate is not expected to change from its current level.

31. This condition has in subsequent portfolio balance models provided an anchor for exchange rate expectations.

32. E.g. Dooley and Isard 1980, 1981), Hooper and Morton (1980), Dornbusch (1980).

33. Canada has been an example of a country with a persistent current account deficit, while Switzerland has normally had a surplus.

TECHNICAL ASPECTS OF THE SIMULATIONS PRESENTED IN PART III

The simulations discussed in the main text have been conducted with the OECD Secretariat's Financial Interlink model. This system incorporates international financial linkages into the previous Interlink System and, in particular, endogenises exchange rates. The present Annex provides a sketch of the structure of the system (Part A) and the technical assumptions underlying the simulations (Part B). It must be stressed, however, that the model is still at an experimental stage and the results derived from it are preliminary[1].

A. THE FINANCIAL INTERLINK MODEL

i) *Basic structure of individual country external sectors*

The basic structure of the external sector for an individual country is set out in equations (1) to (8) in simplified functional notation.

$$
\begin{aligned}
&(1) &&\text{CAPFLOW} &&= \text{C(IRS-IRFOR,EXCHEX/EXCHE,...)*WWD} \\
&(2) &&\text{IRS} &&= \text{I(IRFOR,MONEYS,GDP)} \\
&(3) &&\text{MONEYS} &&= \text{MONEYS(-1)+DFA+ADCE} \\
&(4) &&\text{EXCHX} &&= \text{E(EXCH,....)} \\
&(5) &&\text{BOSD} &&= \text{CBD+CAPFLOW} \\
&(6) &&\text{EXCHE} &&= \text{EXCH/EXCHBASE*(1/EXFOR)} \\
&(7) &&\text{EXCHEX} &&= \text{EXCHX/EXCHBASE*(1/EXFRX)} \\
&(8) &&\text{DFA} &&= \text{BOSD/EXCH}
\end{aligned}
$$

Where: CAPFLOW = net capital flows $; IRS = short term market interest rate; IRFOR = foreign short term interest rate; EXCHE = effective exchange rate; EXCHEX = expected effective exchange rate; CBD = current balance $; MONEYS = broad money stock; ADCE = autonomous domestic credit expansion; DFA = change in foreign reserves (local currency); EXCHX = expected dollar exchange rate; EXCH = dollar exchange rate; BOSD = balance of official settlements $; WWD = world wealth $.

The principal behavioural equation is that for net international capital flows – equation (1) – dependent upon relative yields (short-term interest differentials and the expected rate of appreciation), world wealth and other terms related to international accounting. Foreign interest rates and exchange rates are multi-lateral, being defined through a consistent weighting of all other country rates. World wealth is a common scale factor for all countries, a feature which plays a role in ensuring international consistency (discussed below). Strictly, this assumes that the distribution of world wealth does not change substantially so that the portfolio holders in different countries, who allocate non-country-specific wealth according to the relative attractiveness of various locations, can be aggregated with a fixed-weight scheme. Short-term interest rates – equation (2) – are dependent on foreign rates (for all countries other than the United States) and domestic money demand/supply relationships. Equation (3) determines the money supply through its domestic and external counterparts.

The expected dollar exchange rate – equation (4) – may be specified in a variety of ways. Three have been explored:

- extrapolative time series equations (ARIMA forecasts);
- "quasi-rational expectations" reduced form equations; and
- the imposition of purchasing power parity assumptions.

The version of the model used in this paper employs the first of these, but research is continuing. Equations (5) to (8) are identities which complete the system, on the assumption that domestic credit expansion is exogenous. As in the pre-existing Interlink model, the US dollar is used as the numeraire currency so that the effective exchange rate (equation 6) is defined as the ratio of the domestic currency bilateral dollar rate to a weighted basket of overseas dollar rates. The treatment of the expected effective exchange rate is fully analogous to that of the actual rate, with *expected* bilateral dollar rates replacing actual rates. Current account balances are determined through the international trade mechanisms of the Interlink model.

ii) *International linkages*

The key behavioural equations are specified in terms of domestic variables relative to their foreign counterparts. The latter are defined through a weighting matrix:

(9) $W = [w_{ij}]$

where column j shows the weight of all other countries in country j's foreign variable. Each column sums to unity and there are zeros on the main diagonal. To simplify the analysis in subsequent paragraphs, the determination of capital flows, and ultimately exchange rates via the overall balance of payments relationship, will be discussed in terms of the interest rate differential argument of equation (1). However, the analysis also applies more generally to other arguments of the equation.

When the interest rate IRS increases for country i the yield differential in its favour will rise and, when scaled by world wealth, will imply a capital inflow, the extent of which will depend on the estimated parameter for this argument of equation (1) β_i. This will lead the exchange rate to appreciate in order to maintain external balance. A rise in IRS in country i will imply that all other countries' foreign rates will rise, reducing the yield differential in their favour, the relative extent of which will be determined by W. They will be subject to capital outflows and, hence, downward pressure on their exchange rates. International consistency requires that these outflows (in a common currency) should just match the inflow into country i. This is ensured by a joint restriction on interest rate differential parameters and the weighting matrix. Since there is a common scale factor WWD, then for any country i it is required that:

(10) $\beta_i = \Sigma_j \beta_j w_{ij}$

156

Since $\Sigma_j w_{ij}$ is simply the sum of the ith row of the weighting matrix, it is required that the vector of parameters ß when pre-multiplied by the ith row of W should give $ß_i$. This will hold for all rows if:

(11)   W.ß = ß or

(12)   (W-I)ß = 0

which provides the joint restriction on coefficients and weights. With the weighting matrix given, its eigenvector implies cross country restrictions on coefficients up to a factor of proportionality.

The weighting matrix plays a key role in the transmission of interest and exchange rate disturbances between countries and should, in principle, be estimated. As a starting point Multilateral Exchange Rate Model (MERM) trade weights have been used since, at least to some extent, capital flows will be influenced by current account transactions. However, it is recognized that these do not reflect appropriate international financial weights: in particular, the US dollar will be under-represented by trade weights. This shortcoming has not been rectified in the model used for the simulations in this study, but research to alter the weights is currently under way. This, together with other shortcomings mentioned above:

- the determination of expected exchange rates;
- the absence of explicit treatment of shifts in shares of world wealth and of valuation effects following exchange rate changes; and
- the preliminary nature of estimates for interest rate and capital flow equations;

implies that the results presented are of a highly preliminary nature. However, a large amount of empirical work has already been undertaken and the model does have the advantage of comprehensive international consistency. For these reasons the simulation results presented below will give a very broad indication of the main influences at work.

B. POLICY SIMULATIONS

i)   *A two point cut in US interest rates with the rest of the world floating*

ADCE (autonomous domestic credit expansion) is used as an exogenous instrument to target a two point cut in US interest rates during 1981 and 1982. Other countries are assumed to maintain their baseline rates of monetary growth. Zero intervention is specified, so that BOSD (balance of official settlements in US dollars) is always equal to zero and the exchange rate adjusts to solve the system. That is, the exchange rate varies, altering both current accounts and capital flows to bring this *ex ante* equilibrium condition about. The results, which are reported in Table 1 below, are referred to in Part IV of the main text. The main features which stand out are:

- that while interest rates in other countries adjust sympathetically to the movement in US rates, this is not sufficient to shelter them from exchange rate movements; and
- exchange rate pressures vary between countries depending on interest rate responses and the nodal pattern of influence implied by the weighting matrix.

This latter feature, that the importance of other country interest rates in the own country foreign rate follows a nodal pattern of financial dependence, is of considerable interest. For example, Germany's foreign rate is dominated by the United States. Given its sluggish interest rate response, the shift of the differential term in the capital flow equation leads to a relatively large appreciation of the DM. Other EMS countries' foreign interest rates are dominated by Germany. Consequently, differential pressures on exchange rates arise and, in some cases, effective exchange rates in EMS countries, where trade with Germany is particularly important, actually depreciate (France, Belgium).

ii) *A two point cut in US interest rates under fixed exchange rates*

ADCE is used to target a two point cut in US interest rates. Other countries are assumed to maintain nominal exchange rate targets. This leads to market interest rate adjustments in

Table 1.   **Fully-linked simulation of a two point cut in US short-term interest rates with floating exchange rates**

First year 1981	Percentage deviations from baseline				Level deviations	
	Effective exchange rate	Money supply	Nominal GDP	GDP deflator	Short-term interest rates	Cumulative intervention (billions U.S.$)
North America						
United States	−1.4	3.2	0.2	0.1	−2.0	−
Canada	0.6	−	−	−0.1	−1.1	−
Selected EMS countries						
Germany	0.5	−	0.1	−	−0.2	−
France	−0.2	−	−	−0.1	−0.4	−
Italy	0.6	−	−0.1	−0.1	−0.1	−
Belgium	−0.1	−	−	−0.1	−0.4	−
Netherlands	0.2	−	−0.3	−0.4	−0.3	−
Other						
Japan	0.9	−	−	−	−0.7	−
United Kingdom	0.5	−	−	−0.1	−0.6	−
Switzerland	0.6	−	−0.2	−0.2	−0.1	−
Sweden	0.1	−	−	−0.1	−0.3	−
Second year 1982						
North America						
United States	−3.0	3.7	0.7	0.2	−2.0	−
Canada	1.3	−	−	−0.1	−1.5	−
Selected EMS countries						
Germany	1.2	−	−0.1	−0.3	−0.6	−
France	−0.9	−	0.1	−0.1	−0.7	−
Italy	1.5	−	−0.4	−0.3	−0.3	−
Belgium	−0.2	−	−	−0.3	−0.7	−
Netherlands	0.5	−	−0.9	−1.2	−0.5	−
Other						
Japan	1.6	−	−0.1	−0.1	−1.1	−
United Kingdom	1.2	−	−0.2	−0.3	−0.9	−
Switzerland	2.1	−	−1.1	−0.8	−0.3	−
Sweden	−0.1	−	−	−0.1	−0.6	−

Note : Money supplies are United States M2 ; Canada M3 ; Germany M3 ; France M2 ; Italy M2 ; Belgium M3 ; Netherlands M3 ; Japan M2 + CD ; United Kingdom sterling M3 ; Switzerland M3 ; Sweden M3. Simulations are conducted with the Secretariat Financial Interlink Model (FINLINK).

the rest of the world. But to the extent that these do not offset *ex ante* pressures on exchange rates, reserve changes consistent with pre-determined fixed exchange rates (in this case fourth quarter 1980 parities) are solved for. The results are reported in Table 2 below.

While the results discussed in the text are of interest, they also illustrate a possible bias of the model. The endogenous interest rate responses in the case of fixed exchange rates seem to be rather modest, indicating inadequate sensitivity of capital flow and interest rate parameters. That is, the impact of interest rate changes on capital flows and the consequent impact of money supply changes on interest rates are possibly understated. This feature of the model is currently being researched by the OECD Secretariat.

Table 2.   **Fully-linked simulation of a two point cut in US interest rates :
intervention to fix exchange rates**

First year 1981	Percentage deviations from baseline				Level deviations	
	Effective Exchange rate	Money supply	Nominal GDP	GDP deflator	Short-term interest rate	Cumulative intervention (billions U.S.$)
North America						
United States	–	3.1	0.2	–	−2.0	−4.57
Canada	–	0.5	0.1	–	−1.2	0.49
Selected EMS countries						
Germany	–	0.2	–	–	−0.4	0.92
France	–	0.1	–	–	−0.4	0.37
Italy	–	0.2	–	–	−0.1	0.63
Belgium	–	0.2	0.1	–	−0.5	0.12
Netherlands	–	0.7	–	–	−0.3	0.31
Other						
Japan	–	0.1	0.1	–	−0.7	0.81
United Kingdom	–	0.3	–	–	−0.6	0.38
Switzerland	–	0.3	–	–	−0.1	0.37
Sweden	–	0.3	–	–	−0.4	0.19
Second year 1982						
North America						
United States	–	3.4	0.5	–	−2.0	−8.87
Canada	–	0.7	0.3	–	−1.5	0.63
Selected EMS countries						
Germany	–	0.6	0.2	–	−0.6	1.90
France	–	0.2	0.2	–	−0.7	0.62
Italy	–	0.6	0.1	–	−0.3	1.46
Belgium	–	0.4	0.2	–	−0.7	0.23
Netherlands	–	1.4	0.1	–	−0.6	1.66
Other						
Japan	–	0.1	0.2	–	−1.1	1.42
United Kingdom	–	0.4	0.2	–	−0.9	0.61
Switzerland	–	0.8	0.2	–	−0.2	0.91
Sweden	–	0.6	0.1	–	−0.7	0.37

Note :   Money supplies are as defined for Table 1. Simulations are conducted with the Secretariat Financial Interlink Model (FINLINK).

iii) *A two point cut in German interest rates*

ADCE is used as an exogenous instrument to target a two point cut in German interest rates during 1981 and 1982. Zero intervention is specified for all countries, so that BOSD is always equal to zero and the exchange rate adjusts to solve the system. The results, which are reported in Table 3, are discussed in the main text. The most interesting contrast with the US floating rate simulation is the more homogenous pattern of exchange rate responses within the EMS.

Table 3. **Fully-linked simulation of two point cut in German interest rates with the rest of the world floating**

First year 1981	Percentage deviations from baseline				Level deviations	
	Effective exchange rate	Money supply	Nominal GDP	GDP deflator	Short-term interest rate	Cumulative intervention (billions U.S.$)
North America						
United States	0.5	–	–	–	–	–
Canada	0.1	–	–	–	−0.2	–
Selected EMS countries						
Germany	−2.4	5.5	0.2	–	−2.0	–
France	0.4	–	–	–	−0.6	–
Italy	1.0	–	–	–	−0.1	–
Belgium	0.3	–	–	–	−0.7	–
Netherlands	0.7	–	−0.1	−0.2	−0.5	–
Other						
Japan	0.3	–	–	–	−0.2	–
United Kingdom	0.3	–	–	–	−0.4	–
Switzerland	0.9	–	–	–	−0.1	–
Sweden	0.4	–	–	–	−0.3	–
Second year 1982						
North America						
United States	1.3	–	−0.1	−0.1	−0.1	–
Canada	–	–	–	−0.1	−0.3	–
Selected EMS countries						
Germany	−5.5	8.4	1.3	0.6	−2.0	–
France	1.0	–	–	−0.1	−0.8	–
Italy	1.3	–	−0.3	−0.2	−0.2	–
Belgium	0.7	–	0.1	–	−0.9	–
Netherlands	1.4	–	−0.1	−0.3	−0.8	–
Other						
Japan	0.7	–	−0.1	–	−0.4	–
United Kingdom	0.4	–	−0.1	−0.1	−0.6	–
Switzerland	2.1	–	–	–	−0.2	–
Sweden	1.0	–	−0.2	−0.1	−0.6	–

Note : Money supplies are as defined for Table 1. Simulations are conducted with the Secretariat Financial Interlink Model (FINLINK).

NOTES

1. For a detailed technical description of the "standard" Interlink System, see *OECD Interlink System: Structure and Operation.* This document, updated bi-annually, can be obtained on request from the Economics and Statistics Department of the OECD Secretariat.

BIBLIOGRAPHY

Argy, V. (1982), "Exchange Rate Management in Theory and Practice", *Princeton Studies in International Finance*, No.50.

Balassa, B. (1964), "The Purchasing Power Parity Doctrine A Reappraisal", *Journal of Political Economy*.

Bank of Canada (1975), *Annual Report of the Governor to the Minister of Finance*.

Beenstock, M., A. Budd, and P. Warburton (1981), "Monetary Policy, Expectations, and Real Exchange Rate Dynamics", *Oxford Economic Papers*.

Bilson, J. (1978), "The Monetary Approach to the Exchange Rate, Some Empirical Evidence", *IMF Staff Papers*.

(1979), "Recent Developments in Monetary Models of Exchange Rate Determination", *IMF Staff Papers*.

(1979a), "The Deutschemark/Dollar Rate", in K. Brunner and A.H. Meltzer, eds., *Policies for Employment Prices and Exchange Rates*, North Holland.

(1979b), "A Simple Long-run Model of Exchange Rate Determination", *mimeo*.

Branson, W.H. (1968), *Financial Capital Flows in the U.S. Balance of Payments*, North Holland.

(1977), "Asset Markets and Relative Prices in Exchange Rate Determination", *Sozialwissenschaftliche Annalen des Instituts fur Hohere Studien*.

(1979), "Exchange Rate Dynamics and Monetary Policy", in A. Lindbeck, ed., *Inflation and Employment in Open Economies*, North Holland.

H. Halttunen, and P. Masson (1977), "Exchange Rates in the Short Run: The Dollar-Deutschemark Rate" *European Economic Review*.

and H. Halttunen (1979), "Asset market Determination of Exchange Rates: Initial Empirical and Policy Results", in J.P. Martin and A.D. Smith, eds., *Trade and Payments Adjustment Under Flexible Exchange Rates*, Macmillan.

and W. Buiter (1981), "Macroeconomic Determinants of Real Exchange Rates", *National Bureau of Economic Research*, Working Paper No.101.

Brown, R.N., C.A. Enoch and P.D. Mortimer-Lee (1980), "The Relationship between Costs and Prices in the United Kingdom", *Bank of England*, Discussion Paper No.8.

Buiter, W.H. and M.H. Miller (1981), "Monetary Policy and International Competitiveness: the Problems of Adjust", *Oxford Economic Papers*.

Carse, S., and G.E. Wood (1979), "Currency of Invoicing and Forward Covering: Risk-Reducing Techniques in British Foreign Trade", in J.P. Martin and A.D. Smith, eds., *Trade and Payments Adjustment Under Flexible Exchange Rates*, Macmillan.

Connolly, M., and J.D. da Silveira (1979), "Exchange Market Pressure in Post-War Brazil: An Application of the Girton-Roper Monetary Model", *American Economic Review*.

Cornell, B. (1977), "Spot Rates, Forward Rates, and Exchange Market Efficiency", *Journal of Financial Economics*.

Cumby, R.E. and M. Obstfeld (1980), "Exchange Rate Expectations and Nominal Interest Differentials: A Test of the Fisher Hypothesis", *National Bureau of Economic Research*, Working Paper, No.537.

Dooley, M.P. and P. Isard (1979), "The Portfolio Balance Model of Exchange Rates", *International Finance Discussion Paper No.141*, Federal Reserve Board.

(1980) "Capital Controls, Political Risk, and Deviations from Interest Parity", *Journal of Political Economy*.

Dooley, M.P. and J.R. Shafer, (1983), "Analysis of Short-run Exchange Rate Behaviour: March 1973 to November 1981", in D. Bigman and T. Taya (eds), *Exchange Rate and Trade Instability*, Ballinger.

Dornbusch, R. (1976), "Expectations and Exchange Rate Dynamics" *Journal of Political Economy*.

(1978), "Monetary Policy Under Exchange Rate Flexibility", in *Managed Exchange Rate Flexibility: The Recent Experience*, Federal Reserve Bank of Boston.

(1980), "Exchange Rate Economics: Where do We Stand?", *Brookings Papers on Economic Activity*.

and S. Fisher (1980), "Exchange Rates and the Current Account", *American Economic Review*.

(1981), "Exchange Rate Rules and Macroeconomic Stability" in *Exchange Rate Rules: The Theory, Performance and Prospects of the Crawling Peg*, J. Williamson (ed.).

(1982), "PPP Exchange Rate Rules and Macroeconomic Stability", *Journal of Political Economy*.

Driskill, R.A. (1981), "Exchange Rate Dynamics: An Empirical Investigation", *Journal of Political Economy*.

and S.M. Sheffrin (1981), "On the Mark: Comment", *American Economic Review*.

Eastwood, R.R. and A.J. Venables (1980), "The Macro-Economic Implications of a Resource Discovery in an Open Economy", *mimeo*.

Fleming, J.M. (1962), "Domestic Financial Policies Under Fixed and Under Floating Exchange Rates", *IMF Staff Papers*.

Frankel, J.A. (1979), "On the Mark: A Theory of Floating Exchange Rates Based on Real Interest Differentials", *American Economic Review*.

(1979a), "A Test of the Existence of the Risk Premium in the Foreign Exchange Market vs. The Hypothesis of Perfect Substitutability", *International Finance Discussion Paper No.149*, Federal Reserve Board.

(1979b) "Tests of Rational Expectations in the Forward Exchange Market", *Southern Economic Journal*.

(1981) "On the Mark, Pound, Franc, Yen and Canadian Dollar", *Mimeo*.

(1981a) "On the Mark: Reply", *American Economic Review*.

Franzen, T. and M. Uggla (1978), "Valutaoran Summaren 1977" *Economisk Debatt*.

Frenkel, J. (1976), "A Monetary Approach to the Exchange Rate: Doctrinal Aspects and Empirical Evidence", *Scandinavian Journal of Economics*.

(1978), "Purchasing Power Parity: Doctrinal Perspective and Evidence from the 1920s", *Journal of International Economics*.

(1981), "The Collapse of Purchasing Power Parities during the 1970s, *European Economic Review*.

(1981a), "Flexible Exchange Rates, Prices and the Role of 'News': Lessons from the 1970s", *Journal of Political Economy*.

and R.M. Levich (1975), "Covered Interest Arbitrage: Unexploited Profits?", *Journal of Political Economy*.

(1977), "Transactions Costs and Interest Arbitrage: Tranquil *versus* Turbulent Periods", *Journal of Political Economy*.

Girton, L. and D. Roper (1977), "A Monetary Model of Exchange Market Pressure Applied to the Post-War Canadian Experience", *American Economic Review*.

Gordon, R.J. (1981), "Output Fluctuations and Gradual Price Adjustments", *Journal of Economic Literature*.

Grassman, S. (1973), "A Fundamental Symmetry in International Payments Patterns", *Journal of International Economics*.

Group of Thirty (1980), *The Foreign Exchange Markets under Floating Rates*.

Gylfason, T. (1978), "The Effect of Exchange Rate Changes on the Balance of Trade in Ten Industralized Countries, *IMF, mimeo*.

Hacche, G. and J.C. Townend (1981), "Exchange Rates and Monetary Policy: Modelling Sterling's Effective Rate, 1972-80", *Oxford Economic Papers*, WP.33.

(1981a), "Monetary Models of Exchange Rates and Exchange Market Pressure: Some General Limitations and An Application to Sterling's Effective Rate", *Weltwirtschaftliches Archiv*.

(1981b), "A Broad Look at Exchange Rate Movements for Eight Currencies, 1972-80", *Bank of England Quarterly Bulletin*.

Hansen, L.P. and R.J. Hedrick (1983), "Risk Averse Speculation in the Forward Foreign Exchange Market – An Econometric Analysis", in J.A. Frenkel (ed), *Exchange Rates and International Macroeconomics,* University of Chicago Press.

Henderson, D.W. (1979), "Financial Policies in Open Economies", *American Economic Review, Papers and Proceedings,* Vol.69, No.2.

Hooper, P. and J. Morton (1980), "Fluctuations in the Dollar: A Model of Nominal and Real Exchange Rate Determination", *International Finance Discussion Paper,* No.169, Federal Reserve Board.

Isard, P. (1977), "How Far Can We Push the 'Law of One Price'?" *American Economic Review.*

(1978), "Exchange Rate Determination: A Survey of Popular Views and Recent Models", *Princeton Studies in International Economics,* No.42.

(1980), "Factors Determining Exchange Rates: The Roles of Relative Price Levels, Balance of Payments, Interest Rates and Risk", *International Finance Discussion Paper,* No.171, Federal Reserve Board.

(1981), "An Accounting Framework and Some Issues for Modelling Exchange Rates", *mimeo,* Federal Reserve Board.

Johnson, K.H. (1982), "The Demand for Swiss Monetary Assets", *International Finance Discussion Paper,* No.210, Federal Reserve Board.

Kravis, I.B. and R.E. LIPSEY (1978), "Price Behaviour in the Light of Balance of Payments Theories", *Journal of International Economics.*

Krugman, P. (1978), "Purchasing Power Parity and Exchange Rates: Another Look at the Evidence", *Journal of International Economics.*

Levich, R.M. (1978) "Tests of Forecasting Models and Market Efficiency in the International Money Market", in J.A. Frenkel and H.G. Johnson, eds., *The Economics of Exchange Rates.*

Lybeck, J.A. (1977), "Effekterna av Riksbankens Kreditpolitik pa Konsumtionen, Investeringerna och Importen av Utlandskt Kapital", *Skandinaviska Enskilda Bankens Kvartalsskrift,* nr.1-2.

McCormick, F. (1979), "Covered Interest Arbitrage: Unexploited Profits? Comment", *Journal of Political Economy.*

McKinnon, R.I. (1969), "Portfolio Balance and International Payments Adjustment", in R.A. Mundell and A.K. Swoboda, eds., *Monetary Problems of the International Economy,* Chicago University Press.

(1982), "Currency Substitution and Instability in the World Dollar Standard", *American Economic Review.*

(1983), "Dollar Overvaluation against the Mark and the Yen in 1983", *mimeo.*

and W.E. Oates (1966), "The Implications of International Economic Integration for Monetary, Fiscal and Exchange Rate Policy", *Princeton Studies in International Finance,* No.16.

Magee, S.P. (1973), "Currency Contracts, Pass-Through and Devaluation", *Brookings Papers on Economic Activity.*

Martin, J.P. and P.R. Masson (1979), "Exchange Rates and Portfolio Balance", *National Bureau of Economic Research,* Working Paper No.377.

Meese, R. and K. Rogoff (1981), "Empirical Exchange Rate Models: Are Any Fit to Survive?", *International Finance Discussion Paper,* No.184, Federal Reserve Board.

and K. Singleton (1982), "A Note on Unit Roots and the Empirical Modelling of Exchange Rates", *Journal of Finance.*

Mundell, R.A. (1963), "Capital Mobility and Stabilization Policy Under Fixed and Flexible Exchange Rates", *Canadian Journal of Economic Political Science.*

(1968), International Economics, New York, Macmillan.

Mussa, M. (1979), "Empirical Regularities in the Behaviour of Exchange Rates and Theories of the Foreign Exchange Market", in K. Brunner and A.H. Meltzer, eds., *Policies for Employment, Prices, and Exchange Rates, North Holland.*

Niehans, J. (1975), "Some Doubts about the Efficacy of Monetary Policy Under Flexible Exchange Rates", *Journal of International Economics.*

(1980), "Purchasing Power Parity Under Flexible Rates", in P. Oppenheimer, ed., *Issues in International Economics.*

OECD (1974), *Monetary Policy in France*, Monetary Studies Series.

(1979), *Monetary Targets and Inflation Control*, Monetary Studies Series.

(1982), *Budget Financing and Monetary Control*, Monetary Studies Series.

(1983), *Economic Outlook* No.33.

Poole, W., (1970), "Optimal Choice of Monetary Policy Instruments in a Simple Stochastic Macro Model", *Quarterly Journal of Economics*.

Putnam, B.H. and J.R. Woodbury (1980), "Exchange Rate Stability and Monetary Policy", *Review of Business and Economic Research*, University of Nebraska.

Rose, D., and M. Sheikh (1980), "Impacts of Monetary Shocks in Three Large Canadian Macro-economic Models; RDX2, FOCUS, and DRI", *Bank of Canada*.

Roth, J.P. (1981), "The Demand for Money Under Flexible Exchange Rates: The Swiss Case", *mimeo*, Zurich.

Schiltknecht, K. (1981), "Targeting the Monetary Base", paper presented to the Economic Policy Conference at the Federal Reserve Bank of St. Louis.

Taylor, J.B. (1979), "Staggered Wage Setting in a Macro Model", *American Economic Review, Papers and Proceedings*.

Truman, E.M. (1981), "The New Federal Reserve Operating Procedure: An External Perspective", Federal Reserve Board, *mimeo*.

OECD SALES AGENTS
DÉPOSITAIRES DES PUBLICATIONS DE L'OCDE

ARGENTINA – ARGENTINE
Carlos Hirsch S.R.L., Florida 165, 4° Piso (Galería Guemes)
1333 BUENOS AIRES, Tel. 33.1787.2391 y 30.7122

AUSTRALIA – AUSTRALIE
Australia and New Zealand Book Company Pty, Ltd.,
10 Aquatic Drive, Frenchs Forest, N.S.W. 2086
P.O. Box 459, BROOKVALE, N.S.W. 2100. Tel. (02) 452.44.11

AUSTRIA – AUTRICHE
OECD Publications and Information Center
4 Simrockstrasse 5300 Bonn (Germany). Tel. (0228) 21.60.45
Local Agent/Agent local :
Gerold and Co., Graben 31, WIEN 1. Tel. 52.22.35

BELGIUM – BELGIQUE
Jean De Lannoy, Service Publications OCDE
avenue du Roi 202, B-1060 BRUXELLES. Tel. 02/538.51.69

CANADA
Renouf Publishing Company Limited,
Central Distribution Centre,
61 Sparks Street (Mall),
P.O.B. 1008 - Station B,
OTTAWA, Ont. K1P 5R1.
Tel. (613)238.8985-6
Toll Free: 1-800.267.4164
Librairie Renouf Limitée
980 rue Notre-Dame,
Lachine, P.Q. H8S 2B9,
Tel. (514) 634-7088.

DENMARK – DANEMARK
Munksgaard Export and Subscription Service
35, Nørre Søgade
DK 1370 KØBENHAVN K. Tel. +45.1.12.85.70

FINLAND – FINLANDE
Akateeminen Kirjakauppa
Keskuskatu 1, 00100 HELSINKI 10. Tel. 65.11.22

FRANCE
Bureau des Publications de l'OCDE,
2 rue André-Pascal, 75775 PARIS CEDEX 16. Tel. (1) 524.81.67
Principal correspondant :
13602 AIX-EN-PROVENCE : Librairie de l'Université.
Tel. 26.18.08

GERMANY – ALLEMAGNE
OECD Publications and Information Center
4 Simrockstrasse 5300 BONN Tel. (0228) 21.60.45

GREECE – GRÈCE
Librairie Kauffmann, 28 rue du Stade,
ATHÈNES 132. Tel. 322.21.60

HONG-KONG
Government Information Services,
Publications/Sales Section, Baskerville House,
2nd Floor, 22 Ice House Street

ICELAND – ISLANDE
Snaebjörn Jónsson and Co., h.f.,
Hafnarstraeti 4 and 9, P.O.B. 1131, REYKJAVIK.
Tel. 13133/14281/11936

INDIA – INDE
Oxford Book and Stationery Co. :
NEW DELHI-1, Scindia House. Tel. 45896
CALCUTTA 700016, 17 Park Street. Tel. 240832

INDONESIA – INDONÉSIE
PDIN-LIPI, P.O. Box 3065/JKT., JAKARTA, Tel. 583467

IRELAND – IRLANDE
TDC Publishers – Library Suppliers
12 North Frederick Street, DUBLIN 1 Tel. 744835-749677

ITALY – ITALIE
Libreria Commissionaria Sansoni :
Via Lamarmora 45, 50121 FIRENZE. Tel. 579751/584468
Via Bartolini 29, 20155 MILANO. Tel. 365083
Sub-depositari :
Ugo Tassi
Via A. Farnese 28, 00192 ROMA. Tel. 310590
Editrice e Libreria Herder,
Piazza Montecitorio 120, 00186 ROMA. Tel. 6794628
Costantino Ercolano, Via Generale Orsini 46, 80132 NAPOLI. Tel. 405210
Libreria Hoepli, Via Hoepli 5, 20121 MILANO. Tel. 865446
Libreria Scientifica, Dott. Lucio de Biasio "Aeiou"
Via Meravigli 16, 20123 MILANO Tel. 807679
Libreria Zanichelli
Piazza Galvani 1/A, 40124 Bologna Tel. 237389
Libreria Lattes, Via Garibaldi 3, 10122 TORINO. Tel. 519274
La diffusione delle edizioni OCSE è inoltre assicurata dalle migliori librerie nelle
città più importanti.

JAPAN – JAPON
OECD Publications and Information Center,
Landic Akasaka Bldg., 2-3-4 Akasaka,
Minato-ku, TOKYO 107 Tel. 586.2016

KOREA – CORÉE
Pan Korea Book Corporation,
P.O. Box n° 101 Kwangwhamun, SÉOUL. Tel. 72.7369

LEBANON – LIBAN
Documenta Scientifica/Redico,
Edison Building, Bliss Street, P.O. Box 5641, BEIRUT.
Tel. 354429 – 344425

MALAYSIA – MALAISIE
University of Malaya Co-operative Bookshop Ltd.
P.O. Box 1127, Jalan Pantai Baru
KUALA LUMPUR. Tel. 577701/577072

THE NETHERLANDS – PAYS-BAS
Staatsuitgeverij. Verzendboekhandel,
Chr. Plantijnstraat 1 Postbus 20014
2500 EA S-GRAVENHAGE. Tel. nr. 070.789911
Voor bestellingen: Tel. 070.789208

NEW ZEALAND – NOUVELLE-ZÉLANDE
Publications Section,
Government Printing Office Bookshops:
AUCKLAND: Retail Bookshop: 25 Rutland Street,
Mail Orders: 85 Beach Road, Private Bag C.P.O.
HAMILTON: Retail: Ward Street,
Mail Orders, P.O. Box 857
WELLINGTON: Retail: Mulgrave Street (Head Office),
Cubacade World Trade Centre
Mail Orders: Private Bag
CHRISTCHURCH: Retail: 159 Hereford Street,
Mail Orders: Private Bag
DUNEDIN: Retail: Princes Street
Mail Order: P.O. Box 1104

NORWAY – NORVÈGE
J.G. TANUM A/S
P.O. Box 1177 Sentrum OSLO 1. Tel. (02) 80.12.60

PAKISTAN
Mirza Book Agency, 65 Shahrah Quaid-E-Azam, LAHORE 3.
Tel. 66839

PORTUGAL
Livraria Portugal, Rua do Carmo 70-74,
1117 LISBOA CODEX. Tel. 360582/3

SINGAPORE – SINGAPOUR
Information Publications Pte Ltd,
Pei-Fu Industrial Building,
24 New Industrial Road N° 02-06
SINGAPORE 1953, Tel. 2831786, 2831798

SPAIN – ESPAGNE
Mundi-Prensa Libros, S.A.
Castelló 37, Apartado 1223, MADRID-1. Tel. 275.46.55
Libreria Bosch, Ronda Universidad 11, BARCELONA 7.
Tel. 317.53.08, 317.53.58

SWEDEN – SUÈDE
AB CE Fritzes Kungl Hovbokhandel,
Box 16 356, S 103 27 STH, Regeringsgatan 12,
DS STOCKHOLM. Tel. 08/23.89.00
Subscription Agency/Abonnements:
Wennergren-Williams AB,
Box 13004, S104 25 STOCKHOLM.
Tel. 08/54.12.00

SWITZERLAND – SUISSE
OECD Publications and Information Center
4 Simrockstrasse 5300 BONN (Germany). Tel. (0228) 21.60.45
Local Agents/Agents locaux
Librairie Payot, 6 rue Grenus, 1211 GENÈVE 11. Tel. 022.31.89.50

TAIWAN – FORMOSE
Good Faith Worldwide Int'l Co., Ltd.
9th floor, No. 118, Sec. 2,
Chung Hsiao E. Road
TAIPEI. Tel. 391.7396/391.7397

THAILAND – THAILANDE
Suksit Siam Co., Ltd., 1715 Rama IV Rd,
Samyan, BANGKOK 5. Tel. 2511630

TURKEY – TURQUIE
Kültur Yayinlari Is-Türk Ltd. Sti.
Atatürk Bulvari No : 191/Kat. 21
Kavaklidere/ANKARA. Tel. 17 02 66
Dolmabahce Cad. No : 29
BESIKTAS/ISTANBUL. Tel. 60 71 88

UNITED KINGDOM – ROYAUME-UNI
H.M. Stationery Office,
P.O.B. 276, LONDON SW8 5DT.
(postal orders only)
Telephone orders: (01) 622.3316, or
49 High Holborn, LONDON WC1V 6 HB (personal callers)
Branches at: EDINBURGH, BIRMINGHAM, BRISTOL,
MANCHESTER, BELFAST.

UNITED STATES OF AMERICA – ÉTATS-UNIS
OECD Publications and Information Center, Suite 1207,
1750 Pennsylvania Ave., N.W. WASHINGTON, D.C.20006 – 4582
Tel. (202) 724.1857

VENEZUELA
Libreria del Este, Avda. F. Miranda 52, Edificio Galipan,
CARACAS 106. Tel. 32.23.01/33.26.04/31.58.38

YUGOSLAVIA – YOUGOSLAVIE
Jugoslovenska Knjiga, Knez Mihajlova 2, P.O.B. 36, BEOGRAD.
Tel. 621.992

Les commandes provenant de pays où l'OCDE n'a pas encore désigné de dépositaire peuvent être adressées à :
OCDE, Bureau des Publications, 2, rue André-Pascal, 75775 PARIS CEDEX 16.

Orders and inquiries from countries where sales agents have not yet been appointed may be sent to:
OECD, Publications Office, 2, rue André-Pascal, 75775 PARIS CEDEX 16.

68236-12-1984

OECD PUBLICATIONS, 2, rue André-Pascal, 75775 PARIS CEDEX 16 - No. 42925 1984
PRINTED IN FRANCE
(11 84 01 1) ISBN 92-64-12606-6